"This absorbing book meets a critical need. Although many psychotherapists have been deeply influenced by evolving psychoanalytic thinking, the insularity of most psychoanalytic communities has kept outsiders from this valuable practical knowledge. Dr. Steinberg teaches useful psychoanalytic benefitting concepts, exemplifying their application with personal vignettes, without either oversimplifying complex ideas or patronizing readers. His wisdom, humility, and lucidity make this book a must-read for anyone interested in understanding and helping our fellow human beings."

Nancy McWilliams, *PhD, ABPP, Rutgers Graduate School of Applied & Professional Psychology*

"In this companion piece to his first groundbreaking book, Paul Steinberg once again addresses the insufficient attention paid to psychological factors in the entire range of health care. In addition, he illustrates his exceptional sensitivity in applying psychoanalytic acumen to this work with more seriously disturbed patients and in hospital settings such as Day Treatment facilities. This book merits readership from health care providers in the broadest sense and as well, his psychoanalyst colleagues. Indeed, it should be required reading."

Irwin Hirsch, *PhD, Distinguished visiting faculty, William Alanson White Institute*

From the Foreword:
"There continues to be a desperate need for a 'psychotherapy for the people.' Dr. Steinberg is addressing this need … in an enviable, clear, conversational tone as if he is discussing his ideas and illustrations with us in a personal encounter, or a really well-run seminar. Steinberg has a real gift of illustrating complex concepts with useful clinical narratives."

Joseph Newirth, *PhD, ABPP, Adelphi University*

Applying Psychoanalytic Thought to Contemporary Mental Health Practice

Advances in psychoanalytic theory and technique can be usefully applied in virtually all psychotherapeutic settings, as well as in the management of patients in many nonmental health settings, to enhance understanding of patients. In this book, Steinberg reviews a collection of his own essays, incorporating developments in psychoanalytic theory and new ideas since his essays were published. Chapters clearly describe the evolving psychoanalytic approaches to treatment and illustrate how to use psychoanalytic concepts when working with patients.

A variety of clinical situations are covered, including group psychotherapy, partial hospitalization, and individual psychotherapy. This book provides the foundation of analysis and offers varied clinical experiences appealing to a wide range of practitioners and case examples offering descriptive details and interventions.

This book will be essential reading for all mental health professionals wanting to improve their working relationships with patients.

Paul Ian Steinberg is clinical professor in the Department of Psychiatry, University of British Columbia, and the author of *Psychoanalysis in Medicine: Applying Psychoanalytic Thought to Contemporary Medical Care* (2021).

Applying Psychoanalytic Thought to Contemporary Mental Health Practice

Paul Ian Steinberg

NEW YORK AND LONDON

First published 2022
by Routledge
605 Third Avenue, New York, NY 10158

and by Routledge
2 Park Square, Milton Park, Abingdon, Oxon OX14 4RN

Routledge is an imprint of the Taylor & Francis Group, an informa business

© 2022 Paul Ian Steinberg

The right of Paul Ian Steinberg to be identified as author of this work
has been asserted in accordance with sections 77 and 78 of the Copyright,
Designs and Patents Act 1988.

All rights reserved. No part of this book may be reprinted or reproduced or utilised
in any form or by any electronic, mechanical, or other means, now known or
hereafter invented, including photocopying and recording, or in any information
storage or retrieval system, without permission in writing from the publishers.

Trademark notice: Product or corporate names may be trademarks or registered trademarks,
and are used only for identification and explanation without intent to infringe.

Library of Congress Cataloging-in-Publication Data
A catalog record for this title has been requested

ISBN: 978-1-032-06068-2 (hbk)
ISBN: 978-1-032-06070-5 (pbk)
ISBN: 978-1-003-20058-1 (ebk)

DOI: 10.4324/9781003200581

Typeset in Bembo
by Newgen Publishing UK

Contents

Publication Acknowledgments		ix
Acknowledgments		x
Foreword		xi
Introduction		1

PART A
Psychoanalytic Understanding   9

1   Internal Images and External Bonds: A Little
Psychoanalytic Theory   11

2   Who Is My Patient? The Importance of Relational
Anamnesis in Psychodynamic Formulation   27

3   Understanding and Management of Some More
Severe Disturbances   41

PART B
Group Psychotherapy and Partial Hospitalization
Programs   69

4   Danger from Within: Threats of Violence in Group
Psychotherapy   71

5   Danger from Without: Threats of Violence to Third
Parties in Group Psychotherapy   85

viii   *Contents*

6 Freud in the Clinic: The Psychodynamic Psychiatry
  Service of the University of Alberta Hospital—
  A 30-Year History   99

7 Groups That Support Psychodynamic Group
  Psychotherapy: The Function and Place of Structured
  Groups in Psychodynamically Oriented Day Treatment
  for Personality Disorders   115

8 Hatred and Fear: Projective Identification in Group
  Psychotherapy   130

PART C
Individual Psychoanalytic/Psychodynamic
Psychotherapy   139

9 Clarification and Confrontation: Two Techniques of
  Supportive Psychotherapy   141

10 Coping with Catastrophic Feelings: Supportive
   Therapeutic Relationship with Patients Suffering from
   Chronic, Serious or Life-Threatening Illness—Lessons
   from HIV-AIDS-Related Illness   155

11 Whipped Cream and Other Delights: A Reverie and
   Its Aftermath   165

   Conclusion   185

   Glossary   187
   Index   192

Publication Acknowledgments

I wish to express appreciation to the publishers of the following articles who graciously permitted me to incorporate part or all of the latter in this book. The chapters are listed with their corresponding original versions.

Chapter 1: Steinberg PI (1998). Attachment and object relations in formulation and psychotherapy. *Annals of the Royal College of Physicians and Surgeons of Canada,* 31(1): 19–22; and Routledge, publishers of *Psychoanalysis in Medicine.*

Chapter 2: Steinberg PI (2002). The importance of relational anamnesis in psychodynamic formulation. *Canadian Psychiatric Association Bulletin,* 34(2): 29–32.

Chapter 4: Steinberg PI & Duggal S (2004). Threats of violence in group-oriented day treatment. *International Journal of Group Psychotherapy,* 54(1): 5–22.

Chapter 5: Steinberg PI, Duggal S, & Ogrodniczuk J (2008). Threats of violence to third parties in group psychotherapy. *Bulletin of the Menninger Clinic.* 72(1): 1–18. Reprinted with permission from Guilford Press. Copyright holder: Guilford Press.

Chapter 6: Steinberg PI, Rosie JS, Joyce AS, OKelly JG, Piper WE, Lyon D, Bahrey F, & Duggal S (2004). The psychodynamic psychiatry service of the University of Alberta Hospital: A thirty year history. *International Journal of Group Psychotherapy,* 54(4): 521–538.

Chapter 7: Steinberg PI, Duggal S, Ogrodniczuk J, Bragg K, Handelsman C, MacDonald B, Sayers N, Stovel L, & Hutton K, (2009). The function and place of structured groups in psychiatric day treatment. *Smith College Studies in Social Work,* 79(1): 35–49.

Chapter 8: Steinberg PI & Ogrodniczuk J (2010). Hatred and fear: Projective identification in group psychotherapy. *Psychodynamic Practice,* 16(2): 201–205. Website of journal: www.tandfonline.com/

Chapter 9: Steinberg PI (1989). Two techniques of supportive psychotherapy. *Canadian Family Physician,* 35: 139–1143.

Chapter 10: Steinberg PI (1998). Supportive therapeutic relationship with an HIV-AIDS patient. *Annals of the Royal College of Physicians and Surgeons of Canada,* 31(1): 23–26.

Chapter 11: Steinberg PI (2017). Whipped cream and other delights: A reverie and its aftermath. *Canadian Journal of Psychoanalysis,* 25(2): 88–105.

Glossary: Routledge, publishers of *Psychoanalysis in Medicine.*

Acknowledgments

In *Psychoanalysis in Medicine* I compiled a fairly exhaustive list of individuals to whom I owe a debt of gratitude for developing into the person who wrote that book. I remain as grateful to them now as I was then, but will not repeat the list.

I wish to thank my editors at Routledge, Sarah Gore, Upasruti Biswas and Kanagathara Balaji, for their consistent support, guidance and assistance.

I wish to thank David Brand and Kathy Bragg for reviewing this book for Routledge, and Bea Donald and Judy Beale for being willing to do so.

I wish to thank Joseph Newirth for his Forward, and Irwin Hirsch and Nancy McWilliams for their endorsements.

I wish to thank Dr. John Ogrodniczuk for his helpful contribution to some of the original articles on which this book is based.

I am very grateful to Reece Steinberg for the cover art and Richard Markus for his photographic rendering of it.

I wish to make special mention of Satna Duggal, who, as team leader of the program we led together, was my partner in so many learning experiences and adventures, both clinical and administrative, in a program that had many challenging patients, and, sometimes, colleagues. She also is co-author of some of the original articles on which Section B is based. I also wish to thank Dr. John Rosie, who was an invaluable support for me during those years.

Finally, I would like to thank my family for their ongoing love and support, and, in particular, my wife, for her support of my writing over many years.

Foreword

Joseph Newirth, PhD
ABPP Professor, Derner School of Psychology,
Adelphi University

Paul Steinberg's new book *Applying Psychoanalytic Thought to Contemporary Mental Health Practice* follows in a direct line from Freud's (1919) prescription that psychoanalysis must move out of the rarefied atmosphere of psychoanalytic institutes and into the wider field of mental health, allowing us to provide psychoanalytically informed psychotherapy for a truly expanded population. I would like to paraphrase Freud's (1919) well-known remarks to the Budapest International Psychoanalytic Conference as a way to orient us to Dr. Steinberg's book and his expansion of the possibilities of a "psychotherapy for the people."

Freud cast a glance to a future situation, noting that the therapeutic activities of psychoanalysts are not very far-reaching, as there are only a "handful of us" (p. 166), and even by working very hard one can only devote oneself to a limited number of patients. There are more than a handful of psychoanalysts in the world today, but our numbers are still relatively small: "Compared to the vast amount of neurotic misery which there is in the world, and perhaps need not be, the quantity we can do away with is almost negligible" (p. 166). Freud suggested that to apply psychoanalytic therapy on a larger scale would require "us to alloy the pure gold of analysis freely with the copper of direct suggestion" (p. 168). Observing that current conditions restricted the availability of psychoanalysis to the well-to-do, Freud concluded that whatever form a "psychotherapy for the people" (p. 168) may take, its most effective and important ingredients certainly would remain those borrowed from rigorous and impartial psychoanalysis.

Certainly, this has been Dr. Steinberg's goal, which I believe he has actualized in a very significant way.

A great deal has happened in the world since 1918, which has seemingly increased the "neurotic misery" and suffering of large parts of the population, and as we have become more aware of the mental health needs of the public, practitioners have become increasingly frustrated at the lack of modes of effective treatment. There continues to be a desperate need for a "psychotherapy for the people." Dr. Steinberg is addressing this need, clearly describing the evolving psychoanalytic approaches to treatment and

xii *Foreword*

alloying them with individual and group psychotherapy and, most importantly, illustrating how he uses these abstract, sometimes opaque psychoanalytic concepts in working with patients who are deeply disturbed and often hospitalized.

Dr. Steinberg writes in an enviable, clear, conversational tone as if he is discussing his ideas and illustrations with us in a personal encounter, or a really well-run seminar. In reading his book, I marveled at how clearly he presents complex ideas and again describes how useful they can be in both individual and group psychotherapy. There are many surprises throughout this book; for example, as he describes the evolution of psychoanalytic theory in the first chapter, he moves slightly off-center, describing attachment theory and its contributions to our understanding of the dynamics of the psychotherapy situation, which he then compares to contemporary neo-Kleinian approaches that focus on the

> importance of being attuned with what is happening in the analytic field at any given moment; that is, for the therapist largely to be focusing her attention and therapeutic efforts on precisely what is going on between therapist and patient in the immediate present.
>
> (p. 17)

Steinberg completes this first chapter with a description of psychotherapy with a patient in which he focuses on the importance of the therapist's experience of pressure to react to the patient as a very tangible illustration of the transference–countertransference situation.

The next two chapters in the first section of this book focus on developing skills in interviewing patients and in organizing a diagnostic impression of patients. Again, Steinberg presents this information in an accessible and highly useful way. He acknowledges that interviewing patients in a mental health context can be difficult, and approaches the project with a sense of appreciation for the humanity of patients and of the difficulty of the therapist's job. It is particularly valuable to see Steinberg's illustrations of good interview techniques, suggesting that we should not use simple direct questions, but rather statements that encourage a free associative interview style in which the patient feels safe enough to elaborate their history and emotional experiences. Some of his illustrations made me think of Harry Stack Sullivan (1970/1951), who would introduce a high level of respect and humor in his interviews with patients, which reduced their sense that the anamnesis was an adversarial procedure or a situation in which the patient would become embarrassed, humiliated, or shamed through confessing their failures. Steinberg illustrates how his nondirective approach uses descriptive statements such as "every marriage has some problems," if a patient asserts that he has a fine marriage, which encourages the patient to be a participant in the conversation rather than a subject of investigation. Steinberg carries this humanistic approach into describing the complexity of severe mental disorders, where typically these diagnoses are seen as containing a degree

Foreword   xiii

of hopelessness that discourages clinicians from pursuing therapy with these patients In this chapter, Steinberg integrates the difficult symptom picture of these very disturbed patients with a psychoanalytic understanding of their dynamics and the early developmental issues that underlie these diagnostic impressions. Throughout this section of his book, Steinberg conveys a positive view of the possibilities of helping these patients develop past their limitations and grow into having fuller lives.

The next section of this book focuses on the use of group psychotherapy and partial hospitalization programs. I suspect that this section represents the main purpose of this book, as it is directed at those professionals who work within hospital and partial hospitalization settings with patients who are fairly disturbed and in crisis. It is only as I write this Foreword that I realized the structure of this section, which I did not initially understand, is focused on helping therapists with the inevitable anxieties of working with patients with whom problems of violence or threats of violence are likely to arise, and which can disrupt the group and also terrify the therapists. I think that Steinberg is placing these two chapters first as a way of helping clinicians to feel confident in their ability to deal with crises of violence. In each chapter, Steinberg presents illustrations in which difficult patients challenge their therapists and disorganize the potential safety of the group. These chapters and the illustrations seem directed to helping therapists feel confident in the process and to not blame themselves when such inevitable events occur in the therapy situation. The last chapter of this section is a very useful presentation of the concept and use of projective identification in groups. This represents the heart of this section, describing how the therapist and patient are able to move from the enactment of patients' hatred, fear, and aggression into more symbolic representations of their unconscious patterns, moving from action to experiences of mutual understanding and then to the capacity for self-acceptance. Steinberg presents a rather extensive clinical example which I found both extremely useful clinically and filled with illustrations of complex theoretical points. I think that Steinberg has a real gift of illustrating complex concepts with useful clinical narratives.

The last section of this book is focused on individual psychotherapy, and, as with the previous sections of this book, Steinberg carefully organizes the chapters and contents to help the reader develop a greater understanding and comfort in the use of psychoanalytic concepts, developing and culminating in the last chapter with an extensive illustration of work with a difficult patient that succeeds in a most impressive way. Steinberg is not the kind of person who is drawn to self-aggrandizement; however, this last chapter illustrates the inevitable struggle that occurs for all practitioners. Most importantly, it illustrates the creative potential that a courageous therapist can bring to their work. One of the aspects of Steinberg's book that this case illustrates is how psychoanalytic concepts inform his work, which allows him to be spontaneous and creative rather than, as we often imagine, become constricted and formal in interpretations that are simply explanations. Steinberg shows us how, through his work with this patient, real growth occurs, and in a quite xiv *Foreword*

unusual way describes the patient's growth and development. I would like to quote Steinberg for his quite beautiful description of the positive outcome of a difficult therapeutic journey.

> However, Mr. D also felt that he had the opportunity to think about his own mind, similar to how I thought about it. He began talking more openly about how much he would miss me. He realized that he would have to take the risk of being hurt in a relationship in order to have one. He saw the extent to which he repeatedly had given up on himself, and how that had led to failure and low self-esteem. He realized that he never had allowed himself to think, always asking others for advice, although he found what they offered to be unreliable. He now could think abstractly and interpret proverbs himself, although he never gave himself credit for that. He had been too afraid of rejection to be true to himself, and therefore had given people little opportunity to respond to him in a genuine way. He was more confident and stood up for his point of view in work situations. He rarely felt depressed, handled upsetting experiences more adaptively, and in interpersonal situations was more active. His family relationships were much better; he stood up to his mother when necessary. He accepted that his sister would not change, and protected himself against her. He enjoyed work more now that he was functioning as a leader.
>
> (Chapter 11: p. 175)

I want to say that the reader of this book, whether a beginning mental health professional or a seasoned psychoanalyst, is in for a real treat. Dr. Steinberg's clear exposition of the evolving world of psychoanalysis from Freud's early interpretive approach to contemporary neo-Kleinian and relational approaches that emphasize the importance of enactments, containment, and the therapist's reverie in facilitating growth past the developmental arrests that underlie much of what we understand as psychopathology is a real gift. We owe him a debt of gratitude for his efforts. I believe that he has brought to fruition Freud's insight that we will have to alloy the pure gold of psychoanalysis with the copper of other forms of therapeutic intervention.

References

Freud S (1919). Lines of advance in psychoanalytic therapy. In Strachey J (ed.). *The Standard Edition of the Complete Psychological Works of Sigmund Freud*. Vol. XVII. London: The Hogarth Press and the Institute of Psychoanalysis.

Sullivan HS (1970/1951). *The Psychiatric Interview*. New York and London: W.W. Norton.

Introduction

In my opinion, psychoanalysis has damaged itself in the past through authoritarianism, elitism, promising too much, and not adapting itself and cooperating with other professionals to make itself as useful as possible to other health-care professions and the public. This book and its predecessor (Steinberg, 2021) are part of an attempt to demonstrate what psychoanalysis has to offer to both health-care professionals and their clients and patients. Somewhat ironically, in the last half century, as psychoanalytic theoretical understanding has gradually deepened and this understanding and consequent technical innovations have broadened its clinical applicability, its practitioners have become more tolerant of not knowing, the negative capability first described by the poet Keats and elaborated on by Bion (1970). It is this capacity to tolerate not knowing that makes learning possible.

This book largely follows the format of its sister publication, *Psychoanalysis in Medicine: Applications of Psychoanalytic Thought to Contemporary Medical Care* (hereafter referred to as *Psychoanalysis in Medicine*). The latter's secondary theme, of one's capacity to keep growing, personally and professionally throughout one's career, is also evident in this book.

I consider this book to be a companion volume to *Psychoanalysis in Medicine*. Although that book explicitly has physicians as its target audience, and this book is explicitly aimed at mental health-care providers and their administrators, there is in my opinion a large overlap between the target audiences of these two groups, especially as it relates to taking care of patients as people. To paraphrase Harry Stack Sullivan (1947), we and our patients are much more simply human than otherwise. I actually believe that all providers of health care should find much of interest and utility in both volumes.

The term "mental health-care providers" includes, in its more exclusive sense, counselors, couples and family therapists, family physicians, nurses, some occupational therapists, psychiatrists, psychologists, psychotherapists of every stripe, and social workers, as well as their administrators. In a more inclusive sense, the term comprehends all acupuncturists, chiropractors, chiropodists, dentists, foot health practitioners, geriatric care providers, midwives, occupational therapists, osteopathic doctors, pedorthists, personal care assistants, pharmacists, physical rehabilitation practitioners, physical therapists, physician assistants, physicians in clinical practice, public health practitioners,

DOI: 10.4324/9781003200581-1

2 *Introduction*

rehabilitation counselors, speech therapists, and traditional Chinese medicine practitioners, as well as their administrators. My point in being so inclusive is that all clinicians and administrators are, more or less, responsible for their patients'/clients' mental health, at least to the extent that their patients may present with mental health problems that may affect their experience of their presenting illness, if that is not directly mental health related, or to their reaction to the management of their illness, in addition to the possibility of psychological factors contributing to the predisposition, precipitation, exacerbation, or perpetuation of disease or of the patient's experience of illness, which the clinician needs to consider and sometimes address. I include "administrators" because managers and leaders of hospital and clinic departments (and of hospitals and clinics themselves) no longer usually are practicing clinicians, as in days past, but graduates of university administrative programs, and need to be well informed both about clinical matters, including the mental health aspect of health care, and about the difficulties inherent in group functioning, as all health-care facilities are composed of groups: groups of health-care providers, patients, and administrators, in addition to technical, administrative, and ancillary staff. I believe this book, like *Psychoanalysis in Medicine*, contains ideas that will be helpful not only to the "exclusive" group of mental health practitioners but also to the "inclusive" group.

One concept underlying this whole book is that of the unconscious, and in particular, the unconscious meaning of experience. What we are consciously aware of (which is very little at any given time) and what we readily can summon up to conscious awareness (the pre-conscious) is essentially the tip of the iceberg of our mind. Most people underestimate how much of our mind is occupied by unconscious mental contents. This includes thoughts, feelings, impulses, fantasies, wishes, and fears that we at some point have been to some extent aware of, which have been have been repressed into the unconscious because they are too anxiety-provoking or painful to maintain in conscious awareness. The unconscious also contains the mental mechanisms of defense that we employ to render unconscious what is too uncomfortable to remain conscious. A third area of the unconscious, which currently is an area of very active psychoanalytic exploration, involves aspects of our experience that we have never articulated or been able to mentalize, that is, to think of. This might be because they are too unbearably painful or frightening, such as traumatic experiences, or because they are related to experiences we had in our very early childhood, before we were able to articulate our experience verbally. Freud's discovery or invention of psychoanalysis was largely based on his becoming aware of and exploring the importance of unconscious factors in the genesis of psychiatric symptoms and conditions, personality formation, slips of the tongue and other bungled actions (called parapraxes), dreams, and medical symptoms, such as conversion symptoms (called hysteria back then).

Another important concept which underlies much of what follows is that of unconscious fantasy. This involves feelings, expectations, thoughts,

Introduction   3

fears, and hopes, experienced in unconscious internal relationships between an individual's representation of herself and that of others (called internal objects). These unconscious internal relationships influence our experience of external relationships with other people and can influence what we expect in our interactions with others, how we perceive our interactions with others, and even, through projective indication, can influence the way others actually react to us (Steinberg, 2021).

In the first two chapters, I summarize some ideas about psychoanalytic approaches to understanding individuals, including from a developmental point of view, and how psychoanalysis understands some more severe conditions, as well as some principles of treatment to these conditions. The introduction ends with a snapshot of psychoanalytic psychotherapy, after a few vignettes that also illustrate the type of work I do.

In Chapter 1, I summarize some psychoanalytic theory, focusing on attachment theory and object relations theory, with specific reference to major psychoanalytic theorists, both contemporary and of the past.

In Chapter 2, I note that psychodynamic formulation is a neglected aspect of the education of mental health professionals (MHPs) and therefore of patient management planning. The development of formulation skills is an ongoing process that should continue during one's entire professional life. Clinicians' weakness in formulation may be related partly to limitations in anamnesis, the history one's patient provides, which is remediable. It is crucial to elicit an adequate history of a patient's interpersonal relationships throughout their lifetime to construct a plausible formulation. Various techniques are offered to help reduce patients' defensiveness in giving a history. Knowledge of some psychodynamic theory helps in organizing historical data to make the patient's life experience, including symptoms and character traits, more understandable.

In Chapter 3, I describe a psychoanalytic understanding and psycho-analytically informed management of some more severe psychological disturbances. This includes sexual perversions/paraphilias, substance abuse and other addictive behaviors, severe personality disorders, including patients with psychotic symptoms, and autistic spectrum conditions. Patients with psychosomatic conditions, who would normally be included in this group of conditions, are dealt with in *Psychoanalysis in Medicine* (Steinberg, 2021).

Chapters 4 and 5 deal explicitly with threats made by patients in groups. However, the clinical approach to these situations and the necessary legal considerations are generally applicable to mental health (and other health care and medical) settings when threats occur. In Chapter 4, threats of violence in a group-oriented day treatment program (DTP) are examined regarding the patient's unconscious motivation to make threats and what occurs among patients and staff that fosters these threats. Effects of threats on other patients, the program, and therapists are considered. Psychoanalytically informed management of the threatening patient, the group, and staff reactions are described.

4   *Introduction*

Chapter 5 considers threats of violence toward third parties occurring in psychotherapy groups from a psychoanalytic perspective. A psychoanalytically informed approach to preserve the group work, protect the threatened individuals, maintain the threatening patient's treatment, and protect the group leader legally is described. Reluctance to seek legal advice and inform third parties needs to be resolved. Knowledge of jurisdictional laws pertaining to disclosure is essential.

Chapter 6 describes a full-service outpatient psychiatric service located in a tertiary teaching hospital that is based on psychoanalytic principles, a rare example of the application of psychoanalytic thought in a large government-run facility.

Chapter 7 outlines the functions of the structured psychotherapy groups in a psychodynamic group psychotherapy-oriented partial hospitalization DTP. The structured groups help patients with personality disorders to reflect on themselves. Integration of the structured groups helps to contain patients, teaches them specific skills, makes treatment less intimidating, and provides material for the unstructured groups. The structured groups reduce resistance, modulate anxiety, and support patients' disclosures. Rehabilitative groups help identify conflicts and deficits that contribute to the patients' difficulties. Issues raised in the structured groups are explored in the unstructured psychodynamic psychotherapy groups, making communication among the staff vital. Effective treatment relies on successful integration of the structured and unstructured groups.

Chapter 8 deals with the interpretation of projective interpretation in group psychotherapy. Patients with significant personality disturbance employ a variety of primitive defenses in interpersonal situations that, when unmodified, invariably perpetuate the chronic relational difficulties experienced by these patients. Among such primitive defenses used by patients with personality disorders is projective identification (PI). Ogden (1979) defines PI as a group of fantasies and accompanying object relations having to do with the ridding of the self of unwanted aspects of the self; the depositing of those unwanted parts into another person; and, finally, the recovery of a modified version of what was extruded. In the context of group therapy, PI, if undetected, can have a significant negative impact on the emotional experience and interpersonal interactions among members of the group, including the therapist. Awareness of this potential can enable a group to convert what is a disturbing and potentially destructive experience into one involving learning and therapeutic benefit. Knowledge of the concept of PI is useful for understanding regressive phenomena driven by intense affects such as rage. A therapist's awareness of how to identify, understand, and manage PI is crucial for overcoming what could otherwise become an impasse in group psychotherapy. This article describes a group therapy session illustrating an experience involving PI. I am considering PI both as a defense, that is, an intrapsychic experience, and an interpersonal process. These observations apply to many other kinds of groups of people besides psychotherapy groups.

Introduction   5

Chapter 9 describes two techniques of supportive psychotherapy, clarification and confrontation, which can be used by MHPs in virtually any type of psychotherapy, as well as being usefully employed in many nonmental health clinical situations. Case examples are offered to illustrate the application of these techniques. I discuss what supportive psychotherapy is and what it is not.

Chapter 10 describes the need to consider each patient's personality and psychosocial circumstances when helping patients adapt to the stresses inherent in very serious illness, such as HIV/AIDS-related conditions. An awareness of the patient's attachments and unconscious self- and object-images will help in managing the transference. The physician must also monitor her countertransference and set realistic goals; intervention is needed when a patient becomes suicidal. The clinician should avoid "overtreating" and assuming responsibility that patient or family and friends can bear.

In Chapter 11, I discuss one way to capture the emotional truth that we look for in psychotherapeutic work through the dreamwork that is created in the therapist's reverie. The question of whether disclosure of the reverie represents an unconscious enactment, as opposed to a more disciplined use of reverie, needs to be considered. I reflect on a reverie I had while with a patient, which consisted of a visual image of a sexually provocative record album cover. The patient responded to the reverie's disclosure by describing a dream, which led to an enlivening of the therapy and work involving mourning the loss of the patient's father.

In the envoi, I bid farewell to the reader with some final reflections on how psychoanalytic thought can enhance the provision mental health care.

Vignettes

The first vignette provides an example of a patient's anxiety about containment, communicated indirectly. My patient complained of my wastebasket being hidden in the corner, so it wasn't accessible to her and my other patients, as if I didn't want her or other people putting their waste in my wastebasket. When she asked me if she could use it and I said, "Sure," she interpreted that to mean that I was giving her permission on a one-time basis, as opposed to *carte blanche* to use it whenever she needed to. I was left the impression that she didn't feel I was available to contain what felt like undesirable aspects of herself that she couldn't comfortably hold inside herself. It is as if she heard me saying, "Don't leave your emotional garbage with me," as it would burden me, as opposed to my being willing and at least to some extent able to be a container for what she was having trouble holding on to, that is, her unbearably painful feelings and disturbing thoughts. She also felt unwelcome in contacting me on Zoom (we were meeting remotely during the Covid-19 pandemic), as if she were barging down my door and had not been invited in. There was such a sensitivity to loss, as if something that she felt had been offered inevitably would be taken away. Wishing to keep

6 Introduction

this experience in the present, I decided not to interpret what I thought was the transference, based on my patient's early years with her parents, whom she did not find containing. As if reading my mind, my patient said that her father at least supported her financially, but it seemed like an empty gesture. I suggested that she needed more than only material support.

In this vignette, I recount an experience in which my countertransference hate, perhaps a strong phrase for what I was feeling for this patient, became experienced in a visual illusion concerning the patient's face. One might call it a hallucination from a psychoanalytic point of view. This is another patient who, in retrospect, I felt distaste for, if not actively disliked, from the beginning of the treatment. In the first weeks of treatment, he smelled quite badly, as if he rarely washed. This stopped being a problem within the first month or so. To myself I interpreted his smelling badly as a test, to see if I could stand him, and a provocation, to see if I would respond cruelly. When I eventually made that interpretation, a year into therapy, he did not accept it, and just explained that when he is very depressed, he doesn't care if he smells. His stopping smelling after one month suggested that perhaps at that point he felt some reason to feel less depressed, possibly in part related to starting psychotherapy.

This patient talked nonstop, which I eventually interpreted as expressing a need to be heard that he felt could not be satisfied. Anything I said appeared to be experienced as intrusive and unwelcome. It was difficult to end each session. I suspected, and he later confirmed, that he found the endings abrupt, cruel, and painful. I came to interpret my disliking him in part as an experience of his self-hatred and disdain for himself. I had an odd visual perception, thinking of him as if his face were crumbling when I was not with him, although when I saw him lying on the couch, he did look much older than his stated age, the result, I thought a hard life, including substance abuse. However, looking at him, it also was as if his eyelids, mouth, and nose seemed to be crumbing a little, although this was not evident when I looked closely. I found my visual perceptual disturbance of him to be very curious. I noticed that after treating him for 1½ years, he still looked much older than I, although he was considerably younger, but my experience of seeing him crumbling has gone. Needless to say, I was enjoying treating him much more. Rather than being covertly hostile and overtly deferential, he became much more open about what he disliked about me, and about his comfort in being able to make observations about me, even experiencing our relationship as intimate in some ways. I felt similarly, and found him an apt psychotherapy patient, quite willing and able to reflect on his inner experience. I think he was closer to permitting himself to feel that he was falling apart, and therefore, he didn't need to project into me the experience of crumbling in a physical way.

The final vignette describes an experience in group psychotherapy. One of the benefits of working on a team in a program or psychotherapy group is that two or more heads usually are better than one. If, for example,

Introduction 7

one therapist or leader of a program is unable to effectively respond to something that transpires in a group, another may be better able to. For example, in the DTP described in Chapter 6, once an individual with a severe personality disorder begin making disparaging remarks about DTP, indicating how outdated our psychoanalytic approach was. He went on at length about this in a very sarcastic and demeaning way. He had spent three months in DTP doing very little that could be called psychotherapeutic work. I angrily thought, like a cartoon character, "Why you little …," and felt like wringing his neck, but couldn't think of something constructive or therapeutic to say. I believe my thinking was interfered with by the intensity of my anger. In retrospect, this probably gave an indication of how angry the patient was, and also perhaps a hint about how his anger derailed his own capacity to think. However, my team leader, whose thinking wasn't interfered with at this moment, lightly suggested that the patient should consider how important a question out-of-date thinking was for him, implying that his mode of thinking was out of date in terms of being quite primitive and childlike. He gave a big smile, showing that he understood what she was getting at, implicitly agreeing with her. Due to some vulnerability of mine, that day I was only able to respond with anger (which I did not overtly express, although I'm sure it was evident to some of the patients), and not use what the patient said in a way that was potentially helpful to him, supportive of our program, and potentially useful in helping other patients to engage with what was going on. So it was good that there were several therapists in this large (40+ patients) group, and that one, whose countertransference didn't paralyze her like mine did me, was able to respond effectively.

A Final Comment

Finally, although my two books are presented as having physicians and MHPs, respectively, as their target audiences, I have concluded that there is enough of interest to both groups in each of the books. That is, physicians would benefit from reading this book, and MHPs would benefit from reading *Psychoanalysis in Medicine*. In addition, it occurred to me that not only physicians and MHPs but all health professionals, who of course have to deal with the psychological aspects of their patients' conditions and the management of these conditions, could benefit from reading these books. The above is understandable because the functions of both groups, medical and nonmedical health caregivers, overlap. It Occurs to me that patients who wish to be well informed on what kind of care they are receiving, whether it is medical care, mental health care, or care from other health professionals, could benefit from reading these books in terms of ascertaining what quality and depth of understanding of them is potentially available that they might wish for and would expect their health professionals provide to them.

8   *Introduction*

References

Bion WR (1970). *Attention and Interpretation*. London: Tavistock.

Ogden TH (1979). On projective identification. *International Journal of Psycho-Analysis*, 60: 357–373.

Steinberg PI (2021). *Psychoanalysis in Medicine: Applications of Psychoanalytic Thought to Contemporary Medical Care*. New York and London: Routledge.

Sullivan HS (1947). *Conceptions of Modern Psychiatry*. Washington, DC: William Alanson White Psychiatric Foundation.

Part A
Psychoanalytic Understanding

1 Internal Images and External Bonds

A Little Psychoanalytic Theory[1]

It would be impossible in one chapter to summarize adequately the massive body of psychoanalytic theory that has developed in the last 120+ years. (A book that does an excellent job of this is Ellman [2010]. A shorter, less academic, summary is Mitchell & Black [1995].) My approach here will be briefly to outline some of the most important contributions of the four theoreticians who I believe remain the most influential in contemporary psychoanalytic thinking, Sigmund Freud, Melanie Klein, Donald Winnicott, and Wilfred Bion, and to mention some prominent contemporary theorists. I will refer to excellent introductions by others to their work. Following that, I will go into a little more detail about attachment theory and object relations theory.

Quinodoz (2005) provides an excellent summary of the work of the originator of psychoanalysis. This includes Freud's early work on hysteria, his *magnum opus, The Interpretation of Dreams* (1900/1953), and early applications of psychoanalysis to the psychopathology of everyday life (such as slips of the tongue, forgetting, and bungled actions) and unconscious communication in jokes. Freud emphasized the centrality of sexuality in the etiology of the neuroses. His extended case histories are well worth reading. Freud wrote several important papers on psychoanalytic technique. He made important contributions to the theories of narcissism and mourning and melancholia. His topographic and structural theories of the mind, introduced, respectively, in *The Interpretation of Dreams* and *The Ego and the Id* (1923/1961), form the bedrock of the psychoanalytic understanding of the function and structure of the mind. Freud's later writings reevaluated unconscious motivation, going beyond the pleasure/unpleasure principle to a conflict between the life and death instincts. This helps explain the domination of the destructive component of the mind in sadism and masochism. *Inhibitions, Symptoms and Anxiety* (1926/1959) describes Freud's new approach to anxiety, an affect experienced by the ego when it is faced with danger, which always implies fear of separation from or loss of the object. In this work, Freud revised his theory that repression provoked anxiety, concluding that anxiety provokes repression, with the ego erecting defenses as a means of avoiding anxiety. It is impossible to attempt to summarize Freud's incomparable contributions in one paragraph; all that follows in this chapter is the house that rests on his

DOI: 10.4324/9781003200581-3

12   *Psychoanalytic Understanding*

foundation. Quinodoz (2005) is an excellent introduction; as is true of all great authors, nothing replaces reading them in the original.

Rustin and Rustin (2017) provide an excellent summary of Klein's work. They describe Klein's contributions to child analysis, in particular, to technique, including play therapy, and her concept of epistemophilia, the love of understanding, and its inhibition. Her discovery of the depressive position is related to developing a capacity for mourning and tolerating ambivalence toward the loved object. She conceived of the oedipal development as occurring in the first months of life. Her notions of splitting and projective identification are related to the paranoid-schizoid position. Klein emphasized the destructive aspects of envy and the importance of developing a capacity for gratitude and reparation. Klein's work is instrumental in the development of psychotherapeutic approaches to the psychoses. Klein influenced many important contributors to psychoanalytic theory and technique.

Caldwell and Joyce (2011) provide an excellent summary of Winnicott's work. This includes the observation of infants in a set situation, primitive emotional development, and his very influential ideas on hate in the countertransference, transitional objects, and transitional phenomena. Winnicott described the importance of regression in psychoanalysis and the development of a capacity for concern. He invented the term "good-enough mothering" to emphasize the importance of an average expectable environment in which a child may develop emotionally. Winnicott made important contributions to theories of play and creativity. His understanding of the use of an object is also influential. His experience as a pediatrician influenced his focus on the importance of the mother–infant relationship.

Vermote (2019) provides an excellent summary of Bion's work. Bion pioneered the concept of binocular vision, considering concepts and experiences from different perspectives. He described different basic assumption groups, fight-or-flight, dependency, and pairing, developing Freud's early work on group dynamics. Subsequently, Bion applied his understanding of the irrational thinking of groups to the thought processes of individuals. He developed an approach to the understanding and treatment of patients suffering from psychotic conditions and developed the idea of psychotic and nonpsychotic aspects of everyone's personality. He showed that in psychosis, there is not only catastrophe that happened in the past, but one that goes on in the present, with patients not only attacking the creative link with the analyst but also verbal thought itself. Bion thought of psychosis as a thought disorder, a failure to make emotional experiences mental and process them further. He invented the term "alpha function" to refer to the capacity of a mother or an analyst to help an infant or a patient, respectively, develop the capacity to think.

Bion described transformations in K (knowledge), transformations at the level of thinking, giving a mental representation to experiences. Transformations in O involved of a level of experience that is not yet represented. This involved an area of the mind that cannot be entered with rational thinking but with reverie and relaxed attention. O is difficult to

Internal Images and External Bonds 13

define but refers to psychic truth and unknowable emotional experience. Bion thought transformations in O were more powerful in terms of psychic change. He saw evading psychological pain as leading to psychopathology; he advocated helping patients to have their experience of pain and bear it. He saw the analyst as providing containment for the patient, similar to how a mother provides containment for her infant.

I will refer very briefly to some theorists who have made important contributions to our understanding and treating patients, indicating what some of their major contributions have been. In Great Britain, the following Kleinian authors write about: Joseph (1989), difficult-to-reach patients; Steiner (1993, 2011), psychic retreats; Britton (2003), hysteria, the ego and the superego; and Feldman (2009), the Oedipus complex and projective identification. The Italian psychoanalytic tradition is well represented in *Reading Italian Psychoanalysis* (Borgogno, Luchetti & Coe, 2016). Two prominent contemporary Italian theorists, Ferro (2005, 2018) and Civitarese (2018), write on field theory. *Reading French Psychoanalysis* (Birkstead-Breen, Flanders & Gibeault, 2010) provides a survey for those interested in the distinctive French approach. North American theorists belong to several schools. Harry Stack Sullivan (1953) and Harold Searles (1965) were pioneers in the treatment of severely disturbed and psychotic patients with psychoanalysis. Stephen Mitchell was a pioneer in the relational movement. Christopher Bollas (1987); Levine, Reed and Scarfone (2018); and Donnel Stern (2003) write about the related areas of the unthought known, unrepresented states, and unformulated thought. Thomas Ogden (1979, 1997a, 1997b, 2004) writes on the intersubjective psychoanalytic third, projective identification, and the use of reverie and metaphor. Two prominent South American theorists are Ignacio Matte Blanco (1975, 1998), who applied logic to an understanding of primary and secondary processes of thinking, and Horacio Etchegoyen (1991), writing on psychoanalytic technique. South American contributions to psychoanalytic thought are collected in *The Pioneers of Psychoanalysis in South America* (Lisman-Pieczanki, 2015).

Attachment Theory

I will briefly outline two related psychoanalytic theories that are helpful in understanding people and their difficulties (Steinberg, 1998). Attachment theory holds that an essential need for people is positive human attachments. In fact, the mothering figure's attunement and responsiveness to the infant in the first months of life also is crucial in the early development of the infant's capacity to think. A child with a secure attachment is confident to explore the world as he grows. Children's relationships with their parents are important determinants of the quality of attachments that children eventually form as adults. Deprivation of positive attachments during childhood makes establishing them in adulthood difficult, if not impossible. Being deprived of, losing, or experiencing the threat of losing positive attachments or substitutes for positive attachments makes an adult susceptible to adverse

14 *Psychoanalytic Understanding*

psychological and somatic reactions. Loss, disappointment, or frustration in an important relationship may lead to many reactions, including somatic symptoms, depression, withdrawal, search for a substitute, or hostility, with accompanying guilt. A healthier reaction involves creativity, in pursuits in the arts, an absorbing intellectual interest or hobby, or a vocation, or in finding a constructive solution to a problem in a relationship. Of course, one's parents are not one's only influences in childhood. To the extent that an individual who has been deprived of adequate positive experiences with his parents has meaningful positive contacts with other adults, such as extended family, friends, teachers, leaders of youth organizations such as the scouting movement, and athletic coaches, his less than satisfactory experiences with his parents may be mitigated and his psychological growth enhanced.

If an individual in childhood is deprived of positive human attachments, he may find a substitute. Three types of substitutes may be distinguished. The first group consists of direct somatic satisfaction, either generally oral or genital. It includes substance abuse; overindulgence in food or alcohol; and compulsive, destructive, or self-destructive sexual behavior. The second involves "narcissistic" satisfactions, including the pursuit of power, admiration, fame, or wealth. The third involves the investment of interest in an activity or object. This includes devotion to work, an institution, a social cause, or a group; involvement with a recreational activity; or an attachment to animals, plants, a place, or even inanimate objects. Deprivation of these outlets is also likely to lead to adverse psychological or somatic reactions. All psychological treatments offer the opportunity for a positive human attachment. To what extent the learning specific to any particular form of therapy is therapeutic is an important question. Little psychotherapeutic progress is imaginable outside the milieu of a positive attachment to a therapist; attempts to have computers function as psychotherapists have not succeeded.

Attachment theory can be used in psychodynamic formulation (a psychoanalytic understanding of how a patient got to be the way she is) to organize historical data into predisposing, precipitating, perpetuating, and protective factors, which are understood to affect an individual's development and life situation (Steinberg, 1998, 2002). Impoverished, interrupted, or disturbed early attachments predispose an individual to vulnerability to loss or disappointment in later attachments. Maladaptive styles of attachment learned in early relationships influence the style of relating in adult life and the choice of individuals with whom attachments are formed. Our early relationships are internalized as negative self- and object-images, that is, negative images of the self and others, which are associated with painful affects and a predisposition to psychiatric symptoms. Based on our early attachments, we are familiar with certain ways of relating and with forming attachments to certain types of people. Bollas (1987) describes this beginning in the first weeks of life (if not *in utero*), as the infant and mother encounter each other. We tend as adults to relate in similar ways with similar types of people.

Internal Images and External Bonds   15

A common precipitating factor in the exacerbation of psychiatric symptoms is the loss of, threatened loss of, or disappointment in important attachments. It is important not only to identify these losses, but also to identify their importance and meaning to the patient, based on predisposing factors, such as early attachment patterns. Similarly, ongoing disturbed attachments are often identified as perpetuating factors. Thus, it is necessary to understand their significance to the patient in the context of early attachments. It is important to look for disappointment in, loss of, or threatened loss of an important attachment or substitute for an attachment in trying to understand the onset of a psychiatric or psychosomatic symptom. Temporally associated precipitants for each symptom should be examined in terms of the impact or fantasized impact the precipitating events have had on the patient's attachments.

A history of positive attachments in early life is an important protective factor. Ongoing positive attachments are protective factors and are important when considering a patient's suicide risk. Observations about the attachment between the clinician and the patient, which begins to develop in the first interview, can be used in the formulation. This includes noting the patient's attitude toward the clinician, the characteristic defenses the patient uses, and one's countertransference reactions to the patient. The clinician's emotional reaction to the patient may give important clues to the patient's feelings and the feelings he elicits in others. For example, if the clinician is uncharacteristically experiencing anger when with certain patient, she might wonder whether this represents a feeling the patient is experiencing but cannot express. Alternatively, this countertransference anger might be a clue to the clinician that what she is experiencing with this patient is something many people experience with him.

Jeremy Holmes, in his preface to Bowlby's *A Secure Base* (2005/1998), summarizes Bowlby's thoughts regarding parents providing a secure emotional base on which their children can develop. He notes that mothers and fathers both matter regarding providing a secure base. "[S]ecurity of attachment is an interpersonal, interactive phenomenon, and not simply a matter of the child's inborn temperament ... the same child can be classified ... as secure with one parent and insecure with another" (p. xiv). He notes Bowlby's emphasis on "the primacy of the attachment behavioural response and its role in protection from predation; sensitive care-giving as a foundation for psychological health; the continuing importance of attachment throughout the life cycle" (p. xiii).

Holmes indicates that 20-year prospective studies that look at measures of attachment security, parental sensitivity, exploration, relational competence, and their mental representations throughout childhood can be correlated with attachment disposition in young adulthood as manifested in attitudes toward romantic relationships and the Adult Attachment Interview. These studies demonstrate that paternal contributions are vital to secure, stable, exploratory, balanced, verbally fluent attachment dispositions in adulthood. Holmes observes,

16   *Psychoanalytic Understanding*

combined mother-father scores along multiple dimensions of attachment in childhood are far more predictive of security or insecurity of attachment representation in adulthood than those of either parent alone. However, the preoccupied dimension—adults who give confused, affect-laden, unstructured responses to probes—is strongly correlated with father rejection and insensitivity in mid-childhood, with the maternal contribution being relatively weak.

(p. xv)

He concludes that good-enough fathers help their children to develop clarity of thought and the ability to face up to negative emotions without feeling overwhelmed. He feels that fathers' sensitivity should take the form of "praise, encouragement, and the capacity to sustain positive affect in their offspring … help[ing] their children to cope with curiosity-wariness conflicts" (p. xvi) by being both protective and challenging.

Holmes describes insecure attachment not only in terms of psychological defenses necessary for emotional survival, but also as a constricting factor excluding the insecure individual from the possibility of processing adverse experience. He highlights Fonagy's "reflexive function" (Fonagy et al., 2002) as a protective factor, which, despite adverse childhood experiences like parental separation, bereavement, or even neglect and abuse, enables individuals to remain secure as they grow and to provide security for their offspring. The ability to think and talk about one's experience mitigates long-term negative consequences of early trauma. Holmes notes that Fonagy's concept of mentalization describes crucial developmental processes that enable infants to experience their own and others' minds; develop a capacity to represent the world; and have wishes, beliefs, and aspirations. Mentalization permits individuals to distinguish between external reality and one's personal perspective of reality, as well as to understand that others perceive reality differently. The capacity to mentalize therefore is crucial in developing the ability to interact socially, including the ability to survive the mis-attunement, alliance ruptures, and inevitable minor failures in parent–child relationships.

Holmes notes that Bowlby compared secure parenting and effective psychotherapy, highlighting the contribution of the therapist's role as the patient's companion in the patient's exploration of himself, de-emphasizing the importance of the therapist's interpretations. Diamond et al. (2003) apply the Adult Attachment Interview procedure to the therapeutic relationship. They found that reflexive function improves in the course of therapy; good outcomes appear associated with therapists whose adult attachment scores are not excessively higher or lower than their clients' scores; and therapists' capacities for reflexive function varies depending on the individual patient. This is one facet of the importance of therapist–patient fit. "Each therapist-patient pair appears to generate its own particular attachment atmosphere and capacity for mentalization, or the lack of it" (p. xix). It is heartening to find this work on attachment theory so consistent with contemporary neo-Kleinian thinking, such as that of Ferro (1993), which emphasizes the importance of being attuned with what is happening in the analytic field at any given moment; that is, for the therapist largely to be focusing her attention and therapeutic efforts on precisely what is going on between therapist and patient in the immediate present. Cassidy and Shaver's *Handbook of Attachment* (1999) provides more detail about theoretical, clinical, and research aspects of attachment. Salter Ainsworth et al. (2015) provides empirical support for and expands on Bowlby's concept of attachment with her research on the Strange Situation.

Object Relations Theory

According to object relations theory, unconscious images of the self and others are influenced by interpersonal experiences. The most powerful influences are parenting figures, who in the happiest circumstances are parents who are reliably available, protective, have the child's best interests in mind, and have a generally positive attitude toward the child. A child's self-image largely is based on an internalization of her parents' attitude. The child with parents who feel generally positive toward the child is inclined to grow with a similarly positive attitude toward herself. The converse is true of the unfortunate child whose parents have a more negative attitude. There is not an absolute correlation between parents' attitudes toward their child and the child's attitude toward herself; inborn temperamental factors and unavoidable environmental factors can influence the child's perception of his experience of his parents, which in turn affect the internal images he develops of them. For example, a child who temperamentally is very sensitive and demanding usually will do better with very sensitive, patient, creative parents than with more thin-skinned, rigid ones. (Most children, of course, likely will do better with the former, but the more sensitive and demanding a child is, the more likely he will suffer with the latter.) Unfortunate environments such as living in a war zone, extreme poverty, or displaced persons camps contribute to difficulties parents have in optimally fulfilling their children's needs, no matter how nurturing the parents may be. Other situations, such as maternal postpartum depression, chronic parental medical or psychiatric illness, and frustrating social situations such as long-term parental unemployment, may also interfere with a child's optimal development because of their effects on the parents.

Frustration and loss in important relationships leads to unfriendly internal images of other people ("bad internal objects"), which tend to promote less constructive reactions, whereas a history of satisfactory relationships results in more benign images of others. This in turn favors a more constructive adaptation in adult life, including in relationships and work. The earlier and more severe the loss or frustration occurs, the more likely it is to have a more deleterious effect on internal objects.

The internal object, the unconscious image of the other, is based largely on the child's experience with her parents, seen through the child's eyes.

18 *Psychoanalytic Understanding*

There is controversy regarding the extent to which a child's perception of her parents may be unrealistic. The observation that an individual with a personality disorder can distort early memories may be used in an attempt to relieve parents from some responsibility for how the individual has developed. One can give parents some responsibility for their children's development without blaming them for it, which is not productive and does not further understanding.

Internal images of self and object are subject to modification based on new learning. We tend to project images of our self and our internal objects (our images of the other) onto other people. A sign of relative psychological health is that these projections are not so strong that they interfere significantly with our realistically evaluating other people on the basis of our experience with them and our previous experience of the world. Persons functioning at a low level of psychological development tend to project alternately good or bad "part-objects," unambiguously polarized positive or negative unconscious internal images of, onto other people, with a corresponding unrealistic idealization or devaluation of them. This will be described in greater detail. They experience others as all-good or all-bad, as opposed to tolerating ambivalence, that is, positive and negative feelings concurrently about an individual. In the most severe range of pathology, individuals functioning at a psychotic level project their self- and object representations so unrealistically that they are delusional about how they perceive themselves and others. Their auditory hallucinations can be interpreted as expressions of thoughts, feelings, and impulses of their own that are unacceptable to them and have been evacuated and experienced as belonging to others.

Internal objects influence what we expect in relationships. This is obvious when an individual expects someone to be a certain way when she knows little about that person. Internal objects also influence the way that we perceive other people. Our transference, the way in which we perceive others based on our previous experiences, more or less distorts our perceptions of the other, depending on the extent to which we project our internal self-image or internal objects onto him. An individual may even influence the way someone else relates to her by unconsciously eliciting or provoking certain behaviors on the other person's part. This mechanism, called projective identification, is often accomplished by unconsciously inducing in the other person an affect or impulse that one cannot accept in oneself (Ogden, 1979; Sandler, 1976).

Two defensive tendencies in which interpersonal experiences are repeated instead of remembered involve an individual's projection of either a self- or object-image onto another person, concurrently identifying, respectively, with the Unconscious object or with the self. In the former situation, an individual projects her self-image onto another person and treats that individual as she experienced herself being treated as a child by her parents. The latter situation involves the projection of the internal object (the unconscious image of the other) onto the other person. The individual then reacts to the other person in a similar way to how she reacted to her parents,

Internal Images and External Bonds 19

often unconsciously inviting or pressuring the other person to treat her as her parents did (projective identification). The interpretation of these two forms of interaction, especially in the therapeutic relationship, is important in psychoanalysis and psychoanalytic psychotherapy. The more primitive one's personality development or the more regressed one has become, the greater the tendency to rely on these projections, rather than realistically evaluating other people. The use of these observations is often crucial in the optimal management of "difficult" patients, who can expertly, if unconsciously, influence the attitudes of health professionals toward them, often in an adverse way. To the extent that we remain unaware of how these patients may provoke us, for example, to become enraged with or withdraw from them, our anger or emotional unavailability might distract us from providing our best care (Maltsberger & Buie, 1974).

Individuals who experience frustration in early attachments still need to preserve a positive internal object, an unconscious image of a friendly parent. This may require the defense of splitting, in which a realistically ambivalent attitude toward others is not tolerated. Positive and negative perceptions of and feelings about others are kept separate to prevent the negative feelings from overwhelming the positive. This results in polar opposite positive and negative part-objects, that is, one-dimensional unconscious images of the other, which may be projected into other people in adult life. (By "projected", I mean that the projecting individual experiences the other person, more or less, as corresponding to his unconscious internal image of the other, in this case an unrealistically all-positive or all-negative image.) Similarly, positive and negative aspects of the self may be split and kept separated in the mind. All this may distort one's perception of self and of others in relationships and is characteristic of more severe personality disturbance. (People without such severe personality disturbance may regress to this type of experiencing of self and other when under stress; we all engage in this to some extent.) The projection of an all-good part-object is manifested in idealization and that of an all-bad part-object in devaluation. Both involve unrealistic perceptions of self and others. An individual with these tendencies, Y, may initially idealize a person, Z, with whom he has begun a relationship. This is understood as Y projecting an all-good part-object onto Z. However, it is difficult for Z to live up to the unrealistic expectations inherent in Y's projection. When Y inevitably becomes disappointed, he may then project an all-bad part-object onto Z, resulting in a devaluation as unrealistic as was the idealization.

This pattern, when repeated, results in intense, chaotic, and disappointing relationships. This can occur in relationships involving romance, friendships, and work, but also can occur in health professional–patient relationships. (I write "health professional" because these types of interactions, of course, are not limited to the experiences of mental health professionals (MHPs) only but occur with all types of caregivers.) These oscillating and extreme attitudes toward others and toward oneself are often seen in therapeutic relationships with patients who have severe personality disturbance. This also helps explain many unsatisfactory health professional–patient interactions. It

20   *Psychoanalytic Understanding*

may temporarily be pleasant to be idealized by a patient, although one may be aware of how unrealistic this evaluation is. It is not so pleasant when the idealization is abruptly replaced by a devaluation, often expressed in a very strong terms, and accompanied by a verbal (hopefully not physical, but this is not unknown) attack. At this point, the professional may become aware that the patient's idealization was accompanied by very unrealistic expectations of her, which, when it became clear to the patient that she could not meet, resulted in an abrupt shift in the patient's attitude toward her. Internally, the patient stopped projecting an all-good part-object and instead projected an all-bad part-object onto the health professional. This describes the kind of alternation between positive and negative relationships a professional can experience, for example, with a person with borderline personality disorder. Freud described his understanding of transference, indicating that his patient's falling in love with him was not due to his irresistible charms, but rather to her love unconsciously being transferred onto him from the original object of her love.

Aspects of Personality Functioning

One of the most important discoveries of psychoanalysis has been the concept of internal reality. External reality refers to the consensually agreed-on concrete configuration of the world. For example, two people could agree that a table in a room has four legs. Internal reality refers to the unconscious inner world, populated by images of oneself and other people, not necessarily corresponding to external reality but based on the individual's emotional response to her cumulative experience, especially interpersonal experience. This internal reality also is affected by inborn temperamental factors unrelated to experience in the world. Another concept I wish to mention is that of unconscious fantasy, which is part of internal reality. Unconscious fantasy can influence one's reaction to experiences in the external world. For example, if a child's parents do not show interest in her developing the internal world, that is, are not interested in her thoughts, wishes, interests, and feelings, and generally just expect her to conform to their wishes, dismissing her ideas and initiatives, she may grow up believing that others have no interest in her thoughts or feelings, and no wish to permit her to assume personal agency, making choices about which directions she wishes to pursue in life. With this unconscious fantasy, she likely will be very sensitive to others' reactions to her initiatives and her expression of her thoughts and feelings, with a tendency to assume that they are not interested in them. She also will not be likely to be very adventurous in pursuing her own inclinations and interests. This will have a negative impact both on her developing herself as an individual and her developing satisfying and close relationships with others. In addition, children whose parents do not show interest in their developing internal world tend to identify with the parents, and have, a similar lack of interest in their internal world. This detracts from their developing their cognitive abilities, their capacity for imagination, creativity, and developing interest in both the external world and their own aspirations and wishes. Clearly, under these conditions, a child is disadvantaged regarding realizing her potential.

Internal Images and External Bonds 21

Living a satisfying active life as a human being requires attention to both one's internal and external worlds. The internal world is the source of feelings, ideas, wishes, impulses and fantasies, which provide a richness to life and which we need to inspire us regarding decisions we make about how we live our lives. The external world is a potential source of both opportunities and joy, and danger and pain, and must be perceived, thought and felt about, and accommodated to. One hallmark of relative emotional health is the capacity to distinguish between internal and external reality. This is significantly lost in psychosis, where an individual's feelings and thoughts, part of the internal world, may be experienced as if they were part of the external world, in hallucinations and delusions. However, no one is completely able to distinguish their internal and external worlds; there is inevitably some overlap.

Mechanisms of defense are unconscious attempts to reduce anxiety and other painful feelings. I wish here only to indicate that too heavy reliance on what are called more primitive mechanisms of defense is typical in more disturbed personalities. These defenses, including projection, projective identification, splitting, and denial, interfere with an individual's capacity to test reality. For example, in projection and projective identification, an aspect of the self is not acknowledged as being part of the self but is experienced as part of someone else. In splitting, two aspects of one's perception of another person, for example, are kept separate in the mind. The individual who is splitting may respond at some points to the other person as if the other person were entirely characterized by one part of the split, for example, a tendency toward openness and generosity. At other points, the individual who is splitting may respond to the other person as if he were entirely characterized by the other side of the split, for example, a tendency toward caution about money and relationships. The external reality of the other person, as it were, may be that under some circumstances, she is inclined to be generous and open, but when feeling threatened, she may be more cautious. Rather than perceiving the whole of the other individual, the patient who relies heavily on splitting may only perceive part of it at a time and react to that part. In denial, an individual undoes his perception of some aspect of reality, which is often motivated by the individual experiencing reality as unbearably painful. For example, an investor who has relied too heavily on an investment succeeding may ignore clear signs that it needs to be sold at a loss, with the result that it loses further value, a loss that could have been prevented if the individual had been able to tolerate conscious awareness of the reality of the investment losing value.

These more primitive mechanisms of defense also involve an impoverishment or loss of being in touch with the internal world. In projection and projective identification, aspects of the self, being attributed to someone else, are no longer available to the self. This may include positive attributes, such as a capacity to think, which have been projected in order to be preserved or protected, as the patient might have felt that he would destroy his own capacity to think if he did not find a safe refuge for it outside of himself. Similarly, in splitting, when the individual has disavowed a part of himself that has been split off, he cannot use it.

The personality structures of individuals have been divided arbitrarily into different levels of severity: neurotic (including "normal"), borderline, and psychotic (McWilliams, 2011). Of course, no individual's personality corresponds exactly to any of these categories; rather, it is a question of to what extent an individual's personality

22   Psychoanalytic Understanding

structure most resembles the characteristics of each of these levels. As well, depending on many factors, including the degree of stress one is under, one fluctuates regarding what level one functions at in any given moment, regressing to a lower level of functioning when under significant stress. Three criteria used in determining level of personality structure are reality testing, identity integration, and maturity of defense mechanisms. Reality testing involves a capacity to recognize consensually agreed-upon external reality. Individuals with an adequately integrated sense of identity demonstrate relatively consistent behavior and an inner experience of continuity of the self through time. They are able to describe themselves in some depth, feel a sense of continuity with their past, and can imagine their future directions. They are able to describe people to whom they are close in three-dimensional terms, considering both their positive and negative attributes together.

It is important to note that patients with a neurotic level of personality organization do not necessarily suffer from what used to be called neurotic symptoms, such as conversion, obsessive–compulsive, or phobic symptoms. Patients with a borderline level of personality function do not necessarily have a borderline personality disorder. Patients with psychotic level of personality functioning do not necessarily exhibit florid psychotic symptoms. These different levels of personality functioning do not describe symptoms or specific personality constellations, but rather different levels of development of the personality, each with characteristic defense mechanisms, degrees of identity integration, and capacities for reality testing.

Neurotic level of personality structure is characterized by good contact with reality, relatively intact integration of personal identity, and reliance on "mature" defenses, including altruism, humor, and sublimation (the direction of personally unacceptable or potentially destructive impulses into constructive activities, for example, engaging in competitive sports as a way of coping with aggressive impulses). This structure is also characterized by reliance on "neurotic" defenses that are still relatively mature, including intellectualization (concentrating on the concrete or intellectual aspects of a situation while distancing oneself from the associated uncomfortable feelings), reaction formation, (turning unconscious wishes or impulses that are felt to be unacceptable into their opposites, for example, treating a person in a kindly manner when harboring unfriendly feelings toward her), and repression (the blocking out of conscious awareness of feelings, thoughts, impulses that are unacceptable or threatening to the individual).

Borderline level of personality structure is characterized by adequate reality testing when these individuals are at their best. However, they have a tendency to regress when anxious or threatened and then may demonstrate more impaired reality testing. The identity integration of these patients is not as intact as those at the neurotic level. Their sense of self is somewhat deficient and fragile; under stress it may temporarily fragment. Their experience of themselves is likely to be inconsistent and discontinuous, alternating between polarized positive and negative attitudes toward themselves, as well as toward others. They have difficulty in describing themselves and those close to them in three-dimensional terms, considering both positive and negative aspects of individuals at the same time. As opposed to individuals with psychotic personality organization, borderline individuals may have identity confusion, but they do know that they exist. As well, they are much more likely to react with hostility to questions about their and others' identities than patients at the psychotic level. Borderline patients rely heavily

Internal Images and External Bonds 23

on "primitive" defenses. In addition to the primitive defenses mentioned above, idealization and devaluation are common, as they alternately project positive and negative part-objects onto others, experiencing them alternately as all-good or all-bad.

Patients with a psychotic level of personality organization characteristically have significantly impaired reality testing. Without necessarily being floridly psychotic, they may espouse unrealistic beliefs or think in idiosyncratic ways that interfere with their capacity to perceive and respond to the external world around them, such as tangential thinking, in which their thoughts wander away from the subject at hand without returning to it. They have a very disturbed sense of personal identity, to the extent that they may not be sure they exist. Their descriptions of themselves and others are vague, inconsistent, unrealistic, and superficial. Patients at a psychotic level of personality organization rely on primitive mechanisms of defense in order to protect themselves from terror that they are not able to articulate, including the fear of disintegrating or being swallowed up and disappearing.

For example, I diagnosed a highly trained and, according to him, highly regarded professional with a narcissistic personality disorder, likely with some antisocial features. The presence of dissociation, the unreliability of his memory, a difficulty in commitments, including repeated difficulty in establishing regular times for us to meet when I tried to make arrangements for treatment, and his never remembering any dreams, taken together, suggested a significant level of disturbance of personality functioning. This patient likely functioned between a borderline and a psychotic personality level.

The clinician who is able to identify and consider her patient's level of personality functioning will be better prepared to predict how her patients may respond to interactions with her and deal with the difficulties patients at borderline and psychotic levels are more likely to present her with than will patients functioning at a neurotic level. For example, when a clinician must cancel a patient's appointment, she may expect the neurotic patient to accept this and any disappointment or inconvenience this may entail. She will be prepared for the borderline patient to experience this as a personal rejection and to react with a degree of despair or rage that seems incommensurate with the stimulus. She will not be surprised when the psychotic patient becomes confused or acts as if he didn't even hear what the doctor said and acts as if the appointment had not been cancelled.

I wish to emphasize that many if not most patients who consult the MHPs, especially in the context of public health-care settings, resemble to a significant degree the patients described above as being at a borderline or psychotic level of personality functioning. It is pointless to be discouraged when observing this in a patient and to long for patients functioning at a neurotic level. They just aren't that common! Actually, it is more accurate to suggest that everyone can be found on the neurotic-borderline-psychotic spectrum and when under stress will tend to demonstrate more severe personality pathology. This is consistent with Bion's (1957) discovery of psychotic and nonpsychotic aspects of everyone's personality. Quinodoz's (2003) description of treating "heterogeneous" patients is an example of how psychoanalysis has developed to be able to treat more severely disturbed patients as it has identified more severely disturbed aspects of all individuals (Bion, 1957). In my opinion, it is likely that those who consult MHPs are a more disturbed cohort than was the case in the past. The silver lining is that this means that more disturbed patients have a

24 Psychoanalytic Understanding

better chance of receiving the care they need, if it is available (a big "if"). It is also possible that people as a whole are functioning at a more severe level of personality functioning than in the past. However, if we look back, for example, to Freud's lengthy case histories, which are fascinating and instructive reading (Freud, 1905, 1909a/ 1955, 1909b/1955, 1918/1955), we see much evidence of significant personality disturbance, which Freud to some extent recognized, although psychoanalysis had not yet developed the capacity to understand and therapeutically manage these patients to the extent that it has today. This development of understanding and therapeutic approaches, of courses, is continuous and is available for all MHPs to adapt to their practices.

Note

1 This chapter was adapted from Steinberg PI (1998). Attachment and object relations in formulation and psychotherapy. *Annals of the Royal College of Physicians and Surgeons of Canada*, 31(1): 19–22. Adapted with permission.

References

References to the work of Sigmund Freud are from *The Standard Edition of the Complete Psychological Works of Sigmund Freud*, Strachey J. (ed.). London: Hogarth (referred to herein as *SE*) followed by volume number.]

Bion WR (1957). Differentiation of the psychotic from the non-psychotic personalities. *International Journal of Psycho-Analysis*, 38: 266–275.

Birkstead-Breen D, Flanders S, & Gibeault A (2010). *Reading French Psychoanalysis.* Hove, East Sussex: Routledge.

Bollas C (1987). *The Shadow of the Object: Psychoanalysis of the Unthought Known.* New York: Columbia University Press.

Borgogno F, Luchetti A, & Coe LM (2016) *Reading Italian Psychoanalysis.* London and New York: Routledge.

Bowlby J (2005/1998). *A Secure Base.* London and New York: Routledge.

Britton R (2003). *Sex, Death, and the Superego: Experiences in Psychoanalysis.* London: Routledge.

Caldwell L & Joyce A (2011). *Reading Winnicott.* London and New York: Routledge.

Cassidy J & Shaver PR (1999). *Handbook of Attachment: Theory, Research and Clinical Applications*, 3rd ed. New York and London: Guilford.

Civitarese G (2018). *The Analytic Field and Its Transformations.* Abingdon, Oxon. and New York: Routledge.

Diamond D, Stovall-McClough C, Clarkin J, & Levy K (2003). Patient-therapist attachment in the treatment of borderline personality disorder. *Bulletin of the Menninger Clinic*, 76: 227–259.

Ellman SJ (2010). *When Theories Touch: A Historical and Theoretical Integration of Psychoanalytic Thought.* London: Karnac.

Etchegoyen H (1991). *The Fundamentals of Psychoanalytic Technique.* London: Karnac.

Feldman M (2009). *Doubt, Conviction and the Analytic Process: Selected Papers of Michael Feldman.* London: Routledge.

Ferro A (1993). The impasse within a theory of the analytic field: Possible vertices of observation. *International Journal of Psycho-Analysis*, 74: 917–929.

Ferro A (2005). *Seeds of Illness, Seeds of Recovery: The Genesis of Suffering and the Role of Psychoanalysis*. Hove and New York: Brunner-Routledge.

Ferro A (2018). *Contemporary Bionian Theory and Technique in Psychoanalysis*. Abingdon, Oxon. and New York: Routledge.

Fonagy P, Gergely G, Jurist E, & Target M (2002). *Affect Regulation, Mentalization, and the Development of the Self*. New York: Other Press.

Freud S (1900/1953). The interpretation of dreams. *SE*, IV, pp. xi–338; V, pp. 339–628.

Freud S (1905). Fragment of an analysis of a case of hysteria. *SE*, VII, pp. 3–124.

Freud S (1909a/1955). Analysis of a phobia in a five-year-old boy. *SE*, X, pp. 3–152.

Freud S (1909b/1955). Notes upon a case of obsessional neurosis. *SE*, X, pp. 153–318.

Freud S (1918/1955). From the history of an infantile neurosis. *SE*, XVII, pp. 3–104.

Freud S (1923/1961). The ego and the id. *SE*, XIX, pp. 3–68.

Freud S (1926/1959). Inhibitions, symptoms and anxiety. *SE*, XX, pp. 77–178.

Joseph B (1989). *Psychic Equilibrium and Psychic Change: Selected Papers of Betty Joseph*. London and New York: Tavistock/Routledge

Levine HB, Reed GS, & Scarfone D (2018). *Unrepresented States and the Construction of Meaning: Clinical and Theoretical Contributions*. Abingdon, Oxon. and New York: Routledge.

Lismar-Pieczanki (2015). *The Pioneers of Psychoanalysis in South America*. London: Routledge.

Maltsberger JT & Buie DH (1974). Countertransference hate in the treatment of suicidal patients. *Archives of General Psychiatry*, 30(5): 625–633.

Matte Blanco I (1975). *The Unconscious as Infinite Sets: An Essay in Bi-logic*. London: Karnac.

Matte Blanco I (1998). *Thinking, Feeling, and Being: Clinical Reflections on the Fundamental Antinomy of Human Beings and World*. London: Karnac.

McWilliams N (2011). *Psychoanalytic Diagnosis: Understanding Personality Structure in the Clinical Process*, 2nd ed. New York: Guilford Press.

Mitchell SA & Black M (1995). *Freud and Beyond: A History of Modern Psychoanalytic Thought*. New York: Basic Books.

Ogden TH (1979). On projective identification. *International Journal of Psycho-Analysis*, 60: 357–373.

Ogden TH (1997a). Reverie and interpretation. *Psychoanalytic Quarterly*, 66, 567–595.

Ogden TH (1997b). Reverie and metaphor: Some thoughts on how I work as a psychoanalyst. *International Journal of Psycho-Analysis*, 78, 719–732.

Ogden TH (2004). The analytic third: Implications for psychoanalytic theory and technique. *Psychoanalytic Quarterly*, 73(1): 167–195.

Quinodoz D (2003). *Words That Touch: A Psychoanalyst Learns to Speak*. London and New York: Karnac.

Quinodoz J-M (2005). *Reading Freud: A Chronological Exploration of Freud's Writings*. Hove, East Sussex.

Rustin M & Rustin M (2017). *Reading Klein*. London and New York: Routledge.

Salter Ainsworth MD, Blehar MC, Waters E, & Wall S (2015). *Patterns of Attachment: A Psychological Study of the Strange Situation*. Classic edition. East Hove, Sussex and New York: Psychology Press.

Sandler J (1976). Countertransference and role-responsiveness. *International Review of Psycho-Analysis*, 3: 43–47.

26 Psychoanalytic Understanding

Searles HF (1965). *Collected Papers on Schizophrenia and Related Subjects*. New York: International Universities Press.

Steinberg PI (1998). Attachment and object relations in formulation and psychotherapy. *Annals of the Royal College of Physicians and Surgeons of Canada*, 31(1): 19–22.

Steinberg PI (2002). The importance of relational anamnesis in psychodynamic formulation. *The Canadian Psychiatric Association Bulletin*, April, 34(2): 29–32.

Steiner J (1993). *Psychic Retreats: Pathological Organizations in Psychotic, Neurotic, and Borderline Patients*. London and New York: Routledge.

Steiner J (2011). *Seeing and Being Seen: Emerging from a Psychic Retreat*. London and New York: Routledge.

Stern DB (2003). *Unformulated Experience: From Dissociation to Imagination in Psychoanalysis*. Hillsdale, NJ and London: The Analytic Press.

Sullivan HS (1953). *The Interpersonal Theory of Psychiatry*. New York: Norton.

Vermote R (2019). *Reading Bion*. London and New York: Routledge.

2 Who Is My Patient?

The Importance of Relational
Anamnesis in Psychodynamic
Formulation

Anamnesis: the past history of a disease, including all relevant facts about the patient's environment, experiences, etc. (Funk & Wagnalls, 1959:52).

Introduction

Psychodynamic formulation is an art, the importance of that has been recognized in Canada (Fleming & Patterson, 1999), although it is considered by some to be less crucial in some other countries (Holliman, 1983a, 1983b). In spite of official recognition of the importance of psychodynamic formulation, it appears to be a neglected aspect of mental health education and consequently of patient management planning. Platitudes regarding the importance of completing a psychodynamic formulation for every patient seem more often to be honored in the breach than in the observance. This may be understandable partly in terms of how busy mental health professionals (MHPs) are. A more plausible explanation is that often MHPs are never adequately instructed in this skill, the development of which is an ongoing process that should continue throughout their training and their entire professional lives. Psychodynamic formulation is demanding task, involving clinical skills and theoretical knowledge that MHPs gain only slowly and gradually. In my experience, the need to produce a psychodynamic formulation was the most intimidating part of oral certification examinations. The task is also one of the most intellectually stimulating aspects of mental health practice, one that offers significant benefits in terms of its application, both in psychoanalytic psychotherapy and general patient management (Gabbard, 1994:153–180). Developing skills in psychodynamic formulation involves the opportunity to apply theoretical models of psychopathology to one's entire patient population.

Deficiencies in the basic clinical skill of history-taking limit proficiency in psychodynamic formulation. The capacity to produce a formulation is limited to the extent to which one is able to gather historical data. Histories often do not include sufficient details about important relationships throughout the patient's life to enable clinicians to construct supportable psychodynamic hypotheses about their patients. My experience with trainees leads me to conclude that they often feel that deficiencies in theoretical knowledge limit them. Some trainees feel they can remedy this problem by reading more

DOI: 10.4324/9781003200581-4

28 *Psychoanalytic Understanding*

about psychoanalytic theory. Other trainees take a more passive approach, expecting time alone to provide what they feel is lacking in them. A third group gives up, limiting their formulations to strictly biological considerations. These observations arbitrarily divide trainees into groups; most trainees evince characteristics of more than one group. Trainees in the first group take a highly intellectual approach that may not help them understand better what is affectively important to their patients. The theoretical knowledge they acquire often remains undigested, a lump in their stomachs, bits of which they may regurgitate in an attempt to fit part of a theory to what they have observed in a patient. This phenomenon is most distressing when a trainee assiduously memorizes the bare bones of several psychodynamic approaches and indiscriminately applies isolated aspects of several theories, to a patient, some of which may be difficult to reconcile with others. The resulting formulation, to change metaphors, ends up looking like the work of a modern artist who literally has thrown his paint onto the canvas. It may be a lively and stimulating production but is not coherent, organized representation of the clinician's picture of the patient.

On the other hand, a careful history of the patient's relationships is more likely to permit the clinician to appreciate what is affectively important, not only in terms of the content that the clinician elicits from the patient, but also because of the affect the patient displays when discussing important relationships. The clinician's understanding can be enhanced by considering the quality of the relationship between her and the patient as it evolves during the interview and of the affects and fantasies the clinician experiences during the interview. None of this requires clinicians to be experts on psychoanalytic theory. It does require us to observe our patient astutely, including our patient's reactions to us and the interaction between us and our patient. Having elicited an adequate history, the clinician needs a theoretical approach to organize and make sense of the data. The literature on psychodynamic formulation is growing at an accelerated pace. Much readable material is available to the trainee interested in erecting a theoretical skeleton on which to arrange the flesh of historical data (Steinberg, 1995, 1998; McWilliams, 1999; Weeraseckera, 1993).

Clinical supervisors can encourage trainees to consider what factors in the trainees themselves might interfere with their willingness and capacity to elicit more complete and detailed histories from their patients, particularly histories that outline the quality of the patient's significant relationships. Clinicians may of course ask the same question of themselves. The clinician's own capacity and willingness to tolerate painful affects associated with their own relational vicissitudes is one consideration. Cultural factors may also affect a clinician's willingness to question patients about the quality of her patient's relationships. What needs to be stressed in history-taking as a clinical *sine qua non* for psychodynamic formulation is the importance of a detailed history of interpersonal relationships in all parts of the history. Clinicians need to elicit details that paint a picture of the patient's relationships. We need to ask patients for concrete examples to illustrate the generalizations patient often make about the relationships. We need to explore the patient's superficial and often defensive descriptions of relationships, such as "My marriage is fine"; "I had a happy childhood"; or "My parents were great." One may deal with this defensiveness by acknowledging the positive aspects of the relationship in question and ask for examples: "Please give me an example of what is fine in your marriage." This approach may result in examples being given that both reassure the patient and reduce his defensiveness. It also helps the clinician in her formulation, as something is learned of protective factors. However, what a patient describes as positive in a relationship may not seem as positive to the interviewer, so something may be learned of the patient's interpersonal difficulties this way, in spite of the patient's conscious intention to describe something positive. In addition, the manner in which the patient exhibits his defensiveness to the interviewer is another possible source of information regarding the patient's interpersonal difficulties. Other possible responses include patients becoming overtly defensive, or demonstrating that they are unable to describe their relationships in detail, which leads to other conclusions, for example, regarding the presence of the syndrome of identity diffusion (Akhtar, 1992:27–42).

Patients who are unable to describe relationships in detail often leave the impression that their relationships are not as close or as positive as the patients claim they are, or even that the patient is not really even aware of what a close relationship may entail. Once the patients is allowed to describe positive aspects of the relationship in question, he may be less defensive in describing negative aspects of the relationship. The patient's defensiveness can be reduced further by the clinician indicating that negative aspects of a relationship are "normal": "There is no marriage without disagreements; what is important is how they are resolved." It is rare that a patient absolutely denies any difficulties in relationships. Exploring this denial when it does occur can lead to an assessment of what motivates this defensiveness and how this defense affects the patient in his relationships with others. The following vignettes alternately demonstrate more negative and more positive outcomes in relational anamnesis.

Vignette 1

CLINICIAN (USING QUESTIONS THAT ELICIT SHORT, POSITIVE OR YES-OR-NO ANSWERS): How long have you been married?
PATIENT: Seven years.
CLINICIAN: How many children do you have?
PATIENT: Two.
CLINICIAN: Are you happy in your marriage?
PATIENT: Yes.
CLINICIAN: Do you ever get into fights?
PATIENT: Oh, no.

One may compare the brief, superficial monosyllabic answers elicited from this line of direct questions with the responses to the following questions that

30   *Psychoanalytic Understanding*

invite the patient to paint a picture of his relationship, rather than responding to a specific point.

CLINICIAN (USING MORE OPEN-ENDED NON-DIRECTIVE QUESTIONS THAT INVITE PATIENT TO ELABORATE): Tell me something about your relationship with your wife.
PATIENT: We have our ups and downs. It's a pretty good marriage.
CLINICIAN: Can you give me an idea of some of the strengths of your marriage?
PATIENT: We love each other. We enjoy skiing together and we both are committed to our children. I don't want to give the impression that our marriage has problems. We have a very good marriage.
CLINICIAN: It's clear from what you say that your marriage is a lot of strengths. In the best of relationships, though, I think there are areas of disagreement or differences of opinion. I would be interested in what you can tell me about those, and how they are resolved.
PATIENT: Well, sometimes I think my wife is too close to her mother.
CLINICIAN: In what way?
PATIENT: She's constantly on the phone with her, and seems to want to talk with her whenever we need to make a decision.
CLINICIAN: Can you tell me more about this?
PATIENT: (Jokingly): Sometimes I feel it my wife is as much married to her mother as she is to me. For the number of times we have sex in a week, she might as will be married to her mother.

This type of questioning enables patients to be more open about their concerns in the marriage, in spite of initial defensiveness. Further questioning can clarify the extent and depth of these concerns. *Notice how a nondirective invitation to elaborate on what the patient said resulted in the patient becoming relaxed enough eventually to jokingly volunteer a comment about his and his wife's sex life, which clearly implied dissatisfaction about a significant area of the marriage, something he did not seem inclined to express up to that point. This opens the opportunity to explore to what extent he is frustrated or even angry about how he feels his wife's relationship with her mother affects their marriage. Eventually, of course, clinician and patient will need to look at what the patient feels are both his own and his wife's contributions to difficulties in the marriage, rather than attributing them to his wife's relationship with her mother. This is in contrast with the first series of questions and answers, which seed unlikely to lead to this kind of exploration and important revelation.*

The clinician's countertransference in the interview is also an important potential source of information. He may be aware of the patient's projecting self- and object-representations onto the interviewer during the progress of the interview. Signs of countertransference include idiosyncratic ways in which the clinician treats patient, the clinician experiencing feelings that are not usual to him during the course of the interview, and the clinician experiencing impulses to treat the patient in a manner not characteristic of him. For example, an overly narcissistic patient might behave in a condescending

Who Is My Patient? 31

or superior manner, and the clinician might feel angry or hurt and subsequently experience an impulse to either strike back at or defer to the patient. In this situation, the patient is likely projecting a self-representation characterized by feelings of inferiority, weakness, and helplessness onto the clinician, while identifying with an internal object characterized by feelings of superiority and power. A dependent patient may behave in an overly submissive and passive fashion. This behavior may elicit either irritation or a more sympathetic, kindly, parental reaction from the clinician, who might correspondingly experience an impulse to behave in an impatient manner or to treat the patient in a more gentle and supportive manner. Dependent patients appear to experience themselves as needy, hungry children, and may project either an impatient, unaccepting object-representation onto the clinician or the wished-for, kindly, supportive parental image. The clinician's reaction of course depends to a significant extent on his own personality structure and characteristic reactions to various types of individuals. The more aware a clinician is of his personal tendencies, the more successful he will be in separating out his contribution to the reactions to the patient. The clinician's reaction to the patient can also inform him about the patient. An overly hostile or threatening patient may inspire fear in the clinician, who might respond by becoming more timid and unassertive, perhaps even giving up the initiative in the interview. Conversely, the trainee might respond in a similarly hostile manner. In this case, the patient is likely projecting her frightened self-representation into the clinician, who either responds by attempting to project the frightened self-representation back into the patient or by accepting the projection and experiencing the patient as the threatening object-representation that the patient identified with. One may also compare the self- and object-representations one hypothesizes that are being expressed an interview with the information about early important relationships one gathers in the history. Such a comparison can contribute important material to the psychodynamic formulation.

Clinicians who are aware during the interview of what feelings and impulses patients inspire in them are in a better position not only to use this information in constructing a formulation but also in determining their conduct in the interview. The reaction of a clinician to a patient may inform them of the need for limit setting, confrontation, interpretation, clarification, or simple observation of what the clinician thinks is going on between patient and him, an inquiry as to why the patient thinks this is happening, and whether this represents a pattern for the patient in other relationships. The following vignette offers an example.

Vignette 2

CLINICIAN: What brings you to see me?
PATIENT: My family doctor sent me. I don't think I really need to be here. I don't believe in mental health care anyway. (The clinician experiences a slight sinking feeling and mild irritation with the patient who, far from

32   *Psychoanalytic Understanding*

> being an interesting person to work with, seems to him unwilling even to give a history.)
>
> CLINICIAN: As long as you have come, why don't we look at what concerns your family doctor had in referring you?
>
> PATIENT: I don't think my family doctor understands me very well either, and he isn't really in a position to know whether I need to see a mental health professional. I don't think anyone understands me.

The clinician might either experience this is an invitation to behave in a grandiose manner and respond by attempting to prove to the patient that he can in fact understand this patient. The patient is then likely to respond to the clinician by deflating him and proving him wrong. Alternatively, the clinician may use his ongoing conscious irritation with this patient to be aware that the patient may have difficulties with authority or with caretakers in general, given what the patient has said about mental health care and the family physician. He further may hypothesize that these difficulties may be related to a long-standing feeling of not being understood. In fact, the patient's reluctance to give a history makes the clinician feel that it would be difficult to understand this patient. The clinician feels pressured into accepting a projection of an object-representation of a disinterested, not understanding, rejecting parent. With this awareness, the clinician can continue to attempt to take the history, as opposed to reenacting the rejection with the patient.

> CLINICIAN: You will have to decide how much I am able to understand of your difficulties, but I would like to have an opportunity to try. Can you tell me what concerns you have about yourself?

Some Comments on Relational Psychoanalysis

The most prominent theoreticians in the history of the development of psychoanalytic thought, Freud, Klein, Winnicott and Bion, together with Bowlby, the originator of attachment theory, opened the way for the relational turn in psychoanalysis. This is a movement that is opposed to the classical notion of the analyst's position as one of anonymity, neutrality, and abstinence, which itself has been thought to be an exaggeration and distortion of Freud's original technical recommendations. It is important for the analyst not to be an individual who is known by his patient. To the extent that the patient has information about the analyst, it interferes with the development of a transference based on the patient's fantasies about the analyst, which then can be analyzed, which is an essential source of learning about the patient.

The relational movement has shown, however, that, however anonymous the analyst attempts to be, his patient inevitably discovers much about him (Renik, 1995). Much of this remains outside of the patient's conscious awareness. This is not an argument for not attempting to remain relatively anonymous to one's patients, but rather an acknowledgment that strict anonymity is neither necessary nor possible. When the patient inevitably brings up some realistic aspect of the analyst's life, or an observation she has made about the analyst, it is material the meaning of which to the

Who Is My Patient? 33

patient can then be explored. The concept of neutrality was introduced to encourage analysts to not take sides between different parts of the patient's mind. That is, for example, to neither support the gratification of instincts (the id) nor the prohibition against that (the superego). The classical view of the analyst's job is to explore the patient's intrapsychic conflicts and their origins. I think the relational movement has emphasized that analysts are "for" their patients, but that is that does not mean that they are "against" other people in the patient's lives, for example, being overtly critical of the patient's parents. The patient will provide her point of view, based on her experience of her parents, for example. This does not necessarily correspond to veridical reality, and the analyst is not obliged to agree with the patient as to what really happened. The analyst's job is to explore the meaning to the patient of what they describe as their experience. Abstinence refers to the abstaining from immediate gratifications in the analysis. Technically, that would involve not gratifying the patient with praise or information about the analyst, or being concretely helpful to the patient. Relational psychoanalysis does not propose attempting to gratify patients but recognizes that some gratifications are inevitable and not necessarily harmful. Again, the important thing would be to explore the meaning to the patient of any gratification they wish or have experienced in their relationship with the analyst.

Relational psychoanalysis recognizes the contributions of the analyst's personality to the process of the analysis, as opposed to Freud's earlier notion that the analyst can be like a surgeon or other expert, scientifically and neutrally observing the patient and making objective observations about him. Another metaphor Freud used is that the analyst can be like a reflecting mirror, mirroring back to the patient only what the patient shows him, as if the analyst's personality to some extent does not influence his perception of the patient and what he says to the patient.

Here are some significant relational/interpersonal authors. Stephen Mitchell (1988), an important founder of relational psychoanalysis, describes relational concepts already existing in psychoanalysis. Lewis Aron (1996) describes aspects of mutuality between analyst and patient. Irwin Hirsch (2008, 2015) surveys conscious countertransference enactments and the interpersonal tradition in analysis. Donnel Stern (2003, 2010) describes unformulated experience, dissociation, and enactment. Paul Wachtel (2008) describes the impact of relational theory on the practice of psychotherapy. I also will mention a multivolume series on relational psychoanalysis, which provides some of its most influential papers (Aron & Harris, 2005, 2012; Mitchell & Aron, 1999; Suchet, Harris & Aron, 2007).

Please see Chapter 15, Freud on the ward: Integration of psychoanalytic concepts in the formulation and management of hospitalized psychiatric patients, of my *Psychoanalysis in Medicine: Applying Psychoanalytic Thought in Contemporary Medical Care* (Steinberg, 2021) for more on formulation.

To conclude this section with a metaphor, the size and quality of the house the mason builds depends in part on the amount and quality of construction material. A clinician's psychodynamic formulation can be no better than the historical data the clinician elicits, particularly regarding the individual's interpersonal relationships.

In addition, I am providing a vignette of psychoanalytic psychotherapy. This book is not primarily about psychoanalysis or psychotherapy *per se,*

34   *Psychoanalytic Understanding*

but I thought readers might find it useful to "meet" me as a psychotherapist (albeit a much younger version of me) to get an idea of how I think and work and to apply the above concepts.

Snapshot of a Psychoanalytic Psychotherapy

This is a description of two sessions of psychoanalytic psychotherapy that I undertook with a patient many years ago. It illustrates the emotional pressure on the therapist inherent in psychoanalytic work, and how the difficulties the patient provides the therapist with in their relationship also are opportunities for learning for both patient and therapist, which, because of the intensity and here-and-now quality, has an emotional impact on both.

When I met my patient, Fred, he was a single man in his early thirties who complained of an unsatisfactory relationship with his girlfriend, Daisy. He said he was too easily dissatisfied and found her too demanding and unreasonable. He added that he was never happy and disliked his job in information technology involving video work. He found it hard to force himself to go to work.

Fred described critical, demanding parents who, when he lived at home, always had him do chores but offered no praise. He described his mother as very particular, strict, and snobbish. She controlled him, telling him what to wear and what to say. His mother was always concerned about how he looked, and how he would reflect on her to her relatives. Fred dressed up to keep his mother happy and still avoided saying what would embarrass her, not confiding "private" things, for example, like telling his aunt that he was unhappy in his job, or that he was seeing a psychiatrist. Fred's mother was strict about cleanliness. He resented having to wipe the tiles off after taking a shower. He felt that his bedroom was her room. His mother decorated it with a floral bedspread that he disliked. Fred described her as very controlling. He said his father had little influence and was preoccupied with his work, showing no interest in the children. His father never listened but just badgered Fred, arguing with him about doing the chores. Fred said he hated his father when he was a teenager. There was little emotional warmth from his parents, whom he described as never being satisfied with him. Fred was aware of a similarly critical attitude in himself toward Daisy and complained of her incessant demands and emotional neglect of him. In spite of the relationship being rocky, Fred had loaned Daisy several thousand dollars for her business and was afraid he would never get it back.

My impression was that Fred's problems were largely of a narcissistic nature. He appeared to have grandiose fantasies of success that were never accomplished or even attempted as he moved from one job to another. Such fantasies appeared designed to defend against an awareness of low self-esteem and a feeling of being a failure.

Because I believe it to be central, I will recapitulate some of what has been stated above. Individuals have unconscious images of themselves, called self-images, and of others, called internal objects, which affect their expectations and perceptions of themselves and others. (The term "internal object" seems clumsy to some; "object" refers to the object of one's love.) An individual's images of self and others even can affect how other people react to her. These self-images and internal objects largely are based on one's early experience with caregivers, that is, under usual circumstances, one's parents.

Who Is My Patient? 35

For example, if one has generally friendly, supportive, and interested parents, one's unconscious image of oneself and of others will generally be positive. On the other hand, individuals who were unfortunate enough to have overly critical, unsupportive, uninterested, or distracted parents are more likely to have negative images of themselves and others. Of course, the child's experience of his parents is through the eyes of a child, so the correspondence between the actual experience with the parents and the internal images of self and other is not exact.

Fred's description of his parents, especially his mother, left the impression of his likely developing quite a harsh and demanding unconscious internal image of others, that is, a harsh, critical, demanding internal object. His image of himself appeared to be of a neglected, compliant, and resentful child. One would expect him to project his image of himself and of others onto other people. As noted above, his self-image and internal objects would influence his perception of others, affect the way he relates with them, and influence the way they respond to him. Of course, this all applied to the therapist–patient relationship we were in the process of creating as well.

I saw Fred in psychoanalytic psychotherapy twice weekly for three years. Several months into the therapy, he abruptly demanded to view some videotapes that he saw in my office. When he earlier had asked about them, I indicated that they were teaching tapes that I had made. (Generally, when a patient in psychoanalytic psychotherapy asks a question like this, the therapist does not answer the question, at least not immediately, and often invites the patient to see what comes to his mind about his question. In this case, I decided to answer the question briefly and observe his response.) Fred said he wanted to see me as a teacher, and was interested in whatever I had to say, adding that he would like to see me in a different setting and know me on another level. He then said that he was interested in people's public-speaking ability.

Fred associated to a night school course in which he wanted to know the professor better. Then he said that he was not satisfied with our relationship, was hungry for friends, and was looking for approval and interest in him. He said that he didn't trust his own impressions and had to see people in other settings, for example, to prove that his professor was not such a nice guy. Such a reference to a professor could easily also represent an unconscious reference to Fred's feelings about our relationship, that is, to be a reference to the transference. I indicated that Fred superficially admired the professor, but the question of whether he might dislike the professor if he knew him better came up, so his goal wasn't just to make friends, but perhaps also to devalue the professor. Fred replied that his fantasy was that the professor was just what he thought the professor would be, and would be very interested in Fred as well, so they would become great friends. Fred said that he wanted to see the professor, to be like him, learn from him, and "it would rub off." He hoped that he would become the professor's protégé, adding that he was looking for mentors. I reminded him that there was another aspect, his devaluing the professor. Fred responded that he was looking for evidence that I was not a good therapist, for example, if I fumbled on the videotape. I pointed out that he had the fantasy that he would find a weakness in me in an area in which he was strong, and pointed out his tendency, which I had observed before, to judge people.

Fred agreed that he had a tendency to either admire or denigrate people. I pointed out that if he admires someone, he hopes to get something from him, especially interest and guidance. He said that he never had had this from his parents and couldn't admire

36 Psychoanalytic Understanding

his father. I replied that his fantasies about the professor in part involved a wish for an enthusiastic, caring father whom he could emulate and be close to, and suggested that one of the motivations for his wishing to see my tapes involved a similar wish in his relationship with me. Fred indicated that I might take a special interest in him, invite him for dinner, and get him on the right track in the world. He added that occasionally he wished that I were with him, for example, to help him with Daisy or with his business and whisper in his ear. He imagined that I would be able to advise him regarding the problems he and Daisy had with her children. He objected to Daisy's "strong-arm techniques," which he felt were futile and wanted someone to tell him how to raise her children. (Likely Fred identified with Daisy's children, and his objection to her strong-arm techniques was based on feeling that he been treated similarly by his parents.)

Fred said that information was a cure for everything. I suggested that this didn't take his feelings into account. He replied that if he were fortunate enough to have a good therapist, he would have it made. I suggested that perhaps he felt that then he would be able to stop thinking. Fred said that he felt he was in bad hands with his previous therapist and found that catharsis doesn't work. I replied that he seemed to want an authority to listen to him and to believe in, and seemed to wish to be able to stop functioning as an adult and make decisions, preferring to be cared for, to know that he could rely on someone to do it all for him. He replied that he hated his mother telling him what to do, and rebelled when people told him what to do.

At this point, I interpreted Fred's abrupt demand to view the tape as an attempt to find a substitute for a closer relationship with me, one that he could control. I thought this was an attempt to deal with his longings and feelings of being deprived in relationships, in that he could see me on tape whenever he wanted to. He didn't want to talk about these painful feelings, but rather demanded a concrete solution for them. It was also noteworthy that Fred was willing to accept the tape as a substitute, as if it were the most he could expect. I did not at this point interpret the negative feelings about me that were implied in his remarks. His wish for a tape as a substitute suggested that he felt hopeless about getting what he needed in a real relationship with me. Fred's response to this interpretation was to become sad. I pointed out that his abrupt demand and annoyance at me for persisting in trying to investigate the motivation for the demand for the tape seemed to be a defense against his sadness. Fred replied that he felt that I exposed him as a worthless shit. I asked why he would feel hopeless about having a relationship and feel like a shit for being hungry for a relationship. This may have been a very painful experience for Fred, but a necessary one, in which I think he began to experience feelings about early interactions with his parents, when he was frustrated in his attempts to develop a positive attachment with them and ended up feeling like shit. I also thought this interchange said something about the unconscious motivation for his choice of career; videotapes were a medium in which he might be able to gratify, in fantasy, his wish for a positive relationship with the image of a good parent, without the risks involved in a real relationship and in a situation that he felt he could control completely.

I felt that the abrupt demand at the start of this session likely represented a projection onto me of Fred's self-image, with me experiencing him treating me in the same demanding, critical way that his parents treated him, and with me ending up feeling

Who Is My Patient? 37

helpless and controlled in a manner similar to how he felt with his parents. I did not describe to Fred how I felt under these circumstances, but rather indicated how he treated me, how a person might be expected to respond, and how this appeared to reenact his early relationship with his parents. (Some analysts would be more disclosing to their patients of their feelings in this situation. There is no right technique; so much depends on the analyst's personality and the exact circumstances.) In later sessions, we discussed in what ways Fred similarly interacts with Daisy and how her demands might appear to defend against similar sad and helpless feelings in her, which Fred might contribute to eliciting in her as he did with me.

This is an example of the pressure patients may exert on one with a demand, and the importance of exploring the motivation for the demand, as opposed to either refusing or conforming to it. Another way of putting this is that one must remember that whatever the patient presents the therapist with is "grist for the mill," that is, legitimate material to be understood. This is difficult to remember when the iron is hot, when the therapist is made uncomfortable, either by the material or by the type of interaction in which the material is presented. One may remind oneself in a situation like this that the aim of psychoanalytic psychotherapy is not to give the patient what he requests, but rather to help him understand more about his mind and about his difficulties, including his difficulties in relationships. Physicians, especially family physicians, frequently find themselves confronted by these types of demands from their patients, for example, for the physician to fill out a disability or insurance form for a condition or limitation that the physician feels is exaggerated or not entirely legitimate. The physician's recognizing the pressure she experiences and the accompanying feelings, such as anxiety or anger, can help her to continue thinking about what she feels comfortable doing, what she thinks is the right thing to do, and what is in the patient's best interest, as opposed to being bulldozed into complying with the patient, or, alternatively, refusing in a more unsupportive manner than she would want.

Fred was gratifying to treat because, in spite of the danger of an untoward personal reaction on my part, in situations like this I was able to point out to him what I thought was happening between us in a manner that he was receptive to thinking about. I believe he learned something from this. The pejorative reference to Fred's previous therapist involved, I believe, an invitation for me to become grandiose at the latter's expense, feeling superior to him. This might enable Fred to idealize me temporarily. This reinforced my impression of Fred's narcissistic difficulties and constituted a potential trap for me. If my need to be admired were great enough, I might have accepted the invitation to be grandiose. This would result in my sharing Fred's problem, which would make it difficult for me to help him with it. As well, Fred's idealization, which would function as a defense against painful feelings about himself, would inevitably be succeeded by a devaluation of me when I failed to live up to Fred's expectations.

My temptation to enjoy the idealization can be seen as an experiencing of Fred's wish to be idealized, in addition to narcissistic vulnerabilities of my own. Perhaps, it would be more accurate to say that I briefly accepted the idealization and basked in it. That is, my experiencing ego predominated at that point and identified with and accepted Fred's projection. I was fortunately able to utilize my observing ego in this instance and formulate what was going on between us and within me, rather

38 *Psychoanalytic Understanding*

than linger in the fantasy I was sharing briefly with Fred. I believe Fred's abrupt demand defended against conscious awareness of feelings of hopelessness and sadness about relationships. He projected this painful self-image onto me, identifying with his parents' treatment of him, and pushed me off balance, inducing in me feelings of helplessness and being under attack, the same feelings I think he had to defend against in his experience with his parents. This, in my opinion, is an example of projective identification. The invitation to be grandiose, on the other hand, appears to be a projection of an idealized internal part-object onto me, associated with his fantasy of being a beloved child, his longed-for self-image. In other words, Fred had an unconscious wishful fantasy of a relationship between an idealized parent and a beloved child. This was externalized, with his attempting to feel he was the beloved child with me assuming the role of the idealized parent. Such a fantasy, transient by nature, is gratifying only as long as it lasts; the inevitable disappointment and devaluation leaves the therapeutic relationship worse off than before the idealization.

In a session three months later, Fred described arguing with Daisy, questioning her unnecessary expenses, and observing that she was not keeping her bankbook in balance. Daisy felt insulted. Fred repeatedly reminded her of her financial irresponsibility, which she tended to deny. He had lost all respect for her, adding, "When I get my money back from her …" He indicated that the relationship had died. I thought he was about to say that when he gets his money back from her, he would leave her. Fred indicated that he initially had ignored clues about what Daisy was like, especially her bad temper, her inability to accept advice, and her wish to control. He added that in these ways she was like his mother; it was a familiar relationship. Fred felt that he gave and Daisy took, but wondered if he was coming down too hard on her, with "a strong-arm technique." This sounded reminiscent of his description of Daisy's approach to her own children, about which used to confront her, calling her stupid. Fred apparently felt he had chosen someone he considered stupid and then rubbed it in. He felt he could get away with more with incompetent people; Daisy would put up with him, as she was desperate, and would accept him in spite of his feeling unlovable and unworthy. Fred said he would feel good and teach her. I suggested that as he felt so badly about himself, he attached himself to individuals whom he believed were worse off, so he would feel better by comparison. Fred said that they must have something he wants, as he has lent money both to Daisy's company and to an acquaintance, Joe, for his business, which did not seem like a wise investment either. Neither of his debtors could repay him.

Fred indicated that his mother used to rub in his face how stupid he was. He seemed to recapitulate with Daisy his mother's treatment of him, projecting how stupid he felt with his mother onto his girlfriend and Joe. In this way, he tried to feel in control of these incompetent people the way he felt his mother controlled him. From a concrete point of view, however, his debtors ultimately appeared in control, as they owed him money, so, for example, he did not feel he could leave Daisy until she repaid him. In these relationships, Fred felt he gave rather than received, similar to how he felt with his parents. I believe that Fred used these relationships in order to defend against feeling incompetent, unlovable, and worthless, as he felt in his relationship with his parents. He consoled himself with the fantasy that he was in charge of Daisy and Joe. This appeared to be his understanding of a close relationship, of being in charge.

Who Is My Patient? 39

Fred associated with a former common-law wife, Violet, whom he described as a poor lost soul. She swindled him out of $300. I suggested that he found poor, deprived people onto whom he could project his self-image, while he assumed the role of his controlling, critical mother. However, he concretely still was taken advantage of, similar to how he felt with his mother, who he said demanded but didn't give. Fred said that he was afraid to find a "together" woman who would find something wrong with him. I reinforced how much he struggled to avoid feeling worthless and unlovable. He mentioned that he expected to be alone. The solution seemed to be to fight about how incompetent Violet was, similar to his relationship with Daisy. He recalled how afraid he was to be alone the previous year, when he crawled back to Violet, as he couldn't stand the loneliness and unavailability of sexual contact, which left him with a sense of emptiness. He added how afraid he was of loneliness and of feeling guilty, which kept him with Violet, whom he described as a poor lost soul who needed him and couldn't cope with being alone. I suggested that he was projecting his image of himself onto Violet, and that in her he found a good target, someone who seemed to feel at least as needy as he.

These sessions appeared to demonstrate an unconscious motivation for Fred's choice of romantic partners. I believe he found in his girlfriends a representation of himself onto whom he could project his painful image of himself as a neglected, compliant, and resentful child and relate to each of them as his mother related to him, although in the end, he was the one who was taken advantage of concretely in both relationships, as well as with Joe. Fred appeared to use these relationships to defend against conscious awareness of his feelings about himself. However, this involved a repetition of his early experiences with his parents in his romantic relationships with a similar type of individual and with similar untoward results.

It is unusual for psychoanalysts to have the luxury of hearing how their patients' lives have progressed when treatment is over. Fred contacted me by email decades after termination of therapy, indicating that he had married, was doing fine, and had undertaken training in a more gratifying profession. He added that he was enjoying life immensely, having by then retired from his profession, was spending more time with his wife and adult children, and was avidly pursuing hobbies and interests, while remaining engaged in contract work. Of course, one is pleased to hear that one's patient is doing well, many years after treatment has ended, especially when such follow-up information is not often available.

References

Akhtar S (1992). *Broken Structures: Severe Personality Disorders and Their Treatment.* Northvale, NJ: Jason Aronson.

Aron L (1996). *A Meeting of Minds: Mutuality in Psychoanalysis.* Hillsdale, NJ and London: The Analytic Press.

Aron L & Harris A (2005). *Relational Psychoanalysis. Volume 2: Innovation and Expansion.* Hillsdale, NJ and London: The Analytic Press.

Aron L & Harris A (2012). *Relational Psychoanalysis, Volume 4: Expansion of Theory.* New York and London: Routledge.

Fleming JE & Patterson PGR (1999). The teaching of case formulation in Canada. *Canadian Journal of Psychiatry*, 38: 345–350.

40 *Psychoanalytic Understanding*

Funk & Wagnalls (1959). *Britannia World Language Dictionary*. New York: Funk and Wagnalls.

Gabbard GO (1994). *Psychodynamic Psychiatry in Clinical Practice*, DSM IV edition. Washington, DC: American Psychiatric Press.

Hirsch I (2008). *Coasting in the Countertransference: Conflicts of Self-Interest between Analyst and Patient*. New York and Hove, East Sussex: The Analytic Press.

Hirsch I (2015). *The Interpersonal Tradition: The Origins of Psychoanalytic Subjectivity*. New York and Hove, East Sussex: The Analytic Press.

Holliman, JA (1983a). What do psychiatrists understand about understand by formulation? *The Bulletin of RCP*, 7(8): 140–143.

Holliman, JA (1983b). What do the examiners understand by formulation? *The Bulletin of RCP*, 7(9): 165–166.

McWilliams N (1999). *Psychoanalytic Case Formulation*. New York: Guilford Press.

Mitchell SA (1988). *Relational Concepts in Psychoanalysis: An Integration*. Cambridge, MA and London: Harvard University Press.

Mitchell SA & Aron L (1999). *Relational Psychoanalysis: The Emergence of a Tradition*. Hillsdale, NJ and London. The Analytic Press.

Renik O (1995). The ideal of the anonymous analyst and the problem of self-disclosure. *Psychoanalytic Quarterly*, 64: 466–495.

Steinberg PI (1995). Supportive therapeutic relationship with an HIV—AIDS patient. *The Annals of the Royal College of Physicians and Surgeons of Canada*, 3(1): 23–26.

Steinberg PI (1998). Attachment and object relations in formulation and psychotherapy. *The Annals of the Royal College of Physicians and Surgeons of Canada*, 31(1): 19–22.

Steinberg PI (2021). Psychoanalytic approaches to psychosomatic medicine. In *Psychoanalysis in Medicine: Applying Psychoanalytic Thought in Contemporary Medical Care*. London and New York: Routledge.

Stern DB (2003). *Unformulated Experience: From Dissociation to Imagination in Psychoanalysis*. Hillsdale, NJ: The Analytic Press.

Stern DB (2010). *Partners in thought: Working with Unformulated Experience, Dissociation, and Enactment*. New York and Hove, East Sussex: Routledge.

Suchet M, Harris A, & Aron A (2007). *Relational Psychoanalysis Volume 3: New Voices*. Mahwah, NJ: The Analytic Press.

Wachtel PL (2008). *Relational Theory and the Practice of Psychotherapy*. New York and London: The Guilford Press.

Weeraseckera P (1993). Formulation: A multi-perspective model. *Canadian Journal of Psychiatry*, 38: 353.

3 Understanding and Management of Some More Severe Disturbances

The below quote can be considered an insightful glimpse into the content of this chapter:

> An inability to dream the emotional experience … places the personality in an intolerable emotional storm that has to be acted out and evacuated through projective identification, somatic disorders, addictions, perversions or the like. … what is often referred to as an attack on the mind's linking function is … the consequence of the mind's attempt to survive when threatened by an overwhelming emotional experience [that] the individual cannot 'dream' … these attacks on the awareness of reality are aimed at *avoiding the encounter with the overwhelming pain accompanying excessive emotionality.*
>
> (Bergstein, 2018, italics original)

In this chapter, I wish to outline a psychoanalytic understanding of and make some comments about management of some more severe disturbances, of which many health professionals are not aware. The latter are largely unaware of the possibility of treating some patient who suffer from these conditions with psychoanalysis or psychoanalytic psychotherapy. These patients include psychosomatic disturbances; patients on the autistic spectrum, as well as individuals not on the spectrum who have autistic features; severely traumatized patients; patients with psychotic conditions; addictive individuals; patients with paraphilias/sexual perversions; and patients with eating disorders. Contemporary psychoanalytic thought has made significant strides in understanding the psychological basis for or contributions to these conditions, which has led to varying degrees of success of treatment of these conditions with psychoanalytic treatments. Patients with these conditions have in common significant disturbance in early relationships, which contributes to their difficulties. Space does not permit more than a taste of psychoanalytic thinking about each of these groups of conditions, any one of which deserves a volume to do justice to it.

Advances in these approaches are to a significant extent in an area that is very difficult to work with, which is variously called the unthought known (Bollas, 1987), unrepresented states (Levine, Reed & Scarfone, 2013), and

DOI: 10.4324/9781003200581-5

42 *Psychoanalytic Understanding*

unformulated thought (Stern, 2003). Psychological traumata predisposing individuals to these conditions often occurs in a pre-verbal stage, that is, before the infant or child has words to able to think about what the trauma they have experienced. So the adverse experiences have not being repressed out of conscious awareness because they have never been able to be represented in thought. Although Freud anticipated this, the development of this concept required much work on the part of psychoanalysts over many decades. Bion's concept of the psychotic part of the personality (1957) and Winnicott's concept of the catastrophe that has already occurred (1974) are particularly influential in the development of this line of thinking.

Eshel (2019a) notes, "Wilfred R. Bion and Donald W. Winnicott have exerted a profound influence on the theory and practice of clinical psycho-analysis over the past sixty years" (p. 237), resulting in a paradigm shift in psychoanalysis. She describes Bion's

> new dimension of normal emotional communication within the patho-logical nature of Melanie Klein's conceptualization of projective iden-tification. The patient projects he is or her unbearable, split-off parts and inner experiences into the analyst's psyche, and it is crucial that the analyst—like the mother for her infant—takes in, processes, and modi-fies them, thus enabling the patient to reintroject [reinternalize] them safely. Hence, it can be said that the existence of containing ultimately depends upon what the recipient is able to bear … Successful contain-ment enables both emotional growth and development of the capacity for thinking.
>
> (p. 240)

for both infants and psychoanalytic patients.

Eshel (2019a) describes Winnicott

> moving experientially beyond the space—time confines of traditional clinical psychoanalysis to work with primal processes in the treatment situation and setting, thus reaching and correcting basic self-processes and unthinkable early break down—and enlarging the scope of psycho-analytic practice.
>
> (pp. 250–251)

Winnicott believed that the self cannot make new progress until the envir-onmental failure situation is corrected through the analytic setting and pro-cess. The deeply traumatic origins of the unthinkable, not-yet-experienced breakdown need to be relived and experienced for the first time in the present with the analyst. "The regression to dependence and early psychic processes in treatment calls forth the radical possibility of actually influen-cing and altering the patient's *past and future* [italics in original] in the pre-sent" (p. 253) by allowing the past to *be* the present.

Psychosomatic Disturbance

This is a elaboration of my earlier discussion of psychosomatic conditions (Steinberg, 2021). Aisenstein and Rappoport de Aisemberg (2010) describe four kinds of somatic symptoms: conversion hysteria symptoms, somatic symptoms of "actual neurosis," hypochondriacal symptoms, and organized organic ailments. "Conversion hysteria symptoms are memory symbols converted into the body and underlying unconscious fantasies in which sexuality plays a crucial role" (p. xv). These symptoms imply the existence of the capacity for repression as a defense; a dynamic conscious responsible for symbolization, (which itself suggests the capacity to formulate thoughts and feelings into words and then repress them); and the (Oedipal) capacity for three-person relationships, implying some awareness of other people having separate minds who are able to have relationships with each other, excluding oneself (Britton, Feldman & O'Shaugnessy, 1989). All of these are signs of relative maturity. Patients with somatic symptoms of actual neurosis, hypochondriacal symptoms, and organized organic ailments generally are not thought to have achieved this level of maturity.

Somatic symptoms of "actual neurosis" include the functional disorders of medical practice, that is, medical symptoms not associated with symptoms and signs of recognized medical disease. These symptoms generally do not have symbolic signification, as conversion symptoms do. They usually are accompanied by anxiety. The somatic symptom is viewed as being excessively invested in energy (libido) that might have been directed toward relationships with others, if that had not been thwarted, typically by traumatically adverse early experiences in relationships or by a mismatch between an infant's or child's needs and the parents' emotional resources.

Hypochondriacal symptoms are bodily complaints that are not associated with an organic lesion. They are based on energy (libido) that is not able to be directed toward relationships with others and is therefore narcissistic and directed toward the self, which has not been able to be elaborated psychically. Hypochondriacal preoccupations with parts of the body are not associated with symbolic meanings of the symptoms; preoccupation with hypochondriacal symptoms can be viewed as a displacement onto the body of concerns about the self and the integrity of the self.

Organic ailments refer to psychosomatic conditions in the narrow sense of the word. These are medical conditions whose course is predisposed, precipitated, exacerbated, or perpetuated by psychological factors that have not been formulated symbolically; that is, that the individual is not able to think about. Generally these factors arise in early childhood before the individual has learned to be able to put inner experience into words. Often they are associated with a failure on the parts of parenting figures in helping the infant child to identify inner experience and eventually put words to it, which is an important basis for the capacity to think. This relates to Bion's (1970) theory of containment.

44 *Psychoanalytic Understanding*

Bronstein (2010) suggests that one can see a symptom as a product of psychic conflict with underlying unconscious fantasies (such as a conversion symptom,) or as representing a deficiency or deficit in the patient's psychic structure and the lack of capacity to function symbolically, that is, to think abstractly, including reflecting on one's inner experience, (as in somatic symptoms of "actual neurosis," hypochondriacal symptoms, and organized organic ailments.) Bronstein describes the importance of early sensation-based contact between mother and infant, "where mother functions like the skin, provides the necessary physical containment and support to early, unintegrated aspects of the self" (p. 71). The mothers capacity to lend her "skin" to the baby can be seen as part of her role in processing the infant's unthinkable physical sensations and antecedents of emotions through what Bion (1962) called for a capacity for reverie and alpha function. This helps to give meaning to the baby's inchoate feelings and anxieties, and gradually helps the baby to develop its capacity to think. In mother–infant pairs where this type of physical contact is missing or somehow disturbed, these experiences are disrupted or aborted, with consequent interference in the development of the infant's capacity to think or symbolize. This is felt to make individuals vulnerable to psychosomatic conditions; what can't be thought of may be experienced somatically. The skin, for example, may "become both a vehicle for the expression of raw, unprocessed emotions and acquire a separate life of its own when, in phantasy, it is felt to be the recipient of the infant's projections, [the projections of raw unprocessed emotions,] the embodiment of the object [mothering figure] that the child is identified with" (2010: 72). Itching may then be both "a way of relating to this object-skin … [but] also serves the purpose of resolving the impossible primitive love/hate relationship that has not been mediated by thoughts" (2010: 72). That is, if development of the baby's capacity to think, for example, to gradually be able to identify his emotions, is impaired, his experience of them may be transferred to a part of the body, such as the skin, where they are experienced as bodily sensations, for example, itching, which eventually may represent somatic symptoms. This eventually can result in secondary physical changes based on the continuous abrasion of the skin with itching, or with physical changes of the skin as part of the skin's reaction to the unprocessed emotions being projected into it, which would represent an organic ailment, as described above .

Another group of patients whom I would have described here are patients with psychosomatic conditions, including patients who have medical conditions whose courses affected adversely by psychological disturbance, patients who have an adverse psychological reaction to illness or its management, and patients who have somatic symptoms not thought to be based on medical disease, but rather on psychiatric disturbance, such as patients with somatic symptom disorder, (somatization disorder), illness anxiety disorder (hypochondriasis), and conversion disorder. These patients have been described in my previous book, *Psychoanalysis in Medicine: Applications of Psychoanalytic Thought to Contemporary Medical Care,* to which I refer you,

Understanding and Management of Severe Disturbances   45

as nonmedical mental health professionals frequently encounter these types of patients.

Kalinich (2010) describes patients for whom "touch is a complex, conflict-laden issue," part of whose "history came to write itself on to their skins" (p. 80). One male patient, who suffered from psoriasis, never had had a long-term relationship; women got "under his skin," and he always found something wrong with them. He eventually revealed that his family were Dalits, formerly called Untouchables, from India. His mother was affectionate with his brothers, but never touched him, which he longed for. He then expressed a wish, which he dismissed, that his analyst would touch him. A female patient complained of sexual discomfort and lack of interest in sex, not enjoying being touched. She contracted shingles two days after hearing that her friend was pregnant. The shingles was interpreted by the patient as a compromise to the conflict of both her desire to be pregnant and a defence against it, terrified of what might happen if she were pregnant.

Kalinich describes Anzieu's concept of the skin ego (1995), a bridge between mind, body, world and other minds, which participates in dreams, thought, and speech, providing an imaginary screen on which psychopathology can be represented. Aspects of these patients' life narratives, otherwise split off and unavailable, found their way to the screen and then to the surface of their bodies. "The destructive, non-neurotic elements from the deeply inaccessible unconscious painted themselves on the skin" (p. 87). "Once inserted into the psychoanalytic discourse, the unspeakable could be symbolized and spoken" (p. 88), rendering the symptom unnecessary. "[I]n both patients, the appearance of disease seemed a necessary passage *en route* to psychological health. The communicative function of the skin disorder initiated the process of signification and structure building" (p. 88), that is, being able to symbolize, think about and discuss the conflict or unmet need. The male patient "lived with his family's split-off trans-generational trauma, but could not speak it" (p. 88). The female patient "unconsciously believed her skin's envelope, including the female genital pocket, to be overly porous and vulnerable to disease. Every penetration, every touch, aroused fear. Rage at the offending intruder—organism, brother, mother, father/lover— deadened her desire" (p. 88).

Sechaud (2010) describes how somatization might occur in patients who are not able to complete the work of mourning when confronted with significant loss. Part of the work of mourning includes sublimation, investing in a new object, such as work or artistic activity, a cultural object that has value socially. Somatization in the face of loss, on the other hand, is a return to the body, whose symptoms are not symbolized, unlike hysterical symptoms. The crisis of mourning can lead to a fairly benign and transitory reaction, somatic regression (transient somatic symptoms) that can occur in any sort of psychic organization, or mental disorganizations that give rise to serious illness that may lead to death. Suffering that cannot be experienced emotionally may be experienced somatically, whether or not it is accompanied by an identifiable medical condition.

46   *Psychoanalytic Understanding*

Szwec (2010) notes that it "is generally accepted that children who cannot communicate the refusal of something to someone else have to find some other way of doing so—one that involves the body" (p. 163). Szwec describes "refusals expressed with great violence by children through and by means of their own body—children do not have the psychological wherewithal to make use of negation" (p. 164). These children have symptoms including breath-holding spells, syncopal episodes following apnea, asthma attacks, and infantile anorexia nervosa. Children are from the beginning of life subjected to suppression that parents impose on their urges. This suppression is conveyed through words, facial expressions, and other channels. The child reacts with anger. When the suppression is excessive because the parents are too harsh, the restrictions based on the infant also will be excessive. These prohibitions retard motor functions, aggressiveness, language, and expression of sexuality, such as development of auto-erotic activity. The child might become over-conforming, with a deadening of mental life that can be accompanied by increased likelihood of somatic disorders. They grow up into over-conforming, over-rational people with a split-off emotional life that often is expressed in somatic symptoms. Young children who find it impossible to express their opposition through mental processes like negation may end up expressing it through somatic disorders.

Taylor (2010) provides an example of the development of psychoanalytic understanding in showing

> how some limitations of earlier psychosomatic theories have been surmounted by contemporary theory, which places a greater emphasis on the adverse impact of traumatic events on the symbolizing function of the mind, a capacity that is essential for the cognitive processing and regulation of emotions and thereby helps protect the integrity of the body.
>
> (p. 182)

Taylor describes symbolism in which somatic disease expresses symbolic meanings, such as unconscious representations of repressed sexual and aggressive wishes, that live behind the manifest symbol. With symbolism, the analyst's task is to provide the real meaning for the symbol, thereby making the symbol unnecessary, as the conflict related to the wishes becomes conscious, and no longer needs to be expressed somatically, for example, in a conversion symptom. Symbolization emphasizes the process of linking and meaning-making. With symbolization, the aim of psychoanalytic treatment is to enhance the patient's capacity for symbolization, that is, transforming emotional sense impressions into mental contents that can be used in images, dreams, thoughts and memories.

Taylor concludes that it is the capacity for symbolic functioning that enables human beings to bind or cope with the physical and mental pains that we all inevitably encounter throughout life. This capacity breaks down when adults experience massive psychic trauma. More commonly individuals

Understanding and Management of Severe Disturbances　47

experience serious traumatic events in childhood without a parent able to contain the overwhelming affects and make them bearable for the child.

> Unable to mentally represent the unbearable emotional states so that they can be a 'digested' through dreaming and thinking, the traumatic emotions are dissociated, but are prone to return by way of somatic illness. Psychoanalytic therapy of somatically ill patients requires identification and activation of dissociated emotional states so that unsymbolized trauma, with the aid of the analyst's containing and symbolizing ('alpha') functions, can be transformed the psychic structure.
>
> (p. 195)

Traumatized Patients

People who suffered early repetitive or severe trauma, including those where there was a poor fit between their sometimes great needs and sensitivities and the capacity of their early caregivers to provide for those needs, often say little to their health caregiver about their deep emotional pain. Alternately, they may be very vocal, and express their experience of pain, outrage, and dissatisfaction at every opportunity, and many of the complaints may be directed at their health caregiver. These vocal patients are often described as "borderline" by their health caregivers. Some may present with what seem to be psychosomatic symptoms, and other with overt psychiatric symptoms, including depression, severe anxiety, transient psychotic symptoms, or more subtle disturbances in their thinking. Often referral to a psychoanalyst or psychoanalytic psychotherapist can be helpful. Clinicians should approach these patients in a nonjudgmental, patient, firm manner, offering realistic reassurance only. Dealing with traumatized patients is increasingly relevant to health caregivers, especially in urban settings, who are treating increasing numbers of traumatized immigrants. As well, there is greater recognition of the traumata occurring in daily life in native-born individuals unrelated to immigration.

Ferenczi (1933/1988), in pioneering work that was decades ahead of its time, opposes Freud's abandonment of his "seduction theory"[1] of the etiology of neurosis and experiments with self-disclosure in ways that were antithetical to the (then) widely accepted principle of quite strict analyst anonymity.

Ferenczi describes analytic patients' repressed criticism directed against "professional hypocrisy." The latter consists of analysts having difficulty tolerating some features of a patient after promising to listen attentively to him. Ferenczi suggests that making the source of the analyst's disturbance fully conscious and admitting it to the patient leads to a marked easing off of his (the patient's) condition. This type of self disclosure generally was not done by psychoanalysts back then; now some judicious self-disclosure is frequently practised (Steinberg, 2017). The frank discussion about something

48 *Psychoanalytic Understanding*

left unsaid and insincere in the analyst-patient relationship freed the tongue-tied patient, enabling him to voice his criticisms of the analyst.

> The setting free of his (patient's) critical feelings, willingness on our part to admit our mistakes and the honest endeavour to avoid them in future, all these go to create in the patient a confidence in the analyst. *It is this confidence that establishes the contrast between the present and the unbearable traumatogenic past* (italics in original), the contrast which is absolutely necessary for the patient in order to enable him to re-experience the past no longer as hallucinatory reproductions but as an objective memory.
>
> (p. 200)

Ferenczi is discussing how he discovered that being more open with his patients and to his difficulties with them was helpful. This was in contrast to the authority with which the patient's parents considered themselves to be right in all of their treatment of the child, whose voice could not be heard, and therefore was repressed, or, if the trauma were too great, never represented in thought. Ferenczi realized that maintaining his authority as the "analyst who knows" repeated this trauma, whereas being more open to the patient's point of view was followed by a reduction in symptoms related to the trauma. In 1933, when this was originally published, it was revolutionary. However, Ferenczi's voice was no better heard by the psychoanalytic establishment than the traumatized children he wrote about were heard by their parents (or patients by their analysts, at times). Ironically, Ferenczi was cast into the outer darkness by the analytical establishment; his seminal contributions were only recognized decades later (Aron & Harris, 1993; Harris & Steven Kuchuck, 2015).

> We talk a good deal in analysis of regressions into the infantile, but we do not really believe to what great extent we are right; we talk a lot about the splitting of the personality, but do not seem sufficiently to appreciate the depth of these splits. If we keep up our cool, educational attitude even *vis-à-vis* an opisthotonic patient, [a patient with severe muscle spasms causing hyperextension and spasticity, with an arching of the back; although usually associated with medical conditions, it presumably represents a severe conversion disorder in this example,] we tear to shreds the last thread that connects him to us. The patient gone off into his trance is *a child indeed* who no longer reacts to intellectual explanations, only perhaps to maternal friendliness; without it he feels lonely and abandoned in his greatest need, i.e. in the same unbearable situation which at one time led to a splitting of his mind and eventually to his illness; thus it is no wonder that the patient cannot but repeat now [with the analyst] the symptom-formation exactly as he did at the time when his illness started.
>
> (p. 200)

Understanding and Management of Severe Disturbances 49

Ferenczi concludes that even children of respectable families fall victim to real violence or rape much more often than one might suppose. (As noted above, this was in opposition to Freud's conclusion decades earlier that revelations of sexual abuse were based on the child's fantasies and wishes.) Ferenczi notes that sexually abused children feel helpless and are not able to protest, not even with a thought, against the overpowering force and authority of the abusing adult. He notes that their anxiety, "*if it reaches a certain maximum, compels them to subordinate themselves like automata to the will of the aggressor, to divine each one of his desires and to gratify these: completely oblivious of themselves they identify themselves with the aggressor*" (p. 202). Ferenczi notes that through identifying with the aggressor, the latter disappears as part of the external reality and becomes intrapsychic, that is, part of the child's internal world. One deleterious consequence is that the child internalizes the adult's guilt feelings regarding the abuse. The perpetrator behaves as though nothing had happened, and often becomes over moralistic and severe with the child. Often the child's relationship with a second adult, usually the mother, is not intimate enough for the child to find help from her. Any attempt in this direction is dismissed with the complaints deemed as untrue. In consequence, "The misused child changes into a mechanical, obedient automaton or becomes defiant, but is unable to account for the reasons of his defiance. His sexual life remains undeveloped or assumes perverted forms" (p. 202). Ferenczi emphasizes that "*the weak and undeveloped personality reacts to sudden unpleasure not by defense, but by anxiety-ridden identification ... of the menacing person or aggressor*" (page 203). He adds that the mind of the abused child therefore lacks the ability to maintain itself with stability in the face of unpleasure. This makes him vulnerable to mistreatment in the future, even as an adult, including his relationship with his analyst.

I will add two more quotations from this extremely rich and prescient paper for the reader to contemplate:

> When subjected to a sexual attack, under the pressure of such traumatic urgency, the child can develop instantaneously all the emotions of a mature adult and all the potential qualities dormant in him that normally belong to marriage, maternity and fatherhood. One is justified— in contradistinction to the familiar regression—to speak of a *traumatic progression*, of a *precocious maturity*.
>
> (p. 204)

> In addition to passionate love and passionate punishment there is a third method of helplessly binding a child to an adult. This is the *terrorism of suffering*. Children have the compulsion to put to rights all disorder in the family, to burden, so to speak, their own tender shoulders with the load of all the others; of course this is not only out of pure altruism, but is in order to be able to enjoy again the lost rest and the care and

50   *Psychoanalytic Understanding*

attention accompanying it. A mother complaining of her constant miseries can create a nurse for life out of her child, i.e. a real mother substitute, neglecting the true interests of the child.

(p. 205)

Rappaport de Aisemberg (2010) describes the importance of the relationship between trauma and representation. In psychic trauma (when the traumatized individual has developed a capacity to reflect on her inner experience), there is a representation of the traumatic experience in a structuring transformation that organizes the psyche. That is, the trauma can be mentalized (represented mentally) and thought about, so there is an opportunity to recover from it and put it in the past. In pre-psychic or early trauma, (that is, before the child is capable of mentalizing the trauma and receiving needed support and containment from parenting figures), the traumatic experience has not become represented yet. There is "only a sensorial mark, a reminder that cannot become psychic structure, and that emerges with a compulsion to repetition, seeking binding or meaning." That is, the trauma cannot be thought about, leaving a tendency to repeat the trauma in an attempt to understand it and contain the unbearable feelings associated with it. A third class of trauma, "actual trauma," such as the psychic consequences of the Holocaust among survivors or their descendants, as well as experiences such as wars, social and family violence, and sexual abuse, is associated with post-traumatic alexithymia, ("no words for feelings,") and can be associated with psychosomatic disturbance as a result of these traumas: "Survival is achieved through the body. When a part of the psyche is devastated, only the soma remains as a source of life and survival" (p. 120). What has been lost is the capacity to experience emotion and to think about the trauma, and, in some individuals, some capacity to think in general.

Taylor (2010) notes that contemporary recommendations for the psychoanalytic treatment of traumatized individuals emphasize the need to bring about changes in the organization of emotional schemas. The patient must experience some aspects of the affective core of the dissociative schema in the treatment sessions. Some aspect of the original trauma inevitably re-emerges in the transference, with the potential for re-traumatization with the analyst, who is perceived as the original predator, and provoked to reenact the trauma. In the relationship with the analyst, there is an opportunity to symbolize the dissociated painful emotion by connecting somatic experiences with imagery and language in the context of a new interpersonal relationship with the analyst. Taylor (2010) notes the risk of activating the sympathetic nervous system and the hypothalamic-pituitary-adrenal axis that may aggravate a patient's somatic disorder or even be a threat to life, underlying the importance of the analyst's regulating the intensity of the emotional arousal, with the patient reflecting on the retrieved memories and the meanings the patient has given to them.

Sexual Perversions/Paraphilias

The term "paraphilia" is a diagnostic term based on a constellation of symptoms and behaviors, like other diagnostic categories. In the DSM-5 it replaced term "perversion," which is considered to be politically incorrect because of its judgmental connotations. Nevertheless, I use "perversion" according to its psychoanalytic meaning, that is, indicating an attempt to understand the unconscious motivation and developmental origins of such behavior. No pejorative or judgmental connotations are implied. Similarly, in this book the term "addiction" is not meant to imply a physiological habituation to a substance that results in withdrawal symptoms if ingestion of the substance is abruptly discontinued. "Addiction" is intended to imply the repetitive use of a substance or behavior (such as eating, gambling, promiscuous or compulsive sexual behavior, violence, watching videos/movies or playing video games, or purchasing of items) with the goal of regulating one's emotions or substituting for satisfying relationships, at the expense of more productive behaviours, which generally are subsumed under the triad of work, love and play (Steinberg, 2002).

Carveth's question, "How today may we distinguish healthy sexuality from 'perversion'?" (2010) is relevant today, in this time of increased acceptance of diversity, sexual fluidity and political correctness. For Carveth,

> [c]ontinued use of the loaded term *perversion* is justified when instead of claiming this or that behavior is unnatural or abnormal we mean it entails a deflection away from constructive towards destructive aims ... Perversion in general represents the hijacking of Eros (life, love, and truth) by Thanatos (death, hate, and lies); sexual perversion refers to any form of sexuality hijacked by obstructive aims ... exciting sexuality necessarily entails transgressive elements ... if a couple's sex life is not to descend into boredom, the puritanical superego of each must not be permitted to amplify that of the other such that sublimated forms of transgressive sexual play are inhibited. In a dialectical conception of healthy sexuality each partner simultaneously or in rapid oscillation relates to the other as both an exciting part-object to be selfishly used and a cherished whole object of love and concern.
>
> (p. 298)

Carveth notes that there is positive and negative in both Klein's paranoid-schizoid position (PS) and in her depressive position (D). He suggests that mental health necessarily involves a flexible cycling between PS and D. In this dialectical view, in addition to the extremism, literalism, part-object relations, envy, lack of awareness of the existence of another, and poor-reality testing characterized by PS, there also is passion, intensity and excitement. Similarly, in addition to the capacity for concern, whole object relations, recognition of the Other with a capacity for mourning and guilt, and enhanced

52 *Psychoanalytic Understanding*

reality testing in D, it can also give rise to an excessively dispassionate and unsexy rationality that at times can induce paralysis. Carveth concludes,

> In order to qualify as a perversion as distinct from a mutually acceptable and pleasurable type of transgressive play, the staging of the perverse drama must be excessively costly or risky in the potential physical and/ or social pain and danger to which it exposes the subjects involved. An exciting sexual drama that is mutually fulfilling and non-perverse would be one that, in contrast to the perversion, is not excessively costly or risky, while sufficiently maintaining the elements of transgression, risk, and danger that ... are essential components of sexual excitement. In other words, whereas in creative, transgressive, exciting sexuality, the dialectic between PS and D is maintained, in perversion it breaks down and paranoid-schizoid functioning predominates.
>
> (p. 303)

Regarding psychoanalytic treatment of patients with perversions, Ogden (1996) suggests that

> the analysis of perversion necessarily involves the elaboration and analysis of a perverse transference-countertransference. Both analyst and analysand contribute to and participate in the perverse transference-countertransference in which intersubjective construction is powerfully shaped by the perverse structure of the patient's unconscious internal object world. In the fragment of an analysis that is presented, [Ogden] illustrate[s] the way in which the analyst makes use of his experience in (of) the transference-countertransference in gaining understanding of the perverse scenario that the patient is utilizing as a form of psychic organization, defense, communication, and object relatedness. [Ogden] discuss[es] the analyst's use of his own unobtrusive, mundane thoughts, feelings, fantasies, ruminations, sensations, and so on, in the service of understanding the perverse transference-countertransference, which understanding is utilized in the formulation of transference interpretations. The perversity of the transference-countertransference is viewed as deriving from the patient's defensive use of particular forms of sexualization as a way of protecting himself or herself against the experience of psychological deadness. Compulsive erotization is understood as representing a method of creating an illusory sense of vitality. The subversion of the recognition of the experience of psychological deadness is achieved in part through compulsively enlisting others in the enactment of exciting, erotized, and often dangerous substitutes for the experience of being alive.
>
> (p. 1121)

Ogden (1996) summarizes his understanding of the unconscious basis for perversions:

Understanding and Management of Severe Disturbances 53

1 In healthy development a sense of oneself as alive is equated with a generative loving parental intercourse. Out of this intercourse comes a feeling of aliveness from which the patient derives a sense of the vitality and realness of his or her own thoughts, feelings, sensations, subjectivity, object relations and so on.

2 Perversion of the type being discussed represents an endless, futile effort to extract life from a primal scene that is experienced as dead.

3 Perversion of this sort involves a form of excitement derived from the cynical subversion of the (purported) truth of the aliveness of the parental intercourse which source of vitality is felt to be inaccessible and probably nonexistent. In other words, the seemingly generative, loving parental intercourse is felt to be a lie, a hoax. These perverse individuals introject [that is, internalize] a fantasied degraded intercourse and subsequently engage others in a compulsively repeated acting out of this set of internal object relationships.

4 In this form of perversion, a vicious cycle is generated in which the fantasied intercourse of the parents is depicted as loveless, lifeless, and nonprocreative; the patient attempts in vain to infuse it with pseudoexcitement from which he or she attempts to extract life (or more accurately, attempts to create a substitute for life). Since the fantasied parental intercourse from which the perverse patient is attempting to extract life is experienced as dead, he or she is attempting to extract life from death, truth from falsehood. Alternatively, the patient may attempt to use the lie as a substitute for truth/life.

5 An important method of attempting to infuse the empty primal scene with life (excitement and other substitutes for feelings of aliveness) is the experience of "flirting with danger," tempting fate by "flying too close to the flame."

6 The desire of these perverse individuals is co-opted by and confused with the desire of others leading them more deeply into defensive misrecognitions and misnamings of their experience in order to create the illusion of self-generated desire.

7 Analysis of perversion … fundamentally involves recognizing (naming accurately) the lie-lifelessness that constitutes the core of the transference-countertransference enactment of the perversion. In this way, the patient, perhaps for the first time in his or her life, feels engaged in a discourse that is experienced as alive and real.

8 The initial feelings of aliveness and realness in the analysis arise from the recognition of the lifelessness/lie of the transference-countertransference and consequently are most often frightening feelings of deadness. This experience is different from the deadness of the lifelessness/lie that had not been recognized as a lie and which had been masquerading as truth. Formerly, the lie (the empty intercourse) had to be infused with false/perverse excitement in an effort to bring life to it and acquire life from it. The recognition of the lie is not an experience of sexual excitement but makes possible a state of mind in which sexual aliveness (in the

54 *Psychoanalytic Understanding*

context of whole object relations) [, that is, relationships between individuals in the world, as well as between internal objects, that recognize each other as subjects with their own experience, and are capable of feeling guilt when they hurt someone else,] and generative thinking and discourse might be experienced (1996, pp. 1143–1144).

Eshel (2019b) notes that, "besides castration anxiety is, sexual deviations are desperate attempts to master anxieties of a much earlier phase, when separation from the mother arouses the terror of bodily disintegration, annihilation, and a sense of inner death" (p. 150). She believes that "at the root of severe forms of perversion lie primary desperate attempts in early childhood to overcome the intrusion of brutal situations, of unbearable psychic or psycho-physical violence and abuse, which could be neither endured nor escaped. In such situations of traumatic destructiveness, the infant–child has to split, dissociate, and remove from within itself the sensations of violence, pain, dread, and annihilation, since the significant other, on whom it *depends* introduces terror or reacts to him within indifferent, sadistic, imperviousness rather than providing protection, holding, containment and belief in the possibility of repairing these violent situations" (p. 156). Eshel employs the metaphor of autotomy, referring to living creatures that divide themselves in times of great danger into two parts, one that is left behind to be devoured by the predator, and another that escapes and survives, like a gecko releasing its tail. Eshel concludes that the above child's solution involves "massive dissociative splitting into two disconnected parts, alien to each other, as a means of psychic survival. One part—the second self that escaped—continues functioning in the world, surviving by inertia, emotionally impaired, lacking and dull, lifeless, and alienated from the inner core of its experiences … At times materialistic success or intellectual functioning somewhat compensates for the splitting and the dissociation from the emotional parts that were left behind to be devoured … The other part—the one self that was offered to be devoured—is stuck in that devouring state, suicidally attracted to whatever wounds and preys, to whatever embodies and actualizes … the dark violence, the devastation, devourment, sadism and imperviousness—within the psyche and in self-other relations" (p. 156). So Eshel regards perversion "*as a defense organization—through splitting, externalization, and compulsive sexualization—against a violent, devastating, unbearable, deadening early past situation* … the 'disavowal of annihilating destruction'" (italics original) (p. 158). Eshel believes that in psychoanalytic treatment in general, including that of the patient with a perversion, "if sufficient time is given to presencing and analyst-patient interconnectedness and impact, *the psychic structure of the patient is influenced and changes … within the abiding, deep, and sustaining connection with the analyst's psyche*" (italics original) (p. 175).

Autistic Disturbance

Autism generally is recognized by physicians and psychiatrists as a disturbance of brain function based on brain disease, with a genetic predisposition. I believe the considerable psychoanalytic literature on autism and autistic disturbance is not well known by mental health professionals or physicians. Psychoanalytic treatment of autistic children (Bick, 1968; Meltzer et al., 1975) and Tustin (1981) has led to recognition of autistic aspects of adult patients of various degrees of psychiatric disturbance, similar to the recognition of psychotic aspects of personality in (all) individuals who do not suffer from florid psychotic conditions (Bion, 1957). This has led to psychoanalytic treatment approaches for these adults (Tustin, 1986).

Of course it is accepted that there may be a biological (hereditary or acquired) contribution, whether partial or complete, for the symptoms of individuals with conditions on the autistic spectrum. It is less well known that psychoanalytic researchers have explored psychological and environmental factors that can contribute to autistic symptoms or characteristics even in patients who are not considered to have conditions on the autistic spectrum. To put this another way, every one of us has the capacity to function at an autistic level to some extent. Some do so as a major way of experiencing and interacting with (or, rather, avoiding experiencing and interacting with) the world. Others may do so under stress, and yet others may do so in a restricted sense as part of their "normal" functioning. Autistic symptoms or behavior can be seen not only as signs of pathology, but also as a necessary adaptation to early unbearable experience.

Mitrani (1992) describes patients who experience numbness resulting from the use of "autistic" protections, which involve insulating themselves from their own internal experiences, as well as from the potential healing effects of contact with their analyst, as well as from other relationships. She describes their desperate appeals for therapeutic help in finding an escape from their autistic tomb, the numbness that incarcerates them. Mitrani (2011) describes the analysis of neurotic, borderline and psychotic patients, emphasizing the survival function of autistic mechanisms. These patients, in whom early uncontainable experience have been silently encapsulated, use secretive auto-sensual maneuvers in order to maintain an experience of separate existence in the world. This often involves contact with "autistic shapes," things that are soft and malleable, and experienced as soothing and comforting, and "autistic objects," firm things that give a sense of boundary between the self and the world, described further below. Reassuring autistic mechanisms may also involve a relationship with a part of the world that remains static, such as a routine that is frequently or continuously repeated, as opposed to the unpredictable and ever-changing experiences one has with other individuals, from which patients with autistic features protect themselves. These patients' self-encapsulations may constitute obstacles to emotional and intellectual development, which impair both interpersonal relationships and vocational

56 *Psychoanalytic Understanding*

prospects for these patients. Mitrani demonstrates ways to detect and to modify these mechanisms in a transference-centered analysis.

Ogden (1989) proposes an "autistic-contiguous mode" to conceptualize the most primitive psychological organization. It is a sensory-dominated, pre-symbolic mode of generating experience that provides an experience of the boundedness of human experience and the beginnings of a sense of the place where one's experience occurs. Anxiety in this mode consists of an unspeakable terror of the dissolution of boundedness resulting in feelings of leaking, falling or dissolving into endless, shapeless space. Ogden believes that pathological forms of autism involve hypertrophied versions of the types of defense, form of attribution of meaning to experience, and mode of object relatedness (way of relating to other individuals) characterizing the autistic-contiguous mode. The term "contiguous" refers to the experience of surfaces touching one another, which is a principal medium through which connections are made and psychological organization achieved in this psychological mode.

Ogden (1989) describes two types of experience with objects that constitute important means of ordering and defining experience in the autistic-contiguous mode, which are enlisted in the construction of psychological defense. "Autistic shapes" are "felt shapes" arising from the experience of soft touching of surfaces that makes a sensory impression, for example, if we experience the chair we sit on only in terms of the sensation it makes on our buttocks, with the awareness that it is a chair. For the infant, the objects generating shapes in an autistic-contiguous mode include the soft parts of his own body and the body of the mother, as well as soft bodily substances (including saliva, urine and faeces). Experiences of shape in an autistic-contiguous mode contribute to the sense of cohesion of self and also the experience of perception of what is becoming the infant's experience of something other than himself. Later in development, words like "comfort," "soothing," "safety," "connectedness," "holding," "cuddling," and "gentleness" will be attached to the experience of shapes in an autistic-contiguous mode. By contrast, an "autistic object" is the experience of a hard, angular sensory surface created when an object is pressed hard against the infant's skin. In this form of experience, the individual experiences his surface as armor protecting him against unidentifiable dangers. An autistic object is a safety-generating sensory impression of edgedness that defines, delineates and protects one's otherwise exposed and vulnerable surface shell. Eventually, when the infant develops the capacity for language, words like "armour," "shell," "crust," "danger," "attack," "separateness," "otherness," "invasion," "rigidity," "impenetrability," "repulsion," are attached to the quality of sensory impressions created by autistic objects.

Ogden (1989) suggests that autistic-contiguous anxiety involves the experience of impending disintegration of one's sensory surface or one's rhythm of safety, resulting in the feeling of leaking, dissolving, disappearing or falling into shapeless unbounded space. Manifestations of this type of anxiety include terrifying feelings that one is rotting; the sensation that one's

Understanding and Management of Severe Disturbances 57

sphincters and other means of containing bodily contents are failing and one's saliva, tears, urine, feces, blood, or menstrual fluids are leaking; fear that one is failing, for example, anxiety connected with falling asleep for fear that one will fall into endless, shapeless space. Patients experiencing this form of insomnia may try to relieve this anxiety (their fear of 'falling asleep') by tightly wrapping themselves in blankets and pillows, keeping bright lights on in their bedroom or playing familiar music or soothing podcasts all night. Unconscious mental mechanisms of defense generated characteristic of an autistic–contiguous mode are directed at the re-establishment of continuity of the bounded sensory surface and ordered rhythmicity upon which the early integrity of self rests. During an analytic hour, patients from the most regressed to the most intact may need to reestablish a sensory 'floor' of experience by means of repetitive activities like hair twirling, foot tapping, stroking of the lips, cheek, or ear lobe, humming, intoning, picturing or repeating series of numbers, focusing on symmetrical geometric shapes on the ceiling or wall or using a finger to trace shapes on the wall next to the couch. Such activities can be thought of as self-soothing uses of autistic shapes. Between analytic hours, patients commonly attempt to maintain or re-establish a failing sense of bodily cohesion by means of rhythmic muscular activities including long periods of bicycle riding, jogging, lap swimming, etc.; eating and purging rituals; rocking (sometimes in a rocking chair); head banging (often against a pillow); riding buses and subways or driving a car for hours; maintaining a system of numbers or geometric shapes in one's head or in computer programs that are continually being worked on (i.e. 'perfected'), etc. The absolute regularity of these activities is so essential to the process of allaying anxiety that the individual cannot/will not allow any other activity to take precedence over them.

Psychosis and Allied Conditions

Although Freud did not believe that psychotic conditions could be treated with psychoanalysis, feeling that they were so withdrawn from the world that they could not develop a transference with a therapist, it was subsequently shown that psychotic patients in fact developed very intense transferences. Similarly, the rapid and intense transference experiences therapists can have with borderline patients is well recognized. Attempts to treat patients with schizophrenia and other psychotic conditions with psychoanalysis have been made during most of its history, with increased interest beginning in the 1950s. In the United States, Harry Stack Sullivan (1962) and Harold Searles (1965) were important pioneers in this work, while in the United Kingdom, followers of Melanie Klein, including Hanna Segal (1950), Wilfred Bion (1967), and Herbert Rosenfeld (1987) were prominent, as well as Donald Winnicott (1972). As noted above, one of Bion's important contributions (1957) was in identifying the existence of psychotic aspects of everyone's personality. None of this is to suggest that schizophrenia can be cured with psychoanalysis, but rather that some patients with psychotic conditions,

58 *Psychoanalytic Understanding*

including some schizophrenics, can benefit significantly from psychoanalysis and psychodynamic psychotherapy. Little (1990) has written an account of the analysis of her psychosis. Bollas (2013) describes an intensive psychoanalytic approach to preventing psychotic breakdown when it is imminent.

Steinman (2009) summarizes the history of psychotherapy with schizophrenia and delusional states, and refers to some empirical studies. He describes successful psychoanalytically oriented treatments of patients with delusional or schizophrenic disorders, and provides descriptions of the psychotherapy of delusional states, causes of the delusional orientation and psychotherapeutic techniques and stages in the psychotherapy of delusional states. Steinman notes that while many schizophrenic or delusional patients respond to antipsychotic medication, full or partial hospitalization, and reality-oriented supportive psychotherapy, some do not benefit from this approach and may go through a revolving door of psychiatric hospitalization, drug treatment, day hospital and halfway houses. He finds that a number of allegedly "untreatable" patients diagnosed with schizophrenia, delusional disorder and multiple personality disorder respond to an in- depth exploratory psychodynamic psychotherapy. I would add that some analysts and therapists appear to be especially well-suited to treating the most severely disturbed patients, while other clinicians, not as confident with this group, tend not to treat them. Having said that, there is no question that the level of severity of psychopathology that analysts are able to treat successfully has increased over the decades. As well, our patients are not neatly divided into "less disturbed" and "more disturbed" categories; naturally, there is a spectrum of severity on which every patient finds herself. In addition, as Bion (1957) described, all individuals have a psychotic side of their personality, which may come to the forefront under stress, including the stress of treatment.

Ogden (1980) describes the psychotherapy of a schizophrenic man, viewing schizophrenia "as a form of psychopathology characterized by an intense conflict between wishes to maintain a psychological state in which meaning can exist, and wishes to destroy all meaning and thought as well as the capacities to create experience and to think," with "an enactment of the latter set of wishes in the form of an actual attack on these capacities" (pp. 529–530). Ogden believes "[s]chizophrenic conflict differs from neurotic conflict in that the latter involves tension between coexisting sets of meanings that are felt to be incompatible, while the former involves a conflict between meaning and [an]attack on meaning. In schizophrenia, defensive efforts to deal with meaning can become exhausted and when this occurs, the sphere of conflict shifts from the sphere of psychological representations and meanings to the sphere of the person's capacities for generating such meanings" (p. 530). Ogden describes

> [f]our stages, or types of attempted resolution of the schizophrenic conflict … the stage of non-experience, the stage of projective identification, the stage of psychotic experience, and the stage of symbolic thought. In each stage a different equilibrium is reached between wishes to allow

Understanding and Management of Severe Disturbances 59

meaning and thoughts to exist and wishes to destroy all meaning. In addition, each stage is characterized by a specific form of enactment *beyond the psychological representational sphere,* (italics original) by which the schizophrenic unconsciously limits his own capacity to perceive, experience and think.

(p. 530)

Eating Disorders

Bruch (1980) notes that serious developmental defects underlie anorexia nervosa It generally becomes manifest at a time of developmental crisis, usually when an adolescent girl is confronted with the task of becoming self-reliant and independent, and of growing beyond the immediate family. "The severe cachexia and cessation of sexual functioning have been interpreted as expressing fear of adulthood and its responsibilities, specifically fear of sexual involvement" (p. 169). These fears can be recognized in most or all anorexics, but are the result of early developmental deficits, not the psychodynamic explanation of the illness. What prevents these youngsters from meeting the challenges of adolescence and adulthood, making them withdraw to their own bodies and choose a road of self-starvation in their search for selfhood and personal agency? Bruch suggests that

> the very features that are glowingly described as evidence of superior behavior are indications of serious mal-development. The illness is an effort at declaring independence, a desperate fight against feeling enslaved, not permitted or competent to lead a life of one's own. This effort, instead of solving the underlying problem, only reinforces the difficulties. Changing the body size cannot correct the deficits in overall development or provide the longed-for independence. Hunger itself has a dramatic effect on physiological and psychological functioning. The somatic consequences of starvation are well-known: they represent what are called the classical symptoms of anorexia nervosa. Much of what has been described as "anorectic behavior" closely resembles what goes on in ordinary starving people. Anorexics are reluctant to talk about this and will describe the suffering during the hunger phase only when they are far along in therapy. The enormous psychological effects of hunger have often been confused with the underlying psychological problems.
>
> (pp. 169–170)

Bruch (1969), working with patients with anorexia nervosa and developmental obesity, notes that hunger refers to the physiologic state of severe food deprivation, starvation, or to widespread famine; denotes a psychological experience, the complex, unpleasant, and compelling sensation an individual feels when deprived of food, which results in searching or fighting for food to relieve the torment; and as a metaphor of a state of need in general. She believes that hunger awareness is not innate biological

60 *Psychoanalytic Understanding*

wisdom; learning is required for this biological need to become organized into recognizable patterns. Bruch describes many unconscious and symbolic meanings of food, both in voracious uncontrolled intake and rigid refusal to eat, including, an insatiable desire for unobtainable love; the expression of rage and hatred; a substitute for sexual gratification or indication of ascetic denial; the wish to be a man and possess a penis; the wish to be pregnant, or the fear of it. "Food may help one achieve a sense of spurious power and self-aggrandizement, or serve as a defense against adulthood and responsibility. Preoccupation with food may appear as helpless dependent clinging to parents, or as a hostile rejection of them" (pp. 130–131). Bruch observed that these patients suffered from

> an overriding all-pervasive sense of ineffectiveness, of not being in control of their body and its functions, of mistrusting as a pretense or fraudulent any thought and feeling originating within themselves. They were equally uncertain and confused in their understanding of the behavior of others.
>
> (p.131)

Bruch (1978) describes the anorexic patient using her body for the exercise of control in the process of attempting to establish her own sense of self and identity. Loss of weight and pursuit of thinness is connected with feelings of control and power. The hunger may even be intoxicating. The family background of many of these children involve parents who provide considerable material and cultural benefits to their daughters. However these benefits are experienced as involving excessive implicit demands. These parents highly value achievement in their child, and perceive her as ideal before the onset of the eating disorder. Bruch believes these parents use their child unconsciously to fulfil their own aspirations, that is, use the child narcissistically to gratify themselves, rather than fostering the child's age-appropriate healthy development, including gradual separation from the parents. This makes the child's difficulty developing a sense of individual identity and personal agency understandable. The child may not experience her parents seeing her as a separate individual with her own wishes, preferences and goals. The experience of the child as ideal may represent the child's unwavering conformity to the parents' expectations at the expense of her separate development, until a war of independence is declared, with the final battleground being the child's body. I recall an anorexic patient I treated at the very start of my training, whose family dog's name was an amalgam of her and her parents' names, a concrete representation of the merging and lack of separation and individuation in that family.

Bruch's work

> changed from trying to understand the *why*, the unconscious symbolic motivation of the disturbed eating patterns, to *how* it had been possible for a body function as essential and basic as food intake to be

Understanding and Management of Severe Disturbances   61

transformed in such a way that it could be misused so extensively in the service of non-nutritional needs.

(1969, p. 132)

She discovered that hunger, the recognition of nutritional needs, was not innate but contained important elements of learning:

> something had gone wrong in the experiential and interpersonal processes surrounding the satisfaction of nutritional and other bodily needs, and ... there had been incorrect and confusing early learning which resulted in an inability to recognize hunger and to differentiate "hunger"—*the urge to eat*—from signals of bodily discomfort that had nothing to do with food deprivation, and from emotional tension aroused by a very great variety of conflicts and problems.

(p. 132)

She notes that obese patients are even more inaccurate in recognizing satiety, and that the old charge of obese people having no will power described an important deficit in their functioning related to their not being clearly aware of bodily sensations; one cannot exercise control over a function or need that is not recognized. Bruch concluded that effective treatment required clarifying the underlying conflict situations (as is in traditional psychoanalysis) and helping patients learn to discriminate between nutritional need and other bodily sensations and emotional states, so they acquire the tools necessary for orienting themselves about their own "self," their body and competence, for differentiating themselves from others, and for growing beyond their helpless, submissive passivity or uncritical negativism.

Kadish (2013) describes autistoid encapsulation in anorexia, referring to psychogenic autistic-like defenses, distinct from autism proper, thought to develop in early infancy as a result of a disruption to the earliest mother–infant dyad. "Encapsulation" describes adult patients who maintain a split off encystment or enclave within their psychic structure. All types of encapsulation are considered as the consequence of overwhelming trauma, They develop to ward off anxiety of annihilation. Kadish also describes "secondary-adjunctive" encapsulations in individuals who experience trauma developmentally later, who were relatively psychologically healthy before the trauma was experienced. By "secondary," Kadish implies an ego capable of secondary process (reality-oriented) operations. "Adjunctive" implies that "the encapsulation occurs after the ego has developed, and so is adjunct to psychic structure—like a cyst in healthier flesh" (p. 67). Autistoid and secondary-adjunctive encapsulations are distinguishable. The individual suffering later trauma has developed symbolic mental function prior to it, has a more sophisticated, robust mind, and so is better able to symbolize (and therefore to think about and be more aware of feelings about) the traumatic experience, and with appropriate psychotherapy or psychoanalysis to free herself of the anorexic symptoms. Autistoid anorexics, however, suffering trauma

62 Psychoanalytic Understanding

when mental structure is relatively unformed and symbolic function is not well established, suffer a compromised psychic structure very early on. The secondary-adjunctive anorexic is developmentally relatively healthy before the trauma. In both situations, the unsymbolized contents of the encapsulation must be in some way mentalized, that is, symbolized and mentally processed. The distinction between these two types of encapsulation helps explain differential outcomes in psychotherapeutic treatment of anorexic patients. Recognition of the autistoid patients, who are more severely traumatized because the trauma occurred developmentally earlier, helps in providing them with appropriate psychological treatment, and sometimes in making a realistic prognostications about outcome.

Kadish (2011) suggests that

> anorexia may be understood to be a particular kind of autistoid psychic retreat, a defensive withdrawal to a primitive enclosed part of the self that has been damaged by early infantile trauma, the result of a disruption to the mother-infant pair. This damage can be envisaged as an enclosed "cyst" or "tumour," defensively "sectioned off" from the rest of the individual's psychic life. When a patient takes refuge in an autistoid psychic retreat, she is typically experienced as emotionally cut off by others, including her therapist, thereby making it difficult to establish and maintain a "living" therapeutic alliance. The resulting countertransference, which is a crucial diagnostic tool for establishing the existence of an autistoid retreat, simultaneously challenges the therapist with a range of unsettling feelings that require processing in order to access the anorexic's inner world.
>
> (p.19)

Kadish describes two distinct phases in the psychodynamic psychotherapy of such a patient, with the second phase suggesting emergence from the autistoid retreat. Kadish's ideas about autistoid encapsulation and autistoid retreat appear related to Meltzer's concept of the claustrum (1990) and Steiner's concept of psychic retreats (1993, 2011).

Wooldridge (2018) has edited a psychoanalytically oriented text on eating disorders that deals with welcoming ignored, unspoken and neglected concerns; invisibility and insubstantiality in an anorexic adolescent; primary interactions and eating disorders; narcissism in anorexia nervosa; the dead third in the treatment of anorexia nervosa; eating disorders in the dissociated self; linking psychic and somatic experience in eating disorders; targeting emotional regulation deficits in eating disorders through defense analysis; impaired mentalization and attachment; hyperdeadness and hyperawareness with eating disordered patients; the psychodynamic importance of "cyber" and "in the flesh" friends in psychotherapy with eating disorders; psychoanalytic exploration of pro-anorexia Internet forums; how social and psychological realities converge into an embodied epidemic; and enduring perfectionism.

Addictive Behaviour

Krystal (1978) found a severe disturbance in affective forms and function in drug-dependent individuals. They experienced emotions in vague, undifferentiated somatic form, that is, they experienced sensations, not feelings. They could not put their emotions into words, and so could not use them as signals to themselves. Most of these patients could not articulate feelings. Many affects were expressed as somatic complaints . Krystal concluded that one could prepare some substance-dependent individuals for psychoanalytic psychotherapy with a preliminary stage of the treatment focussing on the patient's affective functions.

Krystal notes, "the interaction between mother and child in the sphere of early affective function vitally affects two areas:

1   Appropriate responses on the part of the mother favor the normal development of affects in the direction of their desomatization and differentiation. [That is, under the mother's influence, infants gradually begin to experience feelings rather than physical sensations and to be able to differentiate different types of feelings from each other. I have referred to this "influence" elsewhere in the book as "maternal reverie."] They [mother's appropriate responses] also promote the progressive development of differentiated affective responses, modulated in their intensity with increasing vocalization, verbalization, and symbolization. This also involves the development of reflective self awareness, and the use of symbols and fantasy for progressive intrapsychic structure formation.
2   The continuation of the symbiotic [mother–infant]relationship without traumatic disruption promotes the attribution of self caring and affective functions to the self representation. With it comes a sense of security and permissibility of striving to attain gratification and comfort." (p. 242).

It follows that disturbances in this process can produce the two problems which we have identified in drug-dependent and psychosomatic patients: (1) an arrest or regression in the disturbance of affect ... termed "alexithymia," [no feelings for words] and (2) an inhibition in the ability to exercise self-caring functions.

"Both of these problems represent a serious handicap in regard to the patient's ability to utilize psychoanalytic psychotherapy. In regard to the inhibition in self-caring functions, we have to deal with the fantasies that underlie the distortions in self and object representations. It follows that *the goal of therapy is not to supply to the patients their missing functions or psychic structures, but to enable them to exercise functions blocked by inhibitions.* In the process of therapy one has to work through the transferences ... in order to enable the patient to renounce his childhood theory of the world and of himself" (pp. 242–243). The theory referred to is

The idea that ... [patients with addictions] suffer from a deficiency disease [having not adequately internalized self-caring and self-soothing

64 *Psychoanalytic Understanding*

functions from mother], and that the analyst must supply to them the loving care of which they were cheated is often and despairingly proclaimed by these patients.

(p. 237)

Waska (2006) describes psychoanalytic patients with addictions, whether to alcohol, gambling, drugs, sex, procrastination or other behaviours, being engaged in some form of repetitive, destructive behavior that is an externalization or projection of their internal struggles. In treating these patients, he finds the transference often colored by acting-out, sadomasochistic dynamics, projective identification, and phantasies of persecution and loss. He found that difficulties in affect tolerance, object substitution, narcissistic rage, and compromise solutions around issues of powerlessness in the analytic work, as well as a depressive element combined with if not overshadowed by paranoid dynamics. Waska describes "phantasies of an [internal] object that is both injured, weak, and needing care as well as disappointing, intimidating, withholding, and aggressive" (p. 59). Parents of addicts are described as prone to fluctuating moods, and being needy, demanding, volatile and controlling. The addict finds a rigid method of dealing with (external) objects characterized by "approach-retreat cycles, passive-aggressive standoffs, retaliation strategies, and a desire to control others through a pattern of strict anti-growth and anti-change ways of relating" (p. 59).

Waska (2006) observes,

With exploration, deeper psychological issues are revealed that fuel the destructive behavior. Patient, consistent interpretation of the internal phantasies, feelings, and defenses that produce these addictions and interpersonal drama provides relief from paranoid and depressive anxieties. This leads to a better understanding of the addiction and a start to eliminating it.

(pp. 60–61)

Waska concludes that analytic understanding and the support of ongoing transference interpretation make growth and change become possible in these patients. The addictions demand a level of perseverance that patient and analyst cannot always bear, but if the psychoanalytic method is utilized, the basis for the destructive, addictive cycle is better understood, and chances of change are more favorable. Psychoanalysis provides the patient hope, support, and a strong opportunity for a shift in the addictive process, not only in its symptoms but also in the underlying psychological basis of the problem. These are complex cases that may fail or only show partial resolution.

Please also see my *Psychoanalysis in Medicine: Applying Psychoanalytic Thought in Contemporary Medical Care* (Steinberg, 2021), pages 144–147, for more on psychoanalytic analytic approaches to trauma and psychosis. See pages 67–69 and 160–162 for more on the development of disturbances in thinking, Chapter 7, Psychoanalytic approaches to psychosomatic medicine, for more

Understanding and Management of Severe Disturbances   65

on psychoanalytic approaches to psychosomatic conditions, and Chapter 4, "My patient is psychotic": Dealing with a patient with a paranoid delusion about her disease, for more on psychoanalytic approaches to psychosis.

Note

1 Freud originally believed the claims of his neurotic patients that they were sexually molested as children, usually by adults familiar to them. His self-analysis and the ubiquity of his patient's complaints convinced him that this was not universally the case. ("I no longer believe in my *neurotica*" [Freud, 1887–1905/1985, p. 264]). Freud concluded that many of these claims were based on childhood fantasies and unconscious wishes. While this may have been true to some extent, it dismissed the inevitable truth that some of these children in fact had been molested, delaying psychoanalytic investigation of trauma for decades.

References

Aisenstein M & Rappoport de Aisemberg E (eds) (2010). *Psychosomatics Today: A Psychoanalytic Perspective*. Abingdon, Oxon. and New York: Routledge.
Anzieu D (1995). *The Skin Ego: A Psychoanalytic Approach to the Self*. New Haven and London: Yale University Press.
Aron L & Harris A (1993). *The Legacy of Sandor Ferenczi*. London: Routledge.
Bergstein A (2018). The psychotic part of the personality: Bion's expeditions into unmapped mental life. *Journal of the American Psychoanalytic Association*, 66(2): 193–220.
Bick E (1968). The experience of the skin early object-relations. *International Journal of Psychoanalysis*, 49: 484–486.
Bion WR (1957). Differentiation of the psychotic from the non-psychotic Personalities. *International Journal of Psycho-Analysis*, 38: 266–275.
Bion WR (1962). *Learning from Experience*. London: Tavistock.
Bion WR (1967). *Second Thoughts*. London: William Heinemann
Bion WR (1970). *Attention and Interpretation*. London: Tavistock.
Bollas C (1987). *The Shadow of the Object: Psychoanalysis of the Unthought Known*. New York: Columbia University Press.
Bollas C (2013). *Catch Them Before They Fall: The Psychoanalysis of Breakdown*. London and New York: Routledge.
Britton R, Feldman M, & O'Shaugnessy E (1989). *The Oedipus Complex Today: Clinical Implications*. London: Karnac.
Bronstein C (2010). Psychosomatics: The role of unconscious fantasy. In Aisenstein M & Rappoport de Aisemberg (eds). *Psychosomatics Today: A Psychoanalytic Perspective*. Abingdon, Oxon. and New York: Routledge.
Bruch H (1969). Obesity and orality. *Contemporary Psychoanalysis*, 5(2): 129–143.
Bruch H (1978). *The Golden Cage: The Enigma of Anorexia Nervosa*. Cambridge, MA: Harvard University Press.
Bruch H (1980). Preconditions for the development of anorexia nervosa. *American Journal of Psychoanalysis*, 40(2): 169–172.
Carveth D (2010). How today may we distinguish healthy sexuality from "perversion"? *Canadian Journal of Psychoanalysis*, 18(2): 298–305.
Eshel O (2019a). *Emergence of Analytic Oneness: Into the Heart of Psychoanalysis*. Abingdon, Oxon. and New York: Routledge.

66 *Psychoanalytic Understanding*

Eshel O (2019b). Pentheus rather than Oedipus: On perversion, survival, and analytic presence in. In Eshel O (2019). *Emergence of Analytic Oneness: Into the Heart of Psychoanalysis*. Abingdon, Oxon. and New York: Routledge.

Ferenczi S (1933/1988). Confusion of tongues between adults and the child—The language of tenderness and of passion. *Contemporary Psychoanalysis*, 24: 196–206.

Freud S (1887–1905/1985). *The Complete Letters of Sigmund Freud to Wilhelm Fliess*. Translated by Masson JM. London: Belknap Press.

Harris A & Steven Kuchuck S (2015). *The Legacy of Sandor Ferenczi: From Ghost to Ancestor*. London: Routledge.

Kadish Y (2011). Autistoid psychic retreat in anorexia. *British Journal of Psychotherapy*, 27(1): 19–36.

Kadish Y (2013). Two types of psychic encapsulation in anorexia. *Psychoanalytic Psychotherapy*, 27(1): 60–76.

Kalinich LJ (2010). A rash of a different colour: somatopsychic eruptions from the other side. In Aisenstein M & Rappoport de Aisemberg (eds). *Psychosomatics Today: A Psychoanalytic Perspective*. Abingdon, Oxon. and New York: Routledge.

Krystal H (1978). Self representation and the capacity for self care *Annual of Psychoanalysis*, 6: 209–246.

Levine HB, Reed GS, & Scarfone D (2013). *Unrepresented States and the Construction of Meaning: Clinical and Theoretical Contributions*. New York and London: Routledge.

Little M (1990). *Psychotic Anxieties and Containment: A Personal Record of an Analysis with Winnicott*. Northvale, NJ: Jason Aronson.

Meltzer D (1990). *The Claustrum*. London: Karnac.

Meltzer D, Bremner J, Hoxster S, Weddell D, & Wittenberg I (1975) *Explorations in Autism*. Perthshire: Cluny.

Mitrani L (1992). On the survival function of autistic manoeuvres in adult patients. *International Journal of Psychoanalysis*, 73: 549–559.

Mitrani JL (2011). Trying to enter the long black branches: some technical extensions of the work of Frances Tustin for the analysis of autistic states in adults. *International Journal of Psychoanalysis*, 92(1): 21–42.

Ogden TH (1980). On the nature of schizophrenic conflict. *International Journal of Psycho-Analysis*, 61: 513–533.

Ogden TH (1989). On the concept of an autistic-contiguous position. *International Journal of Psychoanalysis*, 70: 127–140.

Ogden TH (1996). The perverse subject of analysis. *Journal of the American Psychoanalytic Association*, 44: 1121–1146.

Rappaport de Aisemberg E (2010). Psychosomatic conditions in contemporary psychoanalysis. In Aisenstein M & Rappoport de Aisemberg (eds). *Psychosomatics Today: A Psychoanalytic Perspective*. Abingdon, Oxon. and New York: Routledge.

Rosenfeld H (1987). *Impasse and Interpretation: Therapeutic and Anti-Therapeutic Factors in the Psychoanalytic Treatment of Psychotic, Borderline, and Neurotic Patients*. London: Tavistock Publications.

Searles HF (1965). *Collected Papers on Schizophrenia and Related Subjects*. New York: International Universities Press.

Sechaud E (2010) Particular vicissitudes of the drive confronted with mourning: sublimation and somatization. In Aisenstein M & Rappoport de Aisemberg (eds). *Psychosomatics Today: A Psychoanalytic Perspective*. Abingdon, Oxon. and New York: Routledge.

Segal H (1950). Some aspects of the analysis of a schizophrenic. *International Journal of Psycho-Analysis*, 31: 268–278.

Steinberg PI (2002). Preventing suicide in medical students: a self and relational viewpoint. *Annals of the Royal College of Physicians and Surgeons of Canada,* 35(8): 503–505.

Steinberg PI (2017). Whipped cream and other delights: A Reverie and its aftermath. *Canadian Journal of Psychoanalysis,* 25(2): 88–105.

Steinberg PI (2021). Psychoanalytic approaches to psychosomatic medicine. In *Psychoanalysis in Medicine: Applying Psychoanalytic Thought in Contemporary Medical Care.* London and New York: Routledge, 95–106.

Steiner J (1993). *Psychic Retreats: Pathological Organizations in Psychotic, Neurotic, and Borderline Patients.* London and New York: Routledge.

Steiner J (2011). *Seeing and Being Seen: Emerging from a Psychic Retreat.* Abingdon, Oxon. and New York: Routledge.

Steinman I (2009). *Treating the "Untreatable": Healing in the Realms of Madness.* London and New York: Routledge.

Stern DB (2003). *Unformulated Experience: From Dissociation to Imagination in Psychoanalysis.* Hillsdale, NJ: The Analytic Press.

Sullivan HS (1962) *Schizophrenia as a Human Process.* New York: Norton.

Szwec G (2010). The capacity to say no and psycho somatic disorders in childhood. In Aisenstein M & Rappoport de Aisemberg (eds). *Psychosomatics Today: A Psychoanalytic Perspective.* Abingdon, Oxon. and New York: Routledge.

Taylor GJ (2010). Symbolism, civilization and trauma in psychosomatic theory. In Aisenstein M & Rappoport de Aisemberg (eds). *Psychosomatics Today: A Psychoanalytic Perspective.* Abingdon, Oxon. and New York: Routledge.

Tustin F (1981). *Autistic States in Children.* London: Routledge and Keegan Paul.

Tustin F (1986). *Autistic Barriers in Neurotic Adults.* London: Karnac Books.

Waska R (2006). Addictions and the quest to control the object. *American Journal of Psychoanalysis,* 66(1): 43–62.

Winnicott DW (1972). *Holding and Interpretation.* New York: Grove Press.

Winnicott DW (1974). Fear of breakdown. *International Review of Psycho-Analysis,* 1: 103–107.

Wooldridge T (2018). *Psychoanalytic Treatment of Eating Disorders: When Words Fail and Bodies Speak.* London and New York: Routledge.

Part B

Group Psychotherapy and Partial Hospitalization Programs

One of the benefits of working on a team in a program or psychotherapy group is that two or more heads usually are better than one. If, for example, one therapist or leader of a program is unable to effectively respond to something that transpires in a group, another may be better able to. For example, in our day treatment program (DTP), once an individual with a severe personality disorder begin making disparaging remarks about the DTP, indicating how outdated our psychoanalytic approach was, going on at length about this. He had spent three months in DTP doing very little that could be called psychotherapeutic work. I thought angrily, like a cartoon character, "Why you little ...," and felt like wringing his neck, but couldn't think of something appropriately therapeutic to say.

My thinking was interfered with by my anger. In retrospect, this probably gave an indication of how angry the patient was and also perhaps a hint about how his anger derailed his own capacity to think. However, my team leader, whose thinking wasn't interfered with at this moment, lightly suggested that the patient should consider how important the issue out-of-date thinking was for him, implying that his thinking was out of date in terms of being quite primitive and childlike. He gave a big smile, showing that he understood what she was getting at, implicitly agreeing with her. Due to some vulnerability of mine, that day I was only able to respond with anger, and not use what the patient said in a way that was potentially helpful to him, supportive of our program, and potentially useful in helping other patients to engage with what was going on. So it was good that there were several therapists in this large (40+ patients) group, and one was able to respond effectively.

This is also a good example of how one must be patient with oneself, whether performing individual or group (or, for that matter, family or couples) psychotherapy. What might be the best response you can think of may not occur to you in the heat of the session. In fact, in my experience, the more pressure one is under, the harder it is to think. Fortunately, in our work, there often is a second chance to make the point that eluded one at the first opportunity. It is possible to persecute oneself for not thinking of it straight off. A more constructive response is to consider what was

DOI: 10.4324/9781003200581-6

going on in the session that may have prevented one from thinking of it at the time, and whether something was going on in one's personal life that may have interfered with one's thinking at the time. It helps to accept that sometimes it takes our unconscious minds time to come up with the most felicitous ideas.

For more on psychoanalytic approaches to inpatient and day hospital settings, see Chapter 16, Psychoanalytic approaches integrated into day treatment and inpatient settings, of my *Psychoanalysis in Medicine: Applying Psychoanalytic Thought in Contemporary Medical Care* (Steinberg, 2021).

Reference

Steinberg PI (2021). Psychoanalytic approaches to psychosomatic medicine. In *Psychoanalysis in Medicine: Applying Psychoanalytic Thought in Contemporary Medical Care.* London and New York: Routledge, 95–106.

4 Danger from Within

Threats of Violence in Group Psychotherapy

In this chapter and Chapter 5, it is the psychoanalytic understanding of projective mechanisms and the focus on countertransference considerations that informs the management of the very disturbing experience of threats in the context of group psychotherapy.

Threats of violence are an aspect of group psychotherapy that leaders of groups find threatening and might prefer to ignore. The sparse literature regarding violence and threats of violence in group psychotherapy may reflect the anxiety of practitioners regarding this subject, similar to the paucity of literature on countertransference in the early decades of psychoanalysis. This chapter deals with our experience of threats of violence in psychotherapy groups in the psychiatric day treatment program (DTP) of the University of Alberta Hospital. DTP is led by a clinical coordinator (psychiatrist) and a team leader (nonmedical mental health professional). Threats of violence do occur in DTP, which admits individuals with severe personality disorders (Piper et al., 1996). Most of DTP's patients have a diagnosis of narcissistic or borderline personality disorder or both, and a significant number have antisocial traits. Occasionally, we admit an individual with antisocial personality disorder. One of the difficulties of responding to situations involving threats of violence is the fear and anxiety engendered. The fear is related to the physical danger presented by the threat. The anxiety is related to concerns about how therapists can function in a very difficult and relatively unfamiliar situations. *When discussing fear and anxiety being engendered in psychotherapy situations, especially when there is a question of violence, the concept of projective notification arises. To what extent are group members and therapists intended to feel afraid or anxious? To what extent might this be an unconscious communication of the threatening individual's own fears?*

The observations, conclusions, and interventions discussed here in the context of a partial hospitalization program apply, I believe, to all psychotherapy groups and, for that matter, to all clinical venues.

DOI: 10.4324/9781003200581-7

Literature Review

I found no specific references to threats of violence in the group psycho-therapy literature. In contrast, there is a substantial literature on patient assaults of therapists and mental health personnel (Beck & Roy, 1997). Newman (1997) examines characteristics of emotional abuse experienced by therapists and presents approaches on how to cope with it. He deals with behavioral approaches that allow clinicians to maintain professional decorum with behavioral techniques such as cognitive rehearsal, rational responding, and assertiveness, as well as encouraging judicious use of documentation and supervisory consultations. He deals neither with group psychotherapy nor psychodynamic aspects of predicting or responding to threats. Koopman et al. (1998) describe clinical administrative staff reporting greater acute stress reactions than residents, interns, or research staff after a threatening episode at an outpatient psychiatric clinic. Acute stress symptoms were strongly and positively related to both functional and dysfunctional behavioral change. This article did not deal with group psychotherapy or make suggestions regarding prevention or management of threats.

An observation scale to record aggressive behaviors, defenses, and interventions that occur during a psychotherapy group has been developed (Lanza et al., 1998). The development of the scale appears promising, but the article's discussion of clinical relevance was unfortunately very brief. In this longitudinal study, the rate of assaults on staff on wards taking part in training to learn strategies for coping with violent psychiatric patients was 31% lower after implementation of training. Eight steps for developing a violence pre-vention program are described.

Case Example

The following case example is derived from DTP, an 18-week, all-day psy-chodynamic group psychotherapy-based partial hospitalization program. Our patients suffer from severe personality disorders and comorbid Axis I disorders, especially mood disorders. They attend a variety of unstructured and semi-structured groups four and a half days a week. Confrontation and interpretation are the chief techniques employed. The unstructured groups include a large group in which all patients and therapists attend, and smaller groups in which patients are divided according to their phases of treatment. Each day starts with Large Group, an unstructured group designed to reduce splitting among staff and patients. The semi-structured groups deal with themes such as identity, self-respect, self-discipline, and close relationships. The day ends with a social or recreational group where patients can socialize and inevitably experience difficulties in socialization, which can be discussed in other groups.

Eighteen weeks appears to be a minimum time in which to have a significant psychotherapeutic effect on these patients, who are often limited in psychological mindedness and motivation for treatment. *The latter factors, of course, have become important foci for psychoanalytic and psychodynamic psychotherapeutic treatment in recent decades, rather than being relative contraindications for treatment, as they once were considered. Regarding this, DTP patients with significant personality pathology have similar difficulties to the patients described at the beginning of Chapter 3.* Supervision for DTP therapists consists of meetings of co-therapists after groups, weekly hour-long staff relations groups (SRGs) (O'Kelly & Azim, 1995), and unscheduled discussions among the therapists, the team leader, and the clinical coordinator as needed.

Camille is a 24-year-old, divorced, unemployed, casual clerical worker who is physically tall and large, with a very imposing presence, which can become threatening when she is angry. When she becomes angry, she quickly is enraged; she appears not to have an emotional "rheostat" to enable her to regulate her temper. *Individuals with significant personality pathology often are deficient in affect regulation. Such people are emotionally volatile, frequently and easily express intense affects such as rage or despair, and often receive a diagnosis of borderline personality disorder. The capacity to regulate affect is not inborn; observation of infants in the first weeks and months of life illustrates this. This capacity gradually is internalized from mothering figures as they soothe the baby in any number of ways, including physical care, gentle talking, and labeling the infant's affects. This gradually leads to the infant to being able to identify the latter himself, an important part of the development of the capacity to think. To the extent that an infant does not experience wholesome and competent containing by a mothering figure, many important personality qualities, including affect regulation, will not develop in a satisfactory manner. This leaves the individual seriously disadvantaged in terms of not being able to contain himself adequately when it is important to do so, for example, in public, or when he is angry with his boss. This type of individual will be more likely to be overwhelmed by painful and frightening affects and to tend to develop defenses (that can be maladaptive) in an attempt to avoid experiencing these affects. The associated significant disadvantages include being emotionally cut off and not be able to enjoy intimacy with others and an inability to use affects for their signal function, that is, warning that there may be danger in the external world or when something internally is disturbing them and needs their attention.*

Camille was brought up in a family characterized by abuse and neglect. Her father, an alcoholic who physically abused his wife and five children, was never involved in positive interactions with them. *A history of physical abuse can result in internalizing a destructive object. That is, an unconscious image of the destructive father develops in the child, which is accompanied by both a destructive attitude to oneself and to one's relationships. This may be expressed in a harsh superego, that is, a harsh and punitive attitude toward oneself and a tendency toward harshness in one's relations to others. The harsh attitude toward oneself may be expressed in using others to treat oneself harshly, for example, by undue deference or submission to a partner, friend or even stranger, which is in the realm of masochistic pathology. In Camille's case, she seemed to defend against feeling helpless with and vulnerable to this internal object by projecting these feelings (and self-image) into others, as we shall see.*

74   *Group Psychotherapy and Partial Hospitalization*

Camille's mother was timorous and ineffectual, offering a bit of affection, but too preoccupied by her own difficulties to be very available for sharing positive experiences. *This type of experience with mother can result in an identification with mother, with the development of a frightened, helpless self-image, characterized by deficient personal agency and an inability to take the initiative in pursuing one's interests. As mentioned above, this self-image may be defended against by projecting it into others, identifying with an abusive parent.* An older sister offered more in the way of parenting. Camille's father, in drunken rages, used to interrupt beating her mother to attack the children. Camille remembers being thrown across the room. Camille had no known previous history of violent behavior herself.

Camille had been attending DTP for two months. One day, she was clearly angry and started talking in Large Group even before people had sat down. This developed into a tirade against several patients whom Camille felt were talking about group issues prior to the beginning of the group. When Camille became verbally abusive and threatening, the psychiatrist interrupted her, indicating that this behavior would not help her and was unacceptable in DTP. Camille said that she considered bringing in a gun and shooting some people, and angrily stormed out of the room, after telling the psychiatrist, "Watch your back." The psychiatrist, after some moments of hesitation and fear, left to ascertain whether Camille had left the building and then returned to the group. Patients' associations initially involved their being reminded of their own anger, which sometimes felt like murderous rage. As the psychiatrist became aware of his fantasies of Camille returning with a gun and shooting members of the group, himself in particular, the patients became increasingly anxious, asking for reassurances that this would not happen.

The psychiatrist then called hospital security who involved the police. He certified Camille for emergency assessment regarding dangerousness to others and had the police search her house for weapons. The other patients continued working in Large Group. They talked about their anger at Camille and how her anger reminded them of their own rage and the rage of others, frequently their parents, to which they had been exposed. The therapists were more comfortable once they knew that the security department and the police had been contacted. However, they remained quite anxious during the rest of Large Group, feeling there was no guarantee that Camille would not return with a gun. Not until later was it learned that she had been apprehended, brought to an emergency department, and admitted to a psychiatric hospital.

Camille appeared to have internalized an object representation characterized by abusiveness, hostility, rage, violence, destructiveness, and a lack of tender feelings or warm relatedness. Her self-image appeared to be that of a helpless, frightened, abused, and neglected child. Nonviolent boundary violations by other patients seemed to have precipitated Camille's threat. These interactions may have brought Camille's self-image closer to conscious awareness, both in terms of these violations and the fact that they

Danger from Within 75

were handled nonpunitively. Camille dealt with this increased awareness by projecting her frightened child self-image onto other group members, identifying with her destructive internalized object, and treating group members as her father treated the rest of the family. That is, Camille appeared to defend against experiencing herself as a helpless, abused, neglected, frightened child by evoking these feelings in others, an example of projective identification.

When one is threatened under unfamiliar circumstances, it is difficult to feel secure that one is responding most appropriately. In retrospect, the therapists of DTP thought that rather than merely ensuring that Camille had left the building, the psychiatrist should have involved hospital security and the police immediately. He believed that when Camille left, she was deliberately trying to frighten the members of the group, and that her rage was sufficiently expressed by her manner of leaving that she would be unlikely to return. However, these conclusions were not available to other group members and would not have reassured them. The urgent need of the group appears to have been to secure and to be seen to secure the safety of all group members by involving the police immediately, in order to eliminate the concrete danger that Camille had threatened. This would have provided the group members with the security they needed to continue their therapeutic work. *It is remarkable that the patients and therapists were able to continue working as well as they did in the rest of Large Group.* Patients can be good supervisors. The patients' anxiety and requests for reassurance that they would be protected made it necessary for the psychiatrist to act when he was hesitating.

Initially, the patients appeared to react more strongly to their fear of their own hostility and its erupting into violent behavior than their fear of or anger toward Camille. This likely in part represented a denial of fear related to the current threat. Some anger was expressed at staff for permitting the threat to occur, but many patients were aware that staff could not absolutely prevent this from happening. Considerable anger toward Camille was expressed by patients later in the week.

Subsequently, some patients said that some days previously they had heard Camille mention that she had access to guns and had felt somewhat threatened. It transpired that weeks before the threat they had heard her talk about being so angry that she felt like shooting someone. Back then Camille had indicated in a small group that she had given her guns to a friend for safekeeping, because she did not feel safe having them. In retrospect, both patients and therapists appeared to be too easily reassured by this. We might have had Camille indicate to the police where her guns were stored and ask them to remove them. This action would have indicated to Camille how seriously we took her references to guns. It would also have supported the group members in continuing their psychotherapeutic work without the ongoing question regarding Camille's dangerousness, which was suppressed but continued to affect the patients, and, likely, the therapists. *The revelations occurring some time after the event in question reveal a split between some patients and the therapist(s) in the small groups and the rest of the patients and therapists regarding the information about Camille's access to guns and feeling*

76 *Group Psychotherapy and Partial Hospitalization*

like shooting someone not being shared with the therapists as a whole and then reintroduced into Large Group to deal with Camille's threatening comments. This will be discussed further below.

This intervention (involving the police) would have provided the patients with an example of dealing with a difficult problem and with uncomfortable feelings forthrightly and effectively. The therapists needed to be in touch enough with their own fear of what Camille might do and be willing to confront their fear and Camille's potential aggression directly. This confrontation would have offered Camille an opportunity to work constructively on the difficulty she had in dealing with her rage, not allowing her to persist in retaining violence as an option. This would have been in everyone's interest. Camille would have been obliged to decide whether to work psychotherapeutically on managing her rage or to act it out with threats or violent behavior. Confiscating the guns could be understood as blocking the possibility for acting out, making continuation of psychotherapeutic work possible (Kernberg, 1984).

Camille's continuous refusal to do psychotherapeutic work elicited ongoing frustration in the therapists. This and the therapists' repressed fear contributed to their neglecting to investigate more thoroughly the early reference to Camille's possession of guns. One therapist recalled that in another program, Camille had been involved in a nonphysical, but angry, altercation with staff who had set limits on her regarding accessibility to waiting areas. She felt entitled to wait in the clinic waiting room for a ride after her treatment. Several times other patients complained of her intrusiveness, which was discussed with her. Finally, she was told that the waiting room would not be available to her after her appointments. This precipitated a considerable and prolonged outburst. Although this had been documented, it was not given due consideration when Camille was assessed for suitability for treatment in the DTP.

In the SRG, therapists discussed countertransference reactions, including fear of and rage at Camille. *If therapists have countertransference hate and even death wishes toward suicidal patients (Maltsberger & Buie, 1974), how much more are they likely to have countertransference hate and death wishes toward patients who threaten them or others with violence?* The therapists felt that Camille was being deliberately destructive in making the threat, but also took the threat seriously. Considerable frustration was expressed toward the psychiatrist for not acting immediately to secure the group's safety. Therapists appeared unsettled by the prospect of their leader not being immediately certain of how to handle the situation. For a patient to be discharged from DTP on the basis of making threats is very unusual. Of six cases documented in a two-year period, Camille was the only one who was discharged. She in effect discharged herself, leaving DTP after threatening to assault group members. It was thought that she would not be a workable member of DTP, given her lack of willingness to work up to that point, and it would be infeasible to reintegrate her into DTP because she made such an overt threat.

Source of Threats

Threats of violence in a group can be viewed from the perspective of object relations theory. The threatening patient projects onto other group members a helpless, abused, victimized self-image, usually corresponding to his early experiences with caregivers. Also projected is the accompanying fear. The threatening patient identifies with a destructive internalized object that usually represents one or both parents. The patient's anxiety is reduced with the success of the projection. It is others who appear afraid, so the patient can disavow his own feelings of helplessness and fear. He can also project an internalized object onto the other group members, whose anger (that the patient has actively elicited with his threats) enables him to see the hostility associated with his internalized object outside himself. This reduces the patient's anxiety about his hostility, at the cost of losing support from other group members. They respond with fear and anger that reinforces the patient's hostile attitude. The therapists and other patients identify with the projected self-image and feel threatened, especially if the threat appears realistic, and the projected self-image corresponds closely with their self-image. Therapists should neither accept this projection nor identify with the threatening patient's internalized object. Doing so would result in, respectively, a passive, inadequate response or a hostile, punitive response to the threatening patient. Therapists need to maintain a therapeutic stance, protecting the therapy, the patients, and themselves, by taking appropriate action to secure group members' safety and continue psychotherapeutic work. The occurrence of transference rage is common in DTP but can be contained and worked through if DTP is experienced as secure.

Safety within DTP is dependent on the cohesiveness of the therapists, the therapists' ability to deal with rage and other intense affects, the maintenance of DTP structure (group norms), and the proper timing of therapist absences. Threats become more imminent when therapists are not functioning cohesively and when infractions of patients or anxieties of therapists remain unresolved. A split among therapists in DTP implies a significant anti-leader component among the therapists, which undermines the leadership and interferes with the therapists' optimal functioning. In DTP, all documented threats of violence occurred within a two-year period when serious splits among the therapists occurred. Some seasoned therapists had worked in DTP for an extensive period of time, while more junior therapists had recently joined DTP. The senior therapists were cohesive and had weathered many stresses, including substantial staffing cuts and threats of partial closure of DTP. Fear associated with these changes had spurred the therapists into taking on additional responsibilities while remaining productive during a time of turmoil. When the fear of further cuts diminished, resentment and bitterness arose among these therapists. Resistance and resentment to further changes arose. The junior therapists, who had not experienced the above changes, displayed more energy and a greater appreciation of what they needed to learn than their senior colleagues.

78   *Group Psychotherapy and Partial Hospitalization*

A new psychiatrist-leader was appointed during this time. Therapists were encouraged to be more confrontational and interpretive in their work. Junior therapists adjusted more easily to these expectations, while senior therapists viewed them ambivalently. Eventually, the junior staff felt torn between complying with the leader's instructions and conforming with the senior therapists. This caused anxiety and frustration among the therapists and contributed to a tendency to undermine leadership, as evidenced by guarded communication and restricted input into decision-making on the therapists' part. Discussions became increasingly unproductive and strained. There was limited input into discussion of group themes and process, transference and countertransference issues, and on the nature of interpretations made. Therapists contributed little to the Large Group meetings, leaving the work to the leaders. Little information was brought by the therapists from the small groups into Large Group. DTP works best when there is a continuous flow of themes from Large Group that are worked through in the small groups and then reiterated in Large Group. This fosters therapeutic movement and prevents splits and boundary infractions. When therapists are split, the flow of information within DTP is seriously interrupted, and the small groups become disparate entities, not parts of a comprehensive treatment program.

Also associated with threats of violence were occasions when therapists were stressed due to vacant staff positions, vacations, or illness. The added work and reduced communication allowed the patients with pronounced antisocial tendencies to gain strength, forming a strong subgroup. Because the changes were poorly integrated and not worked through, the antisocial component was able to win over the insecure dependent, borderline, and narcissistic patients. The borderline and narcissistic elements acted out destructive impulses, looking to the antisocial patients to provide support and gratification outside of groups. This led to patients colluding to sabotage therapists and leaders. Similarly, junior therapists colluded with senior therapists in their silence and lack of confrontation of forces undermining the leadership, leaving this work solely to the leaders, and contributing to a split between leaders and therapists.

Cohesiveness is critical to the success of DTP. It is dependent on the maintenance of boundaries and structure. All patients are given complete information on the structure, rules, boundaries, and expectations of treatment. Explanation and written information are provided for patients in a two-hour preparatory session prior to the commencement of treatment. Emphasis is placed on the importance of safety in groups, maintenance of structure, and adherence to rules. Any form of threat may result in immediate discharge. Deviation from some rules might not lead to immediate discharge; patients have an opportunity to learn from their mistakes. But if noncompliance continues, patients may be discharged. Decisions regarding discharge are made during staff meetings where all therapists are invited to express their views. The final decision rests with the leaders. With a cohesive therapist group, a consensus can be reached with therapists respecting decisions

Danger from Within   79

made. A divided therapist group offers restricted input into decision-making. Often, some resentment occurs regarding decisions. Discharges can generate fear and resentment among patients toward staff. When boundaries are not experienced or maintained, general dissatisfaction and insecurity arise among patients. Fear of patient acting out may lead to multiple discharges followed by more admissions to maintain the census. This propagates a vicious cycle of increasing insecurity and resentment among patients and therapists, increasing the risk of further threats. Containing patients and confronting the antisocial elements can be a formidable task, as most acting out is done by borderline and narcissistic patients. An integrated therapist group can contain acting out by these patients and also can confront antisocial elements. This cannot be accomplished when therapists are split; objectivity becomes lost and therapist input is based on countertransference reactions rather than the patients' therapeutic interests. Then, the patients may act out therapists' disavowed destructive impulses.

Camille obviously was resistant to treatment, given her quiet, uncooperative demeanor in groups. Consistent strong confrontation earlier in her treatment may have resulted in her decision to discharge herself or in helping her to work constructively in psychotherapy. Retrospectively, we saw indicators that could have helped predict Camille's threats. Another patient had described having spoken with Camille privately for three hours to convince her not to act on her self-destructive thoughts. He initially was flattered that Camille chose him as a confidant but later felt burdened by this confidence and decided to raise his concerns in group. More emphasis was placed on the boundary violation and the exploration of his resistance in not consulting staff earlier than on Camille's behavior. This was indicative of Camille's capacity for splitting and projecting fear into others, choosing a vulnerable patient in which to confide.

A multidisciplinary team with an openness to self-examination and a willingness to resolve differences of opinion between staff members and leaders functions best and is most effective with patients. This is particularly important in the weekly, one-hour SRG (O'Kelly & Azim, 1995), where openness and honesty within professional boundaries are encouraged. Participation in SRG creates anxiety, as therapists feel professionally vulnerable. During the years when the therapists were split, the SRG became strained and unproductive. One therapist persistently attempted to address issues but failed. This individual was frowned on and perceived to be allying with the leaders, and eventually became increasingly hesitant and ineffectual in these attempts. The anti-leader sentiment among the therapists grew; individuals supporting the leadership were subtly silenced. A parallel process occurred between patient group and therapist group: antisocial elements and anti-leader sentiment, respectively, gained ground. A split staff is difficult to repair, requiring confrontation among the therapists themselves, as opposed to confrontation of therapists by the leaders. Strong confrontation from leaders may frighten therapists, uniting them against the leaders. A carefully supported confrontation among the therapists usually produces a better resolution. Leaders need to ensure that

80   *Group Psychotherapy and Partial Hospitalization*

therapists feel supported in resolving problems with them. Therapist work has to be validated and appreciated when well done. Therapists' suggestions should be respected, even when not acted on. However, leaders sometimes must make decisions that therapists may resent.

DTP was in a vulnerable state for an extended period of time because of many stresses, including the downsizing of the hospital department, the protracted illness of the team leader, the expectations that the new psychiatrist was placing on therapists, and the difficulties of junior and senior therapists in accommodating to each other. During the years of therapist dissension, the anti-leader component gained strength, making it possible for them to elicit support from hospital management, who were distracted in adjusting to change and preoccupied with building up staff morale. Management appeared to have little understanding of the dynamics of running a psychodynamic psychotherapy program. Effective communication between leaders and management, and a collective containment of the anti-leader elements among the therapists would have been more productive. In attempting to appease disgruntled staff and build staff morale, management was somewhat indiscriminate, supporting the anti-leader elements, as opposed to the therapists who quietly performed their work. The principle of isomorphy, that what occurs at any level of a system will gain expression at every other level of the system, may apply here. Therapists expressed considerable resentment toward the administration over a period of years because of cutbacks. Lack of understanding between therapists and the administration also led to therapist resentment. Some therapists appeared threatened by the new psychiatrist's close working relationship with the team leader. All of these factors contributed to an atmosphere in DTP where threats of violence were more likely to occur.

Management Implications

Patients undergo no other psychiatric treatment during their DTP admission, except substance abuse support groups when indicated. This obliges DTP therapists and leaders to deal with threats of violence. An important criterion for predicting violent behavior is a history of past violent behavior. Indications that an individual in group therapy may make threats or become violent need to be considered when assessing patients for admission and need to be carefully explored when they arise in group therapy. Therapists' personal discomfort with threats of violence and concern with disrupting the group's therapeutic process must be secondary to the need to explore whether patients are at risk of becoming violent. Therapists should even explore hints of threats before threats become overt. This is necessary to preserve a sense of safety for group members and is the most productive approach psychotherapeutically. It gives the potentially threatening patient an opportunity to verbalize his impulses and explore their basis, rather than running the risk of the acting out of impulses, which is destructive to the group and unhelpful to therapeutic progress.

Danger from Within 81

In our admission assessment, we inquire about a history of violent or criminal behavior. Often patients describe such incidents in DTP groups that they did not admit during the assessment. Staff should explore the patient's motivation for omitting such incidents. Such deception, in addition to the history of violent behavior, suggests that the patient may be at a higher risk for violent or threatening behavior. The safety of group members must be secure and be seen to be secure for group therapy to be effective. Co-therapists optimally need time to discuss what appropriate action should be taken to secure group members' safety. A group therapist practicing without a co-therapist needs time to reflect on this outside of group. Sometimes this is impossible, because action must be taken immediately, for example, to call the police to apprehend a potentially violent patient. More violent and imminent threats require speedy and decisive action, such as applying to courts for permission to inform police or a threatened third party, dis-charging the threatening patient from the group, or certifying him/her for psychiatric assessment. Sometimes threatening patients need to be admitted to hospital.

We have maintained some patients in DTP and obviated the need for hospitalization by indicating to patients that they cannot continue in group with ongoing threats. We offer the choice between continuing psycho-therapeutic work and talking about the motivation for wishing to harm someone, as opposed to undergoing formal psychiatric assessment regarding dangerousness with the possibility of admission to hospital. It is helpful to juxtapose the opportunities offered in an 18-week, all-day group psycho-therapy program, on the one hand, with the very short-term support avail-able in the hospital, on the other hand. The remediation after threats have occurred must be aimed at the individual patient, the group, and DTP itself. If the threats are containable and the patient can respond to confrontation such that he can continue with psychotherapeutic work, this needs to be the immediate group focus. Otherwise, the patient must be managed psy-chiatrically as described above and/or as an individual who may be charged with criminal behavior. Simultaneously, other patients need to be given the opportunity to deal with how the threats have affected them. Staff may need to schedule additional SRGs to deal with their countertransference, their feelings about how the threat was handled, and how they may have contributed to the threat occurring.

It is essential to deal with the emotional reactions of patients to the threat. Physical safety is a *sine qua non* for the emotional risks that patients need to take in group psychotherapy. This is especially important in programs where patients have experienced physical, sexual, and emotional abuse in the past and can respond with considerable transference fear and hatred to even "minor" threats. Realistic fear needs to be contained by informing patients how their physical safety will be maintained. There is a tension in DTP between patients' rights to be informed about how their safety will be maintained and our policy of not discussing with group members what has happened to patients who have left DTP. We lean toward indicating in

82 Group Psychotherapy and Partial Hospitalization

general how safety will be maintained. Sometimes patients' questions can be defensive in nature, aimed at eliciting reassurance, but at the expense of exploring what the threat means to them. Patients do deserve information but not at the expense of avoiding their therapeutic work. Many group members experience transferences to threatening patients based on their earlier experiences with threats and violence, either having been threatened or violated themselves or having abused others or harboring destructive wishes and fantasies. Patients also need to be able to deal with their feelings about how well therapists have protected them. Containing the threatening patient reassures that person that her persecutory internalized object is not as dangerous as she feels and reduces the pressure on other members of the group to identify both with the internalized object manifested by their anger and with the victimized self-image manifested by their fear. The limit-setting, nonpunitive, decisive group leader who manages threats, securing the group's safety without unduly punishing the threatening member, represents a benign and effective parental figure for patients—including the threatening patient—to internalize. The group leader's adequate handling of the situation, in spite of discomfort and feelings of insecurity, reverses the projection and its effects, making it possible for psychotherapeutic work to continue. This work should focus on patients' experience of the threat and its meaning to them. Reversing the projection implies that patients may be less inclined to accept a projected self- or object-image from the threatening patient. This reversal is based on the projection being blocked by the therapists' confrontation, the threatening patient's "ownership" of the projected self- or object-image, and the opportunity to internalize a more benign self- or object-image from the therapist who deals with the threat effectively but nonpunitively. This process should occur whether or not the threatening patient remains in the group.

Other patients need to be able to discuss their feelings about the threats. Similarly, the solitary therapist needs to consider at length her reactions to the threatening situation. For co-leaders or the therapist team in a program, time needs formally to be set aside to deal not only with their reactions to the threatening patient and to other patients but also with their own and other therapists' reactions to the threatening situation. Issues regarding power, conflict resolution, authority, and domination and submission appear to have played a powerful role in our patients' threats. It is difficult to assess the relative contributions of patient and milieu, apart from indicating that when therapists are not functioning as a coherent team, DTP is more vulnerable to patients who are inclined to become threatening, as therapists are then less likely to confront and contain these patients.

The possibility of therapists' anger being projected into patients, who may act it out, must be dealt with. This can only be done by therapists confronting each other and encouraging verbalization of the dissension among therapists. Staff members need to be encouraged to speak openly and in a timely fashion in team meetings and in SRG regarding any hint of threats among patients. They similarly need to be trained to be sensitive to

Danger from Within

countertransference feelings and to feel safe to discuss them with colleagues. Continuing education of staff along these lines should help obviate threats of violence. Staff must be encouraged to openly discuss difficulties they are having with each other or with the leadership, in order to avoid and resolve splitting. Patients who are seen as potentially threatening need to be carefully assessed before being admitted to DTP or other treatment programs. Our patients are assessed by a DTP therapist and then presented for discussion to the staff regarding admission. In the past, the psychiatrist rarely interviewed patients prior to admission, unless there were medical considerations or the patient was thought to have a mild thought disorder. There is a role for the psychiatrist in interviewing potentially threatening patients to make a risk assessment regarding threats and violence. A strong confrontational approach appears appropriate under these circumstances, to ascertain whether the patient is prepared to take responsibility for previous threatening or violent behavior and to elucidate what his or her present attitude is toward this.

Therapists need to deal both with their own realistic fears and their countertransference. They need to take action partly in order to feel safe enough to work. Therapists can deal with their reactions to threats by introspection, in discussions with a co-leader, in SRG (when the threat occurs in a program with a team), and with his own personal therapist/analyst, if he is seeing one.

It would be difficult enough to deal with threatening patients were therapists and leaders functioning at their best. However, the presence of threats is so distressing and potentially overwhelming that most of us are nowhere near at our best under these circumstances. Nevertheless, threatening situations do come up in clinical venues and have to be dealt with. It is important that solo clinicians and members of teams are able to contain themselves and help to contain each other (in team situations), such that there is the best chance for a satisfactory containment of the threatening patient in a way that protects the therapeutic activity and the physical safety of the group, the program, or the individual therapist and patient.

Conclusion

It is crucial for group therapists to acknowledge their own feelings to themselves. The experience in a therapist of intense fear of or anger toward a patient is a sign that there is a problem that needs to be addressed urgently. Threats of violence are an aspect of group therapy that, naturally, are threatening to group leaders. At times, group leaders may deny the seriousness of the threat in trying to cope with their feelings about it. Patients are then left with the impression that threats can be made with impunity. This is destructive to the therapeutic culture and process; fear and anger increase. Eventually, the threat may be carried out, or some other anti-therapeutic behavior may be permitted, if limits are not clearly set. Even if the threat is not carried out, therapeutic work is interfered with by realistic fear regarding threats of violence and by the loss of trust in therapists who are seen as not able to cope with the threat.

84   *Group Psychotherapy and Partial Hospitalization*

References

Beck PR & Roy R (1997).Violent and destructive behaviour in the therapeutic environment: Guidelines for psychiatrists. *Canadian Journal of Psychiatry*, 42: UI–U6.

Kernberg O (1984). *Severe Personality Disorders*. New Haven, CT:Yale University Press.

Koopman C, Zarcone J, Mann M, Freinkel A, & Spiegel, D (1998). Acute stress reactions to a patient threat. *Anxiety, Stress, and Coping,* 11: 27–45.

Lanza ML, Anderson J, Satz H, Stone J, Kayne HL, Smith K, et al. (1998). Aggression observation scale for group psychotherapy. *Group*, 22: 15–37.

Maltsberger JT & Buie DH (1974). Countertransference hate in the treatment of suicidal patients. *Archives of General Psychiatry*, 30: 625–633.

Newman CF (1997). Maintaining professionalism in the face of emotional abuse from clients. *Cognitive and Behavioural Practice*, 4: 1–29.

O'Kelly J & Azim HFA (1995). Staff-staff relations group. *International Journal of Group Psychotherapy*, 43: 469–483.

Piper WE, Rosie JS, Joyce AS, & Azim HF (1996). *Time-Limited Day Treatment for Personality Disorders*. Washington, DC: American Psychological Association.

5 Danger from Without

Threats of Violence to Third Parties in Group Psychotherapy

Since the California Supreme Court's decisions in the Tarasoff rulings, psychotherapists and physicians are considered to have a duty to warn a potential victim of a potentially dangerous patient. The principles of justice and protection from harm outweigh the principle of confidentiality here. In the first Tarasoff ruling, the court decided that health professionals with reason to believe that a patient may injure or kill someone must notify the potential victim, his/her relatives or friends, or authorities such as the police. It is left up to the health professionals' judgment regarding whom to notify, depending on the circumstances (Tarasoff v Regents of the University of California et al., 1976). The second Tarasoff ruling broadened health professionals' mandate from a "duty to warn" to include a "duty to protect" (Weinstock, Leong, & Silva, 2001). Courts have not made a uniform interpretation regarding the "duty to protect"; when a specific identifiable victim seems to be in imminent and potentially serious danger from a threat of an action by a mentally ill patient, the professional is expected to act (Simon, 2000). Since the Tarasoff rulings, health professionals have been obliged to balance their obligation toward their patients' rights to confidentiality with the rights of third parties to be informed of threats against them during the conduct of treatment.

Knapp and Van de Creek (2000) emphasize the Tarasoff decision as establishing a "duty to protect," as opposed to merely a "duty to warn." They refer to Appelbaum's (1985) three-step procedure regarding responsibilities under Tarasoff. These steps are assessing dangerousness accurately, formulating a management plan, and implementing a management plan. In assessing dangerousness, one must consider past threats of violence, threats to harm others, accessibility of weapons, relationship with the intended victim, membership in a group that condones violence, and lack of adherence to treatment. I would add to that list a history of violent behavior. In formulating a management plan, one must consider warning the intended victim or others likely to apprise the victim of the danger, notifying the police, or taking whatever steps are reasonably necessary. Increasing the frequency of appointments, providing medication for the patient, or referring the patient to a structured program is suggested. It is important to ensure that the treatment plan is implemented. Simon (2001) discusses the duty of

DOI: 10.4324/9781003200581-8

86 *Group Psychotherapy and Partial Hospitalization*

mental health clinicians to foresee, forewarn, and protect against clients' violent behavior. He emphasizes that the risk of harm be serious, imminent, and directed to an identifiable person, adding that the "duty to protect" allows greater treatment latitude than the "duty to warn" alone, emphasizing the need to preserve confidentiality as far as possible.

Perhaps issues of dangerousness are more relevant in recent decades because of societal changes. One is not aware of evidence documenting an increase in violence in society. There is even some suggestion of a decrease in crime in some jurisdictions. However, it appears indisputable that events ranging from the extreme of mass murders to more mundane experiences such as verbal abuse, disrespectful behavior in public, and violent behavior have all increased in frequency in the Western world in the last half century *(to say nothing of the past five years),* and society's attitude toward the more mundane behaviors listed above has become increasingly tolerant and even blasé. *In recent years, there is a tragically unmistakable increase in mass murders, largely in the form of shootings. Equally tragic is the inadequate response on the part of governments to attempt to stem this epidemic.* In addition, recent years have seen a significant increase in the open expression of hatred and violence toward minorities. It would not be surprising for behaviors that become more tolerated in society to tend to manifest themselves more freely in psychotherapy groups or programs open to the public. To give a trivial example, it is common for male patients to wear baseball caps during therapy sessions, which would have been considered unthinkably disrespectful 50 years ago.

Threats in Group Therapy

Since the early 1970s, group therapy has become one of the most frequently used forms of non-pharmacological treatment in public mental health settings. The continued growth of group therapy as a major treatment modality constitutes one of the most significant developments in the mental health field (Kaplan & Sadock, 1993). It is becoming particularly common for group therapy to be used with more severely disturbed patient populations. For example, group therapy has become an integral part of the treatment protocol for patients with schizophrenia (e.g., Granholm et al., 2007). Similarly, in the United Kingdom, group-based partial hospitalization programs are being developed by the Ministry of Health in order to create a network of services for patients with severe personality disorders (Home Office and Department of Health, 2003). I am unaware of laws specifically dealing with mental health professionals' legal responsibilities to third parties following a threat. I understand that common law is largely based on the Tarasoff decisions and subsequent experience in dealing legally with threats.

Clinical Ramifications of Threats in the Group

Group therapists must display strong leadership qualities at times of crisis, including during the propagation of a threat against an individual outside

Danger from Without 87

the group. The group members need to see that the threat is dealt with effectively, to be reassured that no violence will be perpetrated, and that the therapists can contain group members' aggression safely and nonpunitively. Uttering a threat in group therapy involves a diversion from the structure of treatment, which needs to be dealt with in the group. When the threat is to an individual outside the group, the leaders are required to consider the need to undertake a divergence from the group structure, which involves informing individuals outside the group about material brought up in the group, which constitutes a breach of confidentiality.

Diverging from structure can have serious ramifications in group psychotherapy. Complications, sometimes not easy to identify, may result in a temporary rupture involving significant testing and reenactments. When policy is disrupted or changed, reestablishing stability is important. This can be accomplished if there is a strong alliance between the group leaders (in the case of co-led groups), the leaders and the patients, and the leaders and the group as a whole. Diverging from structure also introduces a risk of ruptures and subsequent impasses developing in the therapeutic alliances. This is complex in a group setting in which various relationships have to be repaired, including between leaders and patients, between the leaders, and the relationships in the group as a whole. Group ruptures have been classified into "withdrawal" and "confrontation" subtypes (Safran & Muran, 2000). Both may occur simultaneously, with some group members withdrawing into a passive, hostile silence, while narcissistic, borderline, and antisocial patients express the group's hostility and general dissatisfaction. If the antisocial element is relatively strong, more serious ruptures and impasses are more likely to develop. This may result in a collective disturbance (Steinberg et al., 2004) with considerable acting out, pairing, and subgrouping, which undermine the treatment. The group is forced to go through a cleansing process before hope and trust can be reestablished and stability restored. Discharges from the group, initiated by patients or group leaders, are often an unavoidable part of this process.

A similar process can be seen when the coleaders of a group are not functioning as an organized and cohesive team. Unidentified or unrepaired ruptures between leaders and therapists in a large program can cause serious dysfunction. Although outwardly the group coleaders may appear to be functioning competently, there may be critical but stable conflicts that need to be resolved. We have found this situation to be associated with an increase in the risk of threats of violence in our group program (Steinberg & Duggal, 2004). Early signs of staff discontent with team leaders in multidisciplinary teams involve withdrawal from discussions with team leaders, not providing input into decision-making, and not fully implementing decisions as planned. Team leaders require much resilience and tact to repair these types of ruptures and prevent further splits from developing. Similarly, coleaders of psychotherapy groups require similar qualities in dealing with ruptures and potential splits in groups.

Case Examples

The case examples provided below are derived from psychodynamic psychotherapy groups held within the context of the day treatment program (DTP) of the Department of Psychiatry at the University of Alberta Hospital in Edmonton, Canada. This is an 18-week all-day intensive group psychotherapy program based on psychoanalytic principles. Most of our patients have severe personality disorders, such as borderline personality disorder and narcissistic personality disorder. Many have antisocial personality traits; at any given time, we usually have at least one patient (of about 35) with an antisocial personality disorder. Most of our patients have comorbid Axis I disorders, mood disorders in particular. Patients attend a variety of the unstructured and semi-structured groups on a daily basis 4½ days per week. Confrontation and interpretation are the chief techniques employed in the groups. Identifying data of these patients has been altered for the sake of anonymity.

DTP begins each day with Large Group attended by all staff members and patients. This functions as an unstructured psychodynamic psychotherapy group, and is essential for the cohesion of DTP participants. At the beginning of this group, administrative issues and medication questions are dealt with. Patients spend the remainder of the day in smaller groups of 10–15 participants with one and sometimes two leaders. These groups may be unstructured psychodynamic psychotherapy groups or may be structured in various ways to invite patients to deal with issues such as separation, loss, developing a sense of personal agency, self-discipline, and termination of therapy.

Therapists in DTP are trained on the job. They represent a variety of disciplines, including nursing, social work, occupational therapy, and psychology. The discipline of origin is irrelevant, as the therapists' formal education does not prepare them for the type of work undertaken in DTP. On-the-job training, which lasts for the entire duration of therapists' employment in DTP, consists of meeting with co-therapists after every co-led group, attendance at weekly hour-long Staff Relations Groups (SRGs) (O'Kelly & Azim, 1993), and unscheduled discussions among the therapists, the team leader, and the psychiatrist coordinator as needed. New therapists receive much individual teaching and support from the team leader in the first two years in DTP. An essential component to ongoing staff learning is mutual support and confrontation, which occur on an ongoing basis and are given a regular venue in SRGs.

Prior to admission, a therapist meets with each patient in order to provide an orientation to DTP. Included in this orientation are explicit comments regarding the need for confidentiality, that is, the importance of not disclosing to individuals outside DTP anything patients learn in DTP pertaining to other members. Patients socialize with each other on breaks and at lunch. However, they are told not to discuss group or DTP issues among themselves outside of groups and are not permitted to meet outside

Danger from Without   89

of DTP hours, either during or after their attendance at DTP. Patients are not told routinely in their orientation that threats of violence or violence itself are unacceptable in DTP. If the therapists, when meeting with a patient to discuss suitability for DTP, feel that it is necessary to be explicit to the patient regarding the acceptable limits of behavior, this would be done in the orientation. This most likely would occur with a patient who had a history of making threats, violence, or other illegal behavior, or if the therapist who assessed him had reasons for concern, based on the patient's behavior in the assessment interview. In the cases described below, other DTP patients generally did not seem to be affected personally by threats made by their peers toward individuals outside DTP. They generally did not express resentment about the extra time consumed in group or the extra attention given to threatening patients, although at times they expressed exasperation at the lack of cooperation of the latter regarding their repeating threats, as opposed to performing psychotherapeutic work. The patients were not tolerant of threats or implied threats made toward children and confronted threatening patients strongly about this.

Case 1

Fred, a 35-year-old divorced librarian's assistant with a diagnosis of borderline personality disorder, had a long history of self-mutilating behavior, suicide attempts, and multiple hospitalizations. After completing DTP, he was invited into a psychotherapy Follow-Up Group (FUG), which meets weekly for 1½ hours. This group is reserved for patients who have demonstrated both a capacity for productive work in psychodynamic group psychotherapy and evidence of being able to benefit from more group therapy.

Fred indicated in FUG that he intended to kill his dying father and then himself. Fred's father had allowed Fred's uncle (his father's brother) to sexually abuse him (Fred) when he was a child. Fred subsequently maintained a distant relationship with his father, in spite of Fred's wishes for some closeness with him, especially because he had given up hope of a closer relationship with his mother. Fred's father had been suffering for some years from a neurodegenerative condition, had taken a turn for the worse recently, and was not expected to live more than another few months. Fred indicated that he could not bear to see his father suffering, although there was no indication that his father was suffering more than he had been. There was, however, considerable evidence suggesting that Fred was having difficulty in containing both his rage at his father and his guilt at wishing over the years that his father would die. Fred had conscious fantasies of murdering him. Fred appeared obdurate in his intent to end his father's life. The therapists felt that he was less seriously intent on committing suicide at that time.

After obtaining advice from legal counsel, the group leaders informed Fred's mother of what Fred had threatened, because his father was too ill to come to the phone and was in no position to arrange for protection for himself. Fred's mother took the news calmly and did not sound surprised.

90   *Group Psychotherapy and Partial Hospitalization*

She refused to inform Fred's father, not wanting to upset him, feeling that it would be no use anyway. We had asked her to do this on the advice of legal counsel. We first informed Fred of our intention to call his family. Fred's mother reassured us that Fred would never be left alone with his father during visits. We informed Fred that he would have to make a choice between maintaining his intent to kill his father or continuing in group psychotherapy, as the two appeared mutually incompatible to us. We told him that he was fully entitled to feel like killing his father, and that his task was to come to terms with those feelings in FUG, as opposed to repeatedly stating his intention to act them out. The leaders felt that nothing would be served by certifying Fred and bringing him yet again into hospital, especially because they did not feel that he was actively suicidal, and they believed that adequate arrangements had been made for his father to be protected from him. Fred stubbornly clung to his course of indicating his intention to kill his father and opted to discharge himself from FUG.

One week after Fred discharged himself, he called one of the group leaders, pleading to be readmitted to FUG, promising that he would no longer threaten to harm either himself or anyone else. The leaders agreed to readmit him, which was an exception to usual policy, but one that seemed justified on the basis of Fred's initiative in calling back and reversing his original destructive plans after thinking them through. *Fred's capacity to reflect on his own about his threats, and how his maintaining them had affected his therapy, and his openness to returning and working on this was an encouraging sign. Fred seemed to have taken a step away from action and toward thinking about his impulses and wanting help in doing so. This is an important goal of contemporary psychoanalytic treatment. Whereas originally Freud had described the goal of psychoanalysis to render the unconscious conscious, relieving repressions and recovering lost memories, more recently, the focus has been less on content and more on developing the capacity to think (Ogden, 2004).*

We also were influenced by the considerable progress that Fred, who suffered from a very severe personality disorder, had made in DTP, and our feeling that it would be in Fred's best interest therapeutically to remain in our group. Fred's course for the months he remained in FUG was remarkably stable, given his long history of mood swings; self-mutilations; and suicide threats, gestures, and attempts. The leaders were left with the impression that confronting him with the choice between continuing his therapeutic work in FUG and embarking on a destructive course that he would be prevented from carrying out was useful in managing Fred. Two years after Fred was discharged from the FUG, the DTP leaders had a chance encounter with him in the hospital corridor. He was working at a full-time job, was subjectively well, had lost 100 pounds and no longer appeared overweight, and had not resumed his self-mutilating behavior. From his point of view, he was leading a productive, satisfying life.

Fred's return to group psychotherapy was relatively easy to contain and work through in FUG. The duration of treatment in this group varies between 14 and 18 months. The boundaries and structure are the same as in DTP, but

Danger from Without 91

patients are expected to function more independently and to be more open to confrontation and to reflecting on themselves. Both therapists (the DTP leaders) were in full agreement with respect to having Fred return to FUG. They also had well-established healthy alliances with most FUG members. To foster Fred's constructive return to FUG, strict limits were developed for him to adhere to, and it was made clear to him that his return was conditional. To further involve him within FUG and reestablish an element of trust, Fred was also asked to inform FUG members about what had transpired and to demonstrate a willingness to continue exploring and working through the impending loss of his father. Fred was aware from his previous experience in DTP that he would be confronted by the other patients, and that some anger might be directed toward him. Therapists were also aware that Fred needed to take the initiative and demonstrate a willingness to work, and that the group members needed support from the therapists to deal with their own mixed feelings regarding Fred's return. The leaders also monitored FUG closely for signs that Fred might be scapegoated.

On his return to FUG, Fred informed the group members about what had occurred and about his feelings about the therapists' actions. He felt relieved that his family members were supportive of him, although he was never left alone with his father. The group received this in silence, most members reserving their own thoughts. Only two members responded in supportive terms. It was clear that most members were skeptical of Fred, feeling that he could only reestablish himself in FUG by proving himself somehow, which clearly would take time. Eventually, with encouragement, some members expressed frustration toward the therapists, who were viewed as inconsistent parents, favoring Fred. Some expressed relief that the therapists had taken some constructive action. The real test came when Fred missed a session and returned to announce that his father had died. Because his absence was not addressed, it appeared that the group had not accepted Fred into the group, and there were still unresolved feelings about the decision to readmit Fred. His determination to deal with the loss, without further acting out, probably softened the group members and helped the therapists to assist the group in negotiating the impasse.

Case 2

Sylvia was a 50-year-old widow suffering from dysthymic disorder. She was also diagnosed with narcissistic and histrionic personality disorder. Sylvia announced in a group in DTP that she intended to kill herself. She added that she would kill her beloved great-nephew first, not wishing the great-nephew to survive without her in the care of his (according to Sylvia) unloving parents. Sylvia always described her relationship with her great-nephew as very close. She appeared unwilling to consider how much she might envy the great-nephew for having more favorable family circumstances than she herself had enjoyed as a child. Because Sylvia was a DTP patient, she was able to be monitored closely regarding her suicidal and homicidal intent. As

92   *Group Psychotherapy and Partial Hospitalization*

her discharge date approached, Sylvia continued to be unwilling to look at her reasons for wishing to kill herself and her great-nephew and expressed with increasing determination her intent to do so. The team followed legal counsel's advice and sought a court order giving them permission to inform Sylvia's nephew of the threat to his son.

In Canada and the United States, three criteria are generally necessary for a health professional to be permitted to inform a third party of danger to him or her based on the threat of a psychiatric patient. The first is that an identifiable person needs to be at risk. The second is that the risk needs to be imminent, a qualification that may be interpreted in various ways. The third is that the physician or therapist needs to have learned of this risk in the context of a professional relationship with the patient. Permission is sought from court if it is felt that the risk is not so immediate that delaying disclosure of the risk might endanger the life or health of the individual at risk. If the risk is felt to be more immediate, the individual at risk and the police may be informed without a court order. At a court hearing attended by the psychiatrist involved, his legal counsel, Sylvia, and her legal counsel, permission was granted to inform Sylvia's nephew of the risk to the great-nephew. The nephew indicated that he would not permit Sylvia to see his son alone. Sylvia continued in treatment and at no time following the court appearance appeared to be at serious risk of suicide. Yet her involvement in psychotherapeutic work appeared to be quite limited. The group leaders were left with the impression that Sylvia may have felt that she could utter threats with impunity as a method of dealing with uncomfortable affects, and that taking a legal course of action culminating in a court order was a useful method of confronting her with the limits of her freedom of speech. It is impossible to know whether Sylvia would have carried out her threat to kill her great-nephew.

We decided in Sylvia's case that her threats could not be ignored, either from the point of view of her great-nephew's safety, her treatment, or the potential for legal complications. The DTP staff felt that it was feasible to maintain Sylvia in treatment while indicating that her threats were unacceptable. It was felt that she derived some benefit from the combination of ongoing confrontation regarding her destructive behavior and support in functioning in a more constructive manner.

It required some toleration of some uncertainty and ambiguity on the part of the staff and patients in DTP to continue to contain Sylvia in the program while she maintained her position, continuing to voice thoughts of killing her great-nephew and herself. Although the staff were reassured that her nephew would not permit her to be alone in the presence of her great-nephew, there was of course no guarantee that she would not kill herself while she was in DTP. Bion (1970) developed the poet Keats' notion of "negative capability," the capacity to tolerate not knowing, which although uncomfortable, offers the possibility of continuing to think while not providing one-self with the comfort and security of feeling one knows: "when a man is capable of being in uncertainties, mysteries, doubts, without any irritable reaching after fact and reason" (Keats, 1817). It is challenging for us to allow ourselves to continue thinking, knowing that we do not know. However, taking this course offers the possibility of eventual learning. As soon as one feels he knows, thinking is foreclosed, and no more development can occur. Uncertainty is difficult to bear, especially if the stakes appear to be life and death. It would have been useful to discuss the concept of negative capability with DTP patients and have them describe their experience of not knowing what was going to happen regarding Silvia's threats. This also would have offered an opportunity for individuals in the group to help each other contain uncomfortable feelings, which would be more constructive than what would be for many of them a more usual outlet, acting on them or evacuating them (through projective identification) into others to contain.

For Sylvia to be contained within the treatment environment, it was important to consider the impact of the legal action upon group members. Any mention of "legal action" generates considerable anxiety, because most of our patients not only come from abusive and seriously neglectful backgrounds; many also have been abusive or neglectful to others. Patients are encouraged to talk about destructive aspects of themselves. Most are unable to differentiate between dealing with violent impulses in a constructively therapeutic fashion and planning to act on them. This leaves them in a position in which they feel easily threatened. It was imperative that the group members be made aware of the seriousness of Sylvia's threats. Patients were encouraged to help her work through this.

Considerable patient and staff energy was invested in helping Sylvia to deal constructively with her envy. Patients appeared aware of her resistance to doing therapeutic work and did not overreact when Sylvia informed them about having to go to court with the psychiatrist. Most patients appeared supportive of the psychiatrist's decision. Sylvia presented herself in a manner that appeared manipulative, designed to generate an envious reaction from the group. She presented herself as unique and requiring some special attention. This was unsuccessful; the group shifted from a state of trepidation and anxiety to one of anger at Sylvia. Perhaps, it was less damaging to Sylvia to have made this attempt to attract attention, rather than treating the legal intervention as a narcissistic injury. She completed the 18-week treatment program. Generally, patients were relatively supportive and had an opportunity to deal with the envy and destructive wishes that Sylvia's behavior had evoked.

Three years after discharge, Sylvia spontaneously called the psychiatrist just to let him know that she had figured out on her own the motivation for some difficulties she was having in her relationship with her nephew, which was an issue that had come up during treatment. She appeared clearly to have maintained a positive attachment to the treatment staff, in spite of the legal involvement.

Case 3

Henry, a 26-year-old accountant and married father of two with a diagnosis of narcissistic personality disorder with antisocial traits, was making little progress in DTP. He remained unengaged with most of the patients and all of the therapists, sitting quietly through the groups, doing little therapeutic work. Henry revealed to the group that he and his wife had secured a contract to consult at a school regarding the school's accounting procedures. He indicated in a self-satisfied manner that only his wife was formally acknowledged to be involved in their business. Because they would be working in a school, they were obliged to undergo a check of police records. Henry had a criminal record for having sexually abused a child in the past. He did not believe he would be allowed to enter a school on a regular basis to work. The leaders of the group were anxious about the possibility of Henry abusing the children to which he would have access, although when confronted, he stated outright that he would not do this. He added that he would not be "actively involved." The leaders were concerned about Henry's deception in the securing of the position.

After seeking legal advice, the leaders discussed their concerns with the city Social Services Department. Henry's treatment in DTP concluded shortly thereafter. He expressed little regarding his feelings about the staff's legal involvement in his planned work. He subsequently visited the office of his attending psychiatrist and made vague threats of physical violence toward both that psychiatrist and the psychiatrist of DTP. Legal counsel was again consulted, and application to court was made for a restraining order, such that Henry not be permitted to approach within 500 feet of either of the psychiatrists' homes, should he be aware of their locations. He was also prohibited from returning for assessment or treatment at the hospital Department of Psychiatry in which DTP is located. The Social Services Department was left to investigate and deal with the question of the appropriateness of his involvement with the school.

Several attempts in DTP were made to engage Henry in order to get a clearer sense of how he intended to help his wife without being actively involved. He remained uncooperative. Frequently, group pressure can be utilized to break down resistance to doing therapeutic work. However, group members remained passive when invited to confront or encourage Henry. Either Henry's lack of participation and ongoing resistance had frustrated group members such that they had given up on him, or they were fearful of confronting him. This was difficult to determine because Henry completed treatment before any further action was taken.

I think it is very important for patients in groups to be aware of whatever legal action becomes necessary as a result of destructive behavior in groups such as threats. This enables the patients to feel that the group is being contained, and that destructive impulses need to be talked about but must not be permitted to be acted on. I believe patients seeing group and program leaders taking appropriate initiatives in seeking legal advice and contacting authorities, such as the police, departments of family and children's services, and school principals, adds to the integrity of the group and/or program, as well as modeling an appropriate nonpunitive but effective approach to destructiveness.

Discussion

Therapists and physicians who are confronted with threats to third parties by their patients need to choose from a number of options that will adequately protect the threatened individual, provide legal protection to the therapist or physician, and, when feasible, enable the treatment of the threatening patient to continue. These options include, but are not limited to, warning the threatened third party and/or his relatives, friends, and the police; applying to the courts for permission to inform these individuals; contacting social service agencies for advice when unidentified children may be at risk; and discharging the threatening patient from the group. If the threat is felt to be associated with acute psychiatric disturbance in the patient, consideration should be given to having the patient certified for psychiatric assessment. Expert legal advice provides objective guidelines regarding defensible and appropriate approaches to dealing with threats. It also provides support to therapists and mental health professionals, which in turn enables them to deal with their feelings about the threat and potentially to continue their treatment relationship with the threatening patient.

Fear and anger are understandable and probably almost universal reactions among mental health professionals to threats (Steinberg & Duggal, 2004). This appears to pertain whether the threat is directed toward the clinician, a patient, or an individual outside of a group. It is plausible that when the threat is directed toward a third party, the anger and especially the fear elicited in the therapist(s) and patients may not be as intense as when the threat is directed at them. However, in programs like DTP, in which many of the members have experienced abuse, violence, and threats of violence, threats of violence uttered can elicit extremely strong emotional reactions from other group members. This, of course, may occur in clinicians as well as in patients.

Situations in which the threat is directed toward a member of the group, however uncomfortable they may become, inherently have some practical and psychotherapeutic advantages compared to situations in which threats are directed toward third parties. In the former case, there is no need to consider whether or how to inform the object of the threat; presuming she is in attendance and is aware of the threat as soon as it is made. She can also expect the emotional support of the group members, and both the psychotherapeutic support of being helped by the therapists in dealing with her feelings about the threat and the practical support of receiving reassurance that (and observing how) the threat will be dealt with in a manner so to protect her and the psychotherapeutic process of the group.

As anxiety-provoking as threatening situations may be, in cases when a threat is made to a group member, therapists usually do not have to be involved in extra-group interactions, apart from the possibility of having a threatening patient certified for psychiatric assessment or admission to a psychiatric facility. (Exceptions include when the threatening patient needs

96 *Group Psychotherapy and Partial Hospitalization*

to be assessed for dangerousness by a group leader outside of the group, and, of course, the measures leaders take in discussing the threat among themselves outside the group, as well as SRGs in settings where they exist.) With threats to third parties, therapists must consider involving individuals outside the treatment relationship. It also becomes prudent to seek legal advice, which may make some clinicians anxious and also may incur significant financial expense. We hasten to add that the anxiety (about the group's functioning and the clinician's doing the right thing), fear (about the threat potentially being carried out), financial cost, and potential guilt and grief involved in not appropriately seeking legal advice when a threat is followed by a physical attack or even murder exceed out of all proportion whatever discomfort, inconvenience, and cost may be incurred by seeking legal advice and appropriately informing third parties. A very important part of the process is to seek advice from a lawyer who is experienced in this field. I have concluded from my experience that it is prudent to err on the side of caution and safety and seek legal advice whenever it occurs to me as a serious consideration. I have been gratified by how seriously legal consultants take my concerns, how helpful their advice is from a practical point of view, and how often threatening patients can be contained and their treatment continued, with an approach that combines informing third parties and confronting the patients' threatening behavior in a therapeutic manner. *I have never felt that any lawyer has responded to my concerns with a dismissive attitude, as if to suggest that I am making a mountain out of a molehill. Legal counsel of professional insurance organizations would much rather hear of a potential problem when it is first arising than after some destructive action has occurred, and a clinician who has been accused of some kind of professional deficiency needs to be defended. That, of course, is secondary to the importance of preventing the destructive action from taking place.*

Therapists may hesitate to seek legal advice or to inform third parties for a number of reasons. As threats hopefully are not a common feature in any one therapist's experience, one may be reluctant to tread upon the unfamiliar ground of legal considerations. One may be (misguidedly) concerned about the ramifications of breaching one's patient's confidentiality, if one is not well informed about the limits of therapist–client confidentiality. One may rigidly and mistakenly place a higher priority on one's patient's right to confidentiality than on a third party's need for protection. One may feel, utilizing what might be called a manic defense (Racker, 1968), that one can manage the threatening patient on one's own, without external help or advice.

Therapists who are aware of the laws in their jurisdiction pertaining to third-party disclosure and who are prepared to seek advice in areas (such as the law) that are outside their area of expertise are in a much better position to fulfill their professional obligations. These include offering competent psychotherapy or other treatment, including treatment to the threatening patient when it is possible to maintain the treatment relationship, and (in a group context) helping the group to deal with the threat; ascertaining when it is appropriate to notify individuals and/or agencies outside the group, and doing so; and protecting oneself from a legal point of view. Knowing about the appropriate options for dealing with a threat provides support to therapists in a manner similar to how competence in other areas of their work provides a realistic sense of self-confidence.

Managing threats against third parties in a partial hospitalization program like DTP appears easier than doing so in most other group settings. We have the advantage of being able to assess our patients' potential for violent behavior in an ongoing manner, 4½ days a week. This offers a much greater opportunity for observation, both with respect to time and to number of observers, than, for example, an outpatient psychotherapy group that meets for 1½ hours once a week. Group therapists under the latter circumstances might be obliged to act more quickly upon the utterance of a threat to a third party if they did not expect to see the threatening individual for another week.

One concern involves the risk of becoming so preoccupied by the threatening patient's behavior (i.e., the threat) that the treatment of the patient suffers. A therapist's preoccupation with the danger her patient may represent to a third party can result in a tendency to deny the danger and not continue a needed ongoing assessment assiduously enough. Conversely, one may deal with one's anxiety by assessing the patient in a frequent but ineffective manner, possibly becoming oblivious to other, clinical concerns that need to be addressed. Obtaining an elective, urgent, or emergency psychiatric opinion regarding patient dangerousness should always be a consideration.

Group therapy can take on an unduly behavioral coloring if leaders and patients are preoccupied with ascertaining the extent of a group member's dangerousness. The threatening behavior must be dealt with appropriately to vitiate the threat. The danger is that, especially if the therapist is not satisfied that necessary practical steps have been taken to deal with the threat, she may remain preoccupied with the danger that the threatening patient presents, while not definitively deciding on what measures need to be taken concretely. This also depends on to what extent the therapist's countertransference fear and anger have been consciously experienced and adequately contained (Steinberg & Duggal, 2004). If the therapist remains preoccupied with the threat, she may try to deal with the threat in a concrete, practical manner in order to reassure herself that the danger is under control; that is, in a defensive manner, designed to ward off her own fear. Alternatively, the therapist may act out her anger in an unproductive way, assuming a censorious attitude toward the threatening patient, whether the patient is present or not. Clearly, both practical and countertransference ramifications of the threat need to be dealt with adequately if patients and therapists are to continue in a treatment relationship. It is impossible for therapists to find a place in our minds to engage in our clinical work when we do not feel safe.

98   *Group Psychotherapy and Partial Hospitalization*

References

Appelbaum R (1985). The Tarasoff and the clinician: Problems in fulfilling the duty to protect. *American Journal of Psychiatry*, 142: 425–429.

Bion WR (1970). *Attention and Interpretation*. London: Tavistock.

Granholm E, McQuaid JR, McClure ES, Link, PC, Perivoliotis D, Gottlieh JD, Patterson TL, & Jeste DV (2007). Randomized controlled trial of cognitive behavioral social skills training for older people with schizophrenia: 12-Month follow-up. *Journal of Clinical Psychiatry*, 68: 730–737.

Home Office and Department of Health (2003). *Personality Disorder: No Longer a Diagnosis of Exclusion—Policy Implementation Guidance for the Development of Services for People with Personality Disorder*. London: Home Office.

Kaplan Hl & Sadock BJ (1993). *Comprehensive Group Psychotherapy*, 3rd ed. Baltimore, MD: Williams & Wilkins.

Keats J (1817). Letter to George and Thomas Keats, December 21, 1817. Quoted in Bion (1970).

Knapp S & Van de Creek L (2000). Real life vignettes following the duty to protect. *Journal of Psychotherapy and Independent Practice*, 1: 83–88.

Ogden TH (2004). An introduction to the reading of Bion. *International Journal of Psycho-Analysis*, 85(2): 285–300.

O'Kelly JG & Azim HFA (1993). Staff-staff relations group. *International Journal of Group Psychotherapy*, 43: 469–483.

Racker H (1968). *Transference and Countertransference*. Madison, CT: International Universities Press.

Safran JD & Muran JC (2000). *Negotiating the Therapeutic Alliance*. New York: Guilford Press.

Simon RI (2000). Legal issues in psychiatry. In Sadock BJ & Sadock BA (eds). *Comprehensive Textbook of Psychiatry*, 7th ed. Baltimore, MD: Lippincott, Williams and Wilkins.

Simon RI (2001). Duty to foresee, forewarn, and protect against violent behavior: A psychiatric perspective. In Shafli M & Shafli SL (eds). *School Violence: Assessment, Management, Prevention*. Washington, DC: American Psychiatric Publishing.

Steinberg PI & Duggal S (2004). Threats of violence in group-oriented day treatment. *International Journal of Group Psychotherapy*, 54(1): 5–22.

Steinberg PI, Rosie J, Joyce AS, O'Kelly J, Piper WE, Lyon D, Bahrey F, & Duggal S (2004). The psychodynamic psychiatry service of the University of Alberta Hospital: A thirty-year history. *International Journal of Group Psychotherapy*, 54: 521–538.

Tarasoff v Regents of the University of California et al. 131 *California Reporter*, 14, 551 P 2d 334 (Cal 1976).

Weinstock KR, Leong GB, & Silva JA (2001). Potential erosion of psychotherapists-patient privilege beyond California: Dangers of "criminalizing" Tarasoff. *Behavioral Sciences and the Law*, 19: 437–449.

6   Freud in the Clinic

The Psychodynamic Psychiatry Service of the University of Alberta Hospital— A 30-Year History

Introduction

This chapter describes the Psychodynamic Psychiatry Service (PPS) of the University of Alberta Hospital over its 30 years of development (to 2006). The name of the service itself, including the word "Psychodynamic," given when the service was reorganized in 2001, in the heyday of the drug revolution in psychiatry, was quite unusual and perhaps even provocative. This psychiatric organization consists of three clinical programs—an outpatient clinic and intensive day and evening programs—and an integral evaluation and research unit. PPS is unique in its group psychotherapy clinical orientation, its psychodynamic theoretical orientation, and its integration of an ongoing research program that establishes empirical validation of its clinical work. The productivity and longevity of this psychiatric organization appear to derive from several strengths, including cooperation between leaders of the clinical and research programs; the institution of staff relations groups (SRGs) in the three clinical programs; the operation of the fully integrated evaluation and research program that serves to provide empirical support for the treatment offered; and a unifying ideology characterized by the valuing of both psychodynamic and group-oriented work. Other important factors to the success of PPS include the strengths of the founder of the service and financial and other support of the academic department in which it is housed. This chapter describes the historical development and structure and functioning of PPS, the challenges it has been confronted with, and the responses to those challenges. We conclude with factors contributing to its survival and productivity and with thoughts about the future.

The PPS is the central psychiatric outpatient service within the Department of Psychiatry at the University of Alberta Hospital in Edmonton, Canada. It consists of four integrated units: the psychiatric treatment clinic (PTC), an outpatient program offering comprehensive psychiatric assessment to adults, a range of primarily group-based psychotherapeutic treatments, and psychopharmacological treatment; intensive day treatment program (DTP) and evening treatment program (ETP), offering 18-week group and milieu therapies for those with personality disorders and concomitant Axis I disorders,

DOI: 10.4324/9781003200581-9

100   *Group Psychotherapy and Partial Hospitalization*

especially affective disorders (Piper, Rosie, Joyce & Azim, 1996); and the research and evaluation unit (REU).

We know of few psychiatric services whose main clinical orientation is group psychotherapy and fewer whose theoretical orientation is psychodynamic. The involvement of the leaders in the two core aspects of the program—clinical work and research—has strengthened PPS. The psychiatrist-leaders of the clinical units are actively involved in patient assessments integral to ongoing research and in collaborating with the research staff in project implementation. The clinical and research leaders meet weekly to deal with systemic problems; make decisions regarding service, education, and research; and discuss future directions. They also meet monthly with the therapist coordinators of the clinical staffs to manage service issues. These meetings are important in managing or minimizing splits among and within the PPS programs and in dealing with potential difficulties and strains in the relationships of PPS to the Department of Psychiatry, which administers it, and to the regional health system administrative body, the Capital Health Authority.

There existed, to my awareness, about half a dozen programs in the world similar in structure and function to PPS when I worked there. Few jurisdictions are willing to invest the energy, personnel, and money needed to offer this type of treatment to this patient population. One motivation for including this chapter in this book is the hope that clinicians in a variety of clinical settings may be able to incorporate some of what they read of PPS into their clinical programs and units.

Structure and Functioning

The staff of PTC consists of a psychiatrist/leader and ten staff therapists under a therapist-coordinator. New patients, generally referred by family physicians or self-referred, receive psychiatric assessments on a walk-in basis. Treatment is primarily group based, including long-term intensive therapy, short-term therapy for complicated grief (Piper, McCallum & Azim, 1992), and a variety of supportive groups. Some brief individual psychotherapy is also provided, as well as medications, chiefly antidepressants.

ETP is an intensive 18-week, psychodynamically oriented group therapy program for about 25 patients with comorbid personality disorders, affective disorders, anxiety disorders, and eating disorders, previously described in detail (Nixon, Azim, Ratcliffe & Dyck, 1976; O'Kelly & Piper, 1996; O'Kelly & Azim, 1993). Treatment is provided by a staff of two psychiatrists and five group psychotherapists, including a therapist-coordinator.

Each evening begins with a process-oriented large group for all patients and staff, followed by a variety of small groups, mostly psychodynamic in nature, with some being more psychoeducational, which employ, among other approaches, art, videotape, psychodrama, and exercise. All the work is guided primarily by psychodynamic, specifically object relations, theory, with technical emphasis on limit setting and a here-and-now focus. Much of this description of ETP also applies to the somewhat larger DTP, composed

Freud in the Clinic   101

of about 35 patients and a staff of 2 psychiatrists and 8 group therapists, including a therapist-coordinator. As in ETP, the daily work begins with a large process-oriented group, followed by a variety of unstructured and more psychoeducational groups focusing on themes such as interpersonal relations, the development of self and identity, and constructive communication.

The weekly SRG is an essential component of each of the clinical services (O'Kelly & Azim, 1993). Here the inevitable differences that occur between staff members are aired. Splitting among staff is confronted, and countertransference difficulties are explored and worked on. It is unlikely that our clinical programs could function as effectively as they do without these groups. They not only provide a venue for resolving intra-staff difficulties but also, and importantly, offer opportunities for staff to support each other with positive feedback. Finally, REU conducts ongoing program evaluation and staff performance studies, as well as formal clinical research on both individual and group psychotherapy. The research staff is composed of a coordinator, a master's level psychologist, two psychology technicians, and several grant-supported research assistants.

Development and Challenges

Tensions Between PPS and the Department of Psychiatry

Dr. Hassan Azim joined the Department of Psychiatry at the University of Alberta Hospital in Edmonton in 1973. With a thorough grounding in the principles of the therapeutic community, theories of group psychotherapy, and systems thinking of the 1950s and 1960s, substantial funding and support by the department chair, and a commitment to evaluation and research from the outset, Azim founded both DTP and ETP that year, both based on psychodynamically oriented group psychotherapy. Three years later, he established PTC and REU; together the four units continue to comprise PPS. Tensions between PPS and the larger Department of Psychiatry persisted through the years, but there have been two periods in particular where considerable resistance to the very existence of PPS was mounted. In the first period (1973–1979), psychiatrists within the Department of Psychiatry voiced a number of complaints about PPS. They were upset that inpatients could not be automatically accepted into PTC immediately after hospital discharge. They complained that so much treatment responsibility was given to nonpsychiatrists in PTC. However, such complaints seemed to be derivatives of covert objections that were aimed at the PPS director, Dr. Azim, for becoming too powerful and resourceful, compared to other psychiatrists. In part, these tensions may have been exacerbated by the contrasting orientations—psychodynamic versus biological—of PPS and the department.

This same theme erupted again in the early 1990s. This time the overt objection was that PPS was an unnecessary component of bureaucracy that

102 *Group Psychotherapy and Partial Hospitalization*

resisted integration into the rest of the psychiatry department, that it was too autonomous, and that it required the benefit of hospital administration to make cost-effective decisions. The covert objections were that PPS had become too elite, that the director had become too powerful again, and that in tight economic times, resources had to be shared, particularly since it was thought that so much was being devoted to "the worried well." This resistance involved a prolonged period of quiet opposition and ultimately some systemic changes.

In 1993, PPS lost control of its budget, and Dr. Azim resigned from the university, at which point PPS was administered as four unintegrated and unrelated programs, without an explicitly appointed leader and with questions about its future. Some positions were lost. Monthly meetings of PPS staff as a whole were discontinued. Following these developments, the pressures of resistance from within the department abated somewhat. The administration came to realize, however, that a valued set of clinical services and a productive research team might be lost but deserved to be preserved. The emphasis on integration of all services by the chair of the Department of Psychiatry resulted in much attention being paid to evaluating and redefining the boundaries between PPS and other parts of the department. Perceptions of PPS by others had to be acknowledged and addressed. Two factors were responsible for the successful integration of PPS into the larger department. The PPS staff more actively demonstrated the value of PPS to the larger psychiatric staff group and, at the same time, became more sensitive to other departmental programs and the importance of these linkages in treatment planning for individual patients. Staff developed a greater appreciation of how PPS interacted with other groups in the department and how all program groups were part of the larger whole.

Fortunately, the continuity of PPS was affirmed by the reinstitution of a new director in 2001. This appointment served to boost staff morale and prompted, among other activities, the development of regular PPS-wide in-service meetings and of publication of articles about PPS (Steinberg & Duggal, 2004; Steinberg, Duggal & Ogrodniczuk, 2008; Steinberg, et al., 2009; Steinberg & Ogrodniczuk, 2010; Steinberg, et al., 2004). The academic strengthening of PPS in turn enhanced the psychotherapy training program for residents in the Department of Psychiatry of the University of Alberta. Increasing numbers of medical students and psychiatry residents from Edmonton and other Canadian medical schools from Vancouver to St. Johns choose to spend elective rotations in PPS, learning about group psychotherapy and group dynamics.

The Integration of the Psychiatric Treatment Clinic

Throughout its early years, until 1986, the PTC was quite unique in relation to other aspects of the Department of Psychiatry and to the other components of PPS. Therapists, drawn from the disciplines of nursing, occupational therapy, psychology, and social work, conducted psychiatric assessments traditionally done by psychiatrists and residents in other areas of the department. Further exemplifying its uniqueness, assessments and treatments were provided on a walk-in basis, with no prior appointment or referral from another professional required. The clinic had operated with its own budget according to its own needs, sometimes with little regard or respect for that of the department. Staff in PTC felt a loyalty to it and its psychiatrist-leader and pursued their own ideology. For example, if a child therapy specialist was needed, one was sought, even if it meant replacing a departing social worker with a psychologist, without regard to hospital policy. Alienation between PTC and DTP and ETP arose in the context of negotiating patient appointments. PTC staff became frustrated and envious of the other staff, who were perceived as having the luxury of scheduled appointments for referrals from PTC. The occasional refusal of these referrals would exacerbate their frustration. PTC staff, in turn, felt considerable pressure conducting initial assessments without the protective barrier of scheduled appointments.

Meetings at several levels attempted to reduce splitting between the programs. Now PTC enjoys a less estranged relationship with other components of PPS and the department, with improved flow of patients between components. The integration of PTC within PPS is supported by monthly meetings of the leaders and therapist coordinators of the four components of PPS.

Splits Within the Day Treatment Program

DTP had experienced a quick succession of three psychiatrist-leaders in the years prior to 1982, after which one psychiatrist led the program for most of the time since. Before then DTP had become a divided system. Both the daily large patient–staff group and the SRG were characterized by stubborn silences, verbal fighting, and unresolved tensions among the staff. Staff loyalties were seriously split between the series of new program leaders, on one side, and the one staff therapist, on the other, whose psycho-drama group was perceived as the primary locus of clinical work. Other staff infighting ensued, such as a significant disagreement about whether and how adolescents should be treated within DTP.

To manage the destructive idealization and compartmentalization of the psychodrama group, its focus was changed, with less emphasis on dramatic role-playing. Patients were encouraged to link the work in this group to other parts of DTP, facilitate programmatic integration, and reduce devaluing and idealizing of different program components. This intervention succeeded, resulting in and partly facilitated by the resignation of the psychodrama group therapist who was serving as a fight leader. With the appointment of the new psychiatrist, who more closely identified with the ideals of the founder of PPS (Dr. Azim) than his several predecessors, the splits in the program tended to heal.

104   *Group Psychotherapy and Partial Hospitalization*

Difficult Transition in the Evening Treatment Program

ETP expanded significantly in the late 1980s from a patient census of 11, treated by 1 psychiatrist and 4 therapists to a census of some 30 patients, with 3 additional therapists. During this time, however, a therapist who had frequent conflicts with the psychiatrist/leader and who had recently left ETP committed suicide. This event had a very jarring effect on the staff, resulting in a complete turnover of therapists and ultimately the resignation of the psychiatrist/leader in 1989. While his successor had a psychodynamic orientation, he had little experience in group psychotherapy. His initial suggestions regarding redirection in therapy were often greeted by staff with a stony silence. The staff were still loyal to their departed leader and were not confident that the new psychiatrist knew what he was doing.

In late 1990, the psychiatrist's position was rendered more difficult when a borderline patient brought a lawsuit against him as well as an ETP therapist and the hospital. While the latter two suits were quickly settled out of court, the psychiatrist was left to defend the suit alone for the subsequent seven years. At the same time, other stressors, including severe cutbacks in the health-care system and a resultant reduction in staff, occurred. With increasing patient morbidity, ETP's existence seemed in jeopardy.

SRG proved most valuable in containing the anxieties from these several sources. There the psychiatrist/leader tried at all times to model openness (O'Kelly & Azim, 1993; Yalom, 1985) and invited the therapists to be candid in exploring their concerns, while continuing to work under very difficult circumstances. During this time, psychiatrist/leader also received immeasurable support from his colleagues, the psychiatrist/leaders, in the weekly team leaders meeting. His writing a series of papers highlighting the program components had a cathartic effect, as well as boosting team morale in facing the ongoing challenges (O'Kelly & Azim, 1993; O'Kelly & Piper, 1996; O'Kelly, Piper, Kerber & Fowler, 1998) All this allowed the psychiatrist/ leader and the therapists an opportunity to modify and adapt a therapeutic approach more suited to the changing patient population.

Increasing Morbidity in Psychodynamic Psychiatry Service

The composition of the patients in PPS has changed over the years, as higher functioning patients have found other psychodynamic treatment resources in the region. At present, over half of the patients in DTP have a diagnosis of borderline or narcissistic personality disorder or both. Many have antisocial traits; a few have full-blown antisocial personality disorder. This population is challenging to treat, especially with respect to their motivation to understand their interpersonal difficulties, their capacity to tolerate uncomfortable affects and frustration, and their limited impulse control and psychological mindedness. One manifestation of this higher level of pathology is the increasing occurrence of physical threats enacted by DTP patients (Steinberg

Freud in the Clinic   105

& Duggal, 2004; Steinberg, Duggal & Ogrodniczuk, 2008). This evolution in patient pathology has had a negative impact on therapists' morale, especially when they fail to acknowledge and accept the limitations inherent in working with these patients.

With increased patient morbidity, the staff have been encouraged to shift their technical work in the direction of greater interpretative and confrontational interventions, but they have experienced this shift primarily as an invitation to do more sophisticated psychotherapeutic work than they have felt capable of doing. This led to some initial resistance to change from a more supportive, less confrontational approach. The emotionally intense responses by patients to the confrontations seemed to further staff resistance to change. Staff needed both support and teaching to help develop new approaches to their work with patients, as well as to enhance their capacity for reflection of both transference and countertransference reactions. The SRG and in-service training on topics such as projective identification helped facilitate these changes.

Integration of the Research and Evaluation Unit

The existence of REU as an integral element of PPS has been quite unique and unprecedented. From 1978, it started to conduct small-scale evaluations of the treatment programs offered to patients in the three clinical programs. These data began to support the effectiveness of the programs and also to identify aspects that needed revision or development, as shown in a series of early studies (Azim & Joyce, 1986; Dyck, Joyce & Azim, 1984). In general, therapists in the clinical programs welcomed REU's efforts to collect data on intervention activities and patient responses and were enthusiastic about applying findings to improve the developing clinical services. An early trial of a manual-based psychotherapy in the PTC examined the process and outcome of a time-limited individual therapy model (Joyce & Piper, 1990). Staff of REU started to provide regular seminars for clinical staff during this study; a new director of REU was recruited. This appointment led to a dramatic transition from conducting small-scale program evaluative studies of primarily local relevance and interest to conducting methodologically rigorous and generalizable large-scale psychotherapy clinical trials. A 15-fold increase in major funding from external sources accrued over the next 15 years, supporting five major studies. Fortunately, PPS was able to provide the considerable resources necessary for carrying out such projects, including (a) program leaders who support the integration of clinical and research activities, who welcome having their treatments evaluated, and who participate directly in research projects; (b) experienced therapists who can tolerate the demands of contemporary research methodology, including the use of therapy manuals, close monitoring of clinical work, feedback regarding therapeutic technique on the basis of adherence assessments, dealing with patients who have been assigned rather than selected, and completing rating forms about the therapy process; (c) experienced intake assessors who can

106   *Group Psychotherapy and Partial Hospitalization*

appropriately screen, prepare, and refer patients to the treatments being studied; (d) stable programs with high volumes of patients; (e) research staff in permanent positions of some stability; and (f) external research grants that cover part of the costs of complex projects.

In 1985, the research unit tested REU's research resource potential by embarking on a randomized clinical trial investigating the efficacy of short-term individual psychotherapy. The resources of PPS proved to be more than sufficient, leading to successful completion of the project. The trial represented the first of a series of such studies of time-limited, dynamically oriented therapies, each involving a large number of patients, typically 150–250, and a period of data collection of 3–5 years. The studies were consistently funded by provincial or federal granting agencies. They included a controlled trial of short-term individual therapy for a mixed outpatient population (Piper, Azim, McCallum, & Joyce 1990); a controlled trial of short-term group therapy for patients with complicated grief (Piper et al., 1992); a controlled trial of day treatment partial hospitalization for patients with mood and personality disorders (Piper et al., 1996); a predictor study of evening treatment partial hospitalization for patients with mood and personality disorders (McCallum, Piper & O'Kelly, 1997); and two aptitude-treatment interaction trials that involved two personality variables and two forms (interpretive and supportive) of short-term therapy, one project addressing individual therapy for a mixed outpatient population and the other project addressing group therapy for patients with complicated grief (Piper, McCallum, Joyce, Rosie, & Ogrodniczuk, 2001).

As the trials progressed over the years, they became more complex and more clinically informative. In addition to addressing basic questions about treatment effectiveness, the studies investigated mediating process variables such as therapist technique, patient work and patient affect, and moderating patient personality variables such as psychological mindedness and quality of object relations. The weekly seminars associated with the projects were attended by clinicians, researchers, and clinician-researchers from a wide range of disciplines, reflecting the multidisciplinary composition of PPS. The research generated a large number of publications, including four books (Piper et al., 1992, 1996, 2001; McCallum & Piper, 1997). Overall, PPS has fostered a spirit of inquiry that has been conducive to conducting high-quality clinical research. That facilitation of excellent research is systemic to PPS is evidenced by its continuation after the departure of the director in 1997 and the transfer of REU leadership to a new director. The research unit continues to conducting clinical trials that follow in a programmatic way from previous investigations.

The program of research on time-limited, psychodynamically oriented therapies has been characterized by comprehensive assessments of treatment outcome and the assessment of patient characteristics relevant to productive therapy process and treatment benefit. This ensures that the studies have immediate clinical applicability and thus facilitates the support of the clinical staff. The research program encompassed modalities of individual

Freud in the Clinic   107

therapy (Piper et al., 1990: Piper, McCallum, & Azim, 1992); group therapy for patients with complicated grief (Piper et al., 1992); and intensive, group-oriented partial hospitalization treatment (McCallum & Piper, 1997; McCallum, Piper & O'Kelly, 1997; Piper, Rosie, Joyce, & Azim, 1996).

The integration of REU has not proceeded without difficulties, however. In addition to conducting clinical trials, REU collects data on staff activity and caseload characteristics relevant to annual therapist performance evaluations. As a result, there have been negative feelings expressed about being "evaluated" by REU. This concern reemerges whenever a new investigation is launched. In addition, there have been tensions associated with implementing treatments as called for by the research protocol. Technical manuals are developed by the research unit, and therapists are expected to show strong "adherence" to them. Feelings about the researchers' intrusion on the therapy process and the rigidity of the treatment manuals are expressed in the weekly seminars associated with each project. In general, these tensions between the clinicians and researchers are resolved through active collaboration and compromise during each research endeavor. The research team, for example, revised their therapy manuals, allowing for greater therapist flexibility, functioning more as guidelines than prescriptions for the therapeutic interventions. Clinicians were asked and supported for their input regarding development of the therapy manuals and other aspects of the research protocols. They, in turn, came to have a greater appreciation of the importance of technical consistency in the context of research.

Changes in Approach

Treatment approaches within the clinical programs have evolved over the years, particularly as the patient population has changed. In DTP, for example, psycho-educative aspects inherent in psychodynamic therapy recently have been acknowledged and integrated into the program (McWilliams, 2003). New semi-structured groups dealing with topics such as critical thinking, self-discipline, the integrity of the self, and development of an identity have been created. A follow-up psychotherapy group has been added for those patients who could benefit from more psychologically intensive work. Such program changes can, of course, introduce unforeseen problems and conflicts. Some patients, for example, envied those who were accepted into the new follow-up group. Others who were not invited felt that this signified that they needed to do no other work and were deemed cured. Therapists sometimes became advocates for their patients regarding acceptance into the follow-up group. As with other emotional reactions to changing aspects of the program, these reactions served as grist for the therapeutic mill within DTP.

We have not always been successful at accurately conveying to external systems what we do with our patients, creating misperceptions about elitism, and resulting in a tendency to be isolated in the 1980s and the early 1990s. We rejected inappropriate referrals without sufficient explanation to the referral source. These rejections further confirmed the view of PPS as an elitist,

108   *Group Psychotherapy and Partial Hospitalization*

ivory tower organization catering only to the "worried well." Sometimes, we were viewed as exercising favoritism, accepting inappropriate referrals from some sources but not from others. In order to encourage appropriate referrals and to indicate an openness to accepting new patients, we have designed brochures describing each clinical program, highlighting which types of patients are appropriate for which programs and distributing them to Edmonton family physicians and new referral sources. We have become more conscientious in contacting our referral sources to discuss referrals and rejections.

Factors Contributing to the Survival and Productivity of PPS

Cooperation among leaders of the constituent programs of PPS has been essential for PPS to function well and indeed to survive. This involves regular meetings, collaborating in each other's clinical programs and in research, and being willing to confront problems in the system and problems with each other. The judicious use of authority by PPS leaders has been an important source of stability in PPS, as has mutual support (including confrontation, when necessary) of PPS leaders. SRGs are an essential part of the maintenance of each clinical program. These meetings ensure that the team leaders and coordinators in each program are aware of the work problems facing the front-line staff and the means to resolve them. The regular meetings of PPS leaders help to ensure a harmonized response to policy directives and proposals from the level of the encompassing system, that is, the administration of the University of Alberta Hospital.

A unifying ideology, both psychodynamic and group oriented, has been central to PPS's success. Application of psychoanalytic concepts to our thinking about the therapy groups we offer in each program, and the relationship of the four components of PPS to each other, as well as to the relationship of PPS to the Department of Psychiatry and to the regional health authority, has been essential to the maintenance and success of PPS. Such knowledge has led us to implement the crucial remedies of regular staff meetings at all levels, including SRGs, and to attempt the judicious use of authority throughout PPS (Rosie, Azim, Piper, & Joyce, 1995).

When issues arise in any of the components of DTP and ETP, we have become more vigilant in bringing them back to the process-oriented large group for continued working through. This enhances both the depth of the psychotherapeutic work done on here-and-now issues and its breadth in terms of the number of patients and staff who can contribute to the exploration and benefit by it. The large group in particular offers an occasion for patients and staff to cooperate and examine issues that otherwise might be lost.

Combining pharmacotherapy and psychotherapy within the partial hospital treatment programs has been a challenge. While medication often stabilizes our patients, making them more amenable to intensive group

Freud in the Clinic   109

therapy (O'Kelly & Piper, 1996; Steinberg, 2007), it also provides an opportunity for some patients to become involved in enactments. Addressing the acting out behavior in group, often with the support of other patients, can improve compliance and allow patients to delve further into psychodynamic issues.

The latter refers to unconscious conflicts and emotional pain about disturbances in interpersonal relations and psychic deficiency states that our patients largely are unable to articulate verbally and are expressed in action, often destructive and/or self-destructive in nature. Although at times these were acted out outside of group, they were more easily dealt with when expressed in group. For example, a patient might convey that they were angry by behaving in a manner likely to provoke other members of the group and the staff. It usually would fall to the staff to invite the subject patient and the patients reacting to him to think about what was transpiring. Many patients usually are able to relate to this type of situation and help the subject patient become aware of his anger and the effect on others of how he is evacuating it.

By "psychic deficiency states," I am referring to the types of difficulties in thinking, feeling, and impulse control (described in Chapter 5 of Psychoanalysis in Medicine, *summarized here):*

> *significant disturbances of ... thought processes ... [including] the maintaining of mutually contradictory beliefs or thoughts without awareness of the contradiction; beliefs that [are] obviously false but [do] not qualify to be called delusions; a tendency to dissociate or derail thinking when an emotionally intolerable thought [is] approaching consciousness; and abrupt changes of subject to avoid articulating an emotionally disturbing thought. Other disturbances in thinking [include] twisting the meaning of a word the therapist [uses] to render meaningless what she [is] trying to express; hairsplitting about the meaning of a word until what was emotionally important about the discussion [is] lost; and responding in a tangential or irrelevant manner to the discussion.*

Disturbances of ... thought content include "becoming paranoid or grandiose when under stress" (Steinberg, 2021:68).
Difficulties with affect regulation include

> *volatility of affect ... [such as] rapidly becoming upset, enraged, despairing or elated; affective numbness ... feeling little affect, or becoming affectively numb when an emotionally disturbing thought [arises]; or a characteristically superficial expression of affect that [is] unresponsive to current circumstances, for example, consistently appearing cheerful or calm. Difficulty containing impulses ... [may be] manifest by a tendency to action rather than reflection on how one [feels] and discussion of what [is] transpiring in one's inner experience*
> (Steinberg, 2021:69)

for example, abruptly leaving a psychotherapy group that is upsetting; quitting a treatment program impulsively; not showing up for individual, family, or group psychotherapy; or becoming enraged in a psychotherapy session and expressing it in an

110　*Group Psychotherapy and Partial Hospitalization*

intense manner. Sometimes, patients act in impulsive and destructive ways outside of psychotherapy sessions, such as leaving their partners, getting into physical fights, or relapsing into substance abuse.

It is a challenge to view a patient simultaneously as both "a disturbed person and diseased organism" (Docherty et al., 1977), a sometimes daunting task in the heat of an intense therapy situation. Involving therapists in the instrumental task of tracking prescriptions and patient medication compliance has helped integrate treatment modalities while adding a check to our system (Nixon et al., 1976).

That the PPS is located in Canada is not incidental to its success. We are fortunate in enjoying comprehensive health-care coverage, including psychiatric treatment for everyone, regardless of financial status. The vast majority of our patients have little or no capacity to pay privately for mental health care; they have available to them all the treatment resources of PPS. Moreover, the staff, both psychiatric and nonmedical, are secure regarding being paid for their work. These conditions are an important basis for good morale that should not be taken for granted, especially when compared to other health-care systems.

Concepts of Group Functioning

The concepts about group functioning introduced by Bion (described briefly in Chapter 1) were not mentioned or in evidence during my time in DTP. Either these concepts had been forgotten and neglected by the time I arrived, or the staff never were any more familiar with them then than I was. In my opinion, this was a theoretical deficiency of PPS staff, supplementation of which would have enhanced the functioning of the many psychotherapy groups extant in PPS. In addition, wider familiarity with Bion's contributions to current psychoanalytic theory and technique would have enhanced the individual therapy being offered at PTC.

I will elaborate here a bit on Bion's concepts of groups. Bion (1961), originally in studying groups in a military psychiatric rehabilitation unit during the Second World War, made a very original contribution to group theory and practice. He essentially focuses on the process of what was going on in the group between the group members, in particular in the relationship between the group members and the leader. This is as opposed to making interpretations regarding the content of what is brought up in the group. He describes work groups that fulfill the task for which they became a group. This is an ideal outcome of group formation, be it a psychotherapy group or any other form of group meeting for the purpose of doing work. He called this "work group." Bion notes that groups often are diverted from their work because of intense emotional interactions in the group that may result in the group becoming a "basic assumption" (BA) group, that is, a group dominated by a BA. In BA groups, the group's anxieties divert them from the work of the group to a defensive attempt to reduce the anxieties. Bion described three BA groups, fight-or-flight, dependency, and pairing.

Bion (1961) describes members of groups functioning in the BA of dependency (baD), considering the leader as the only person to be regarded but at the same time

Freud in the Clinic 111

showing by their behaviour that they don't believe the leader knows his job. Benefit is felt not to come from the group members but only from the leader, so members of the group feel they are being cheated or starved (that is, most of the time) unless they are being addressed by the leader. Members throw all their cares on the leader and sit back and wait for him to solve all their problems. This results in an experience of dissatisfaction; not only are their problems not solved by the leader, but there is no opportunity for group members behaving this way to learn from the experience of thinking.

In groups dominated by the BA of pairing (baP), a couple of patients monopolize the session and mostly ignore the rest of the group. The group has a peculiar air of hopefulness and expectation. This finds expression verbally in ideas that the couple will put an end to neurotic disabilities, that is, will solve the problems of the other members of the group, and then an improved group, a new kind of community, will be developed. The hope engendered is as opposed to feelings of hate, destructiveness, and despair (the experiencing of which the hope defends against). For the hope to be sustained, it is essential for the group to imagine that its leader should be (and remain) unborn. This is a person or idea that will save the group, but this fantasy can only be maintained by a hope that will never be fulfilled. Bion suggests that pairing groups meet for the purpose of maintaining the existence of the group, rather than performing the function the group was intended to do.

Members of groups dominated by the BA of fight-or-flight (baF) experience the group as having something to fight or run away from. The leader of the group is expected to afford an opportunity for flight or aggression; if he makes demands that the group do something else, he is ignored. Essentially, there is a paranoid quality to this group, which finds an enemy outside of itself.

Bion describes characteristics common to all BA groups. He describes BA activity as instantaneous, inevitable, and instinctive. In contrast with work group function, the work of the group for which the group has been created, BA activity makes no demands on the individual for a capacity to cooperate, but depends on the group members' possession of a "valence" (Bion, 1961:153) that Bion describes as an instantaneous, involuntary combination of one individual with another for sharing and acting on a BA. All BA functioning opposes work group function. Emotions associated with BAs include anxiety, fear, hate, and love.

Bion notes that the fight-or-flight group also serves to preserve the group, while the dependency group has gathered in order to attain security from one individual on whom they depend.

> *The three basic assumptions satisfy different needs: a sense of protection by and reference of the leader in the case of baD; of effective action and strength in the case of the baF; and the hopeful expectancy of an unborn, future saviour (a Messiah) in baP … The three basic assumptions serve to preserve the group on an unconscious level and in order to do this they go against the interests and welfare of individuals.*
>
> *(Vermote, 2019:55)*

Work groups, by contrast, maintain contact with reality and solve problems in a rational, scientific manner.

112 *Group Psychotherapy and Partial Hospitalization*

Bion distinguishes between groups operating on a BA level whose members share feelings corresponding to baF, baP, or baD groups, and what he called a sophisticated or work group level that deals with reality. The work group, not entertaining unrealistic fantasies as BA groups do, is formed through cooperation and rewarded for doing a task. One can see conflicts in groups between tendencies toward a BA and toward work.

Bion compared some of the functioning of BA groups to psychotic functioning. This led him to apply his observations on groups to individuals, eventuating in his idea that there is a psychotic and nonpsychotic part of everyone's personality (Bion, 1957). This is an influential concept that is very helpful in both understanding patients and the different levels of functioning one can see them engaging in and in therapeutically addressing more severely disturbed parts of individuals' personalities.

I wanted to give the reader a taste of Bion's ideas about groups. One can consider how these concepts may throw light on psychotherapy groups, other work groups, or, for that matter, social groups, in which one participates. Reading Bion's Experiences in Groups *(1961) may revolutionize the thinking about group functioning of clinicians unfamiliar with his work.*

Future Prospects and Conclusions

One motivation for choosing the name "Psychodynamic Psychiatric Service," in an era dominated largely by advances in psychopharmacology and by the growing influence of pharmaceutical companies, was to acknowledge the importance of a psychoanalytically based understanding our patients— their unconscious conflicts, unmet needs, and psychological strengths and deficits—irrespective of the treatment offered. Hopefully, the continued survival and growth of PPS represent part of a swing in the pendulum back to a more balanced biopsychosocial approach to treatment that values the inclusion of a psychodynamic understanding of the patient. Indeed with regard to the training of new psychiatrists, there are signs of this happening, at least in Edmonton. All psychiatric residents in the Department of Psychiatry may spend a block of time at PPS. This should increase their level of psychotherapeutic skills and the sophistication of their grasp of psychodynamic theory and, consequently, lead to more engagement in psychodynamic psychotherapy in their careers than previously. Such a development harkens back to the vision and energy of Dr. Hassan Azim, without whom PPS likely never would have been founded as an early oasis of group psychotherapy and psychodynamic psychiatry in Western Canada.

Post Script

I learned while this book was in press that after half a century of development, the DTP described in this chapter, experience in which much of Section B of this book is based, is being closed by the health authority; a sad end of a significant psychoanalytically informed contribution to the treatment of serious psychiatric disturbance available to the public free of charge.

References

Azim HFA & Joyce AS (1986). The impact of data-based program modifications on the satisfaction of outpatients in group psychotherapy. *Canadian Journal of Psychiatry*, 31: 119–122.

Bion WR (1957). Differentiation of the psychotic from the non-psychotic personalities. *International Journal of Psycho-Analysis*, 38: 266–275.

Bion WR (1961). *Experiences in Groups and Other Papers*. London and New York: Routledge.

Docherty JP, Marder SR, Vam Kammen DP, & Sins, SC (1977). *Psychotherapy and pharmacotherapy: Conceptual issues*. *American Journal of Psychiatry*, 134: 529–533.

Dyck RJ, Joyce AS, & Azim HFA (1984). Treatment noncompliance as a function of therapist attributes and social support. *Canadian Journal of Psychiatry*, 29: 212–216.

Joyce AS & Piper WE (1990). An examination of Mann's model of time-limited individual psychotherapy. *Canadian Journal of Psychiatry*, 35: 41–49.

McCallum M & Piper WE (Eds.). (1997). *Psychological Mindedness: A Contemporary Understanding*. Mahwah NJ: Lawrence Erlbaum Associates.

McCallum M, Piper WE, & O'Kelly J (1997). Predicting patient benefit from a group-oriented, evening treatment program. *International Journal of Group Psychotherapy*, 47: 291–314.

McWilliams N (2003). Educative aspects of psychoanalysis. *Psychoanalytic Psychology*, 20: 245–260.

Nixon GW, Azim HFA, Ratcliffe VD, & Dyck RJ (1976). Descriptions of an evening program. Unpublished manuscript.

O'Kelly JG & Azim HFA (1993). Staff-staff relations group. *International Journal of Group Psychotherapy*, 43: 469–483.

O'Kelly JG & Piper WE (1996). Group dynamics and medication in evening treatment. *Continuum*, 3: 85–94.

O'Kelly JG, Piper WE, Kerber R, & Fowler J (1998). Exercise groups in an insight oriented evening treatment program. *International Journal of Group Psychotherapy*, 48: 85–98.

Piper WE, Azim HFA, McCallum M & Joyce AS (1990). Patient suitability and outcome in short-term individual psychotherapy. *Journal of Consulting and Clinical Psychology*, 58: 383–380.

Piper WE, Joyce AA, McCallum M, Azim HFA, & Ogrodniczuk JS (2001). *Interpretive and Supportive Psychotherapies: Matching Therapy and Patient Personality*. Washington, DC: American Psychological Association.

Piper WE, McCallum M, & Azim HFA (1992). *Adaptation to Loss through Short-Term Group Psychotherapy*. New York: Guilford Press.

Piper WE, McCallum M, Joyce AS, Rosie JS, & Ogrodniczuk JS (2001). Patient personality and time-limited group psychotherapy for complicated grief. *International Journal of Group Psychotherapy*, 51: 525–552.

Piper WE, Rosie JS, Joyce AS, & Azim HFA (1996). *Time-Limited Day Treatment for Personality Disorders: Integration of Research and Practice in a Group Program*. Washington, DC: American Psychological Association.

Rosie JS, Azim HFA, Piper WE, & Joyce AS (1995). Effective psychiatric day treatment: Historical lessons. *Psychiatric Services*, 46: 1019–1026.

Steinberg PI (2007). The use of low dose neuroleptics in the treatment of patients with severe personality disorder: An adjunct to psychotherapy, *British Columbia Medical Journal*, 49(6): 306–310.

114 *Group Psychotherapy and Partial Hospitalization*

Steinberg PI (2021). *Psychoanalysis in Medicine: Applying Psychoanalytic Concepts to Contemporary Medical Care.* London and New York: Routledge.

Steinberg PI & Duggal S (2004). Threats of violence in group-oriented day treatment. *International Journal of Group Psychotherapy*, 54(1): 5–22.

Steinberg PI, Duggal S, & Ogrodniczuk J (2008). Threats of violence to third parties in group psychotherapy. *Bulletin of the Menninger Clinic*, 72(1): 1–18.

Steinberg PI, Duggal S, Ogrodniczuk J, Bragg K, Handelsman C, MacDonald B, Sayers N, Stovel L, & Hutton K (2009). The function and place of structured groups in psychiatric day treatment. *Smith College Studies in Social Work*, 79(1): 35–49.

Steinberg PI & Ogrodniczuk J (2010). Hatred and fear: Projective identification in group psychotherapy. *Psychodynamic Practice*, 16(2): 201–205.

Steinberg PI, Rosie JS, Joyce AS, O'Kelly JG, Piper WE, Lyon D, Bahrey F, & Duggal S (2004). The psychodynamic psychiatry service of the University of Alberta Hospital: A thirty year history. *International Journal of Group Psychotherapy*, 54(4): 521–538.

Yalom IK (1985). *The Theory and Practice of Group Psychotherapy*, 3rd ed. New York: Basic Books.

Vermote R (2019). *Reading Bion.* London and New York: Routledge.

7 Groups That Support Psychodynamic Group Psychotherapy

The Function and Place of Structured Groups in Psychodynamically Oriented Day Treatment for Personality Disorders

Bion (1961), originally in studying groups in a military psychiatric rehabilitation unit during the Second World War, made a very original contribution to group theory and practice. He essentially focuses on the process of what was going on in the group between the group members, in particular in the relationship between the group members and the leader. This is as opposed to making interpretations regarding the content of what was brought up in the group. He describes work groups that fulfill the task for which they became a group. This is an ideal outcome of group formation, be it a psychotherapy group or any other form of group meeting for the purpose of doing work. He called this "work group." Bion notes that groups often are diverted from their work because of intense emotional interactions in the group that may result in the group becoming a "basic assumption" group, that is, a group dominated by a basic assumption. In basic assumption groups, the group's anxieties divert them from the work of the group to a defensive attempt to reduce the anxieties. Bion described three basic assumption groups, fight-or-flight, dependency, and pairing.

Bion noted that a basic assumption is that people come together as a group for purposes of preserving the group. He believed that groups know only two techniques of self-preservation, fight or flight. In a fight-or-flight group, an enemy outside the group is selected, and the group's energy goes toward imagining fighting this enemy or fleeing from it. In a group dominated by the basic assumption of dependency, the members looked to a leader, not always the identified leader of the group, to take care of them, devolving responsibilities for themselves and for the group onto this leader. In a group dominated by the basic assumption of pairing, the group fantasy is that two individuals in the group get together, and it is assumed that the relationship is a sexual one. There is a shared fantasy that the product of this union will be a savior of the group, delivering them from their anxieties and fears, although the savior never arrives.

Introduction: The Day Treatment Program (DTP)

There is some redundancy between this introduction and the first paragraphs of Chapters 4 and 5. However, I believe there is enough of a different perspective, given the fact that the original article on which this chapter is based had multiple authors, to justify including this introduction. As well, this

DOI: 10.4324/9781003200581-10

116 *Group Psychotherapy and Partial Hospitalization*

chapter includes quite a bit of detail regarding DTP that is not contained in other chapters.

Day treatment is a form of partial hospitalization that can be helpful for patients with personality disorders who do not require inpatient care, but may benefit from more intensive care than is possible on an outpatient basis (Ogrodniczuk & Piper, 2001). Day treatment differs from other forms of partial hospitalization, day hospital and day care, in the amount of emphasis that it gives to active treatment and rehabilitation of patients (Piper, Rosie, Joyce, & Azim, 1996). Treatment is concerned with the optimal recovery of the individual and aims to alleviate symptoms, promote recovery from illness, and/or facilitate insight and intrapsychic integration. *Now I would add that treatment also involves the initiation of an ongoing process of psychological growth, involving expansion of a capacity for thinking and feeling in particular, that could be continued in individual psychotherapy or psychoanalysis after discharge.* Rehabilitation focuses on assisting the individual in accommodating to disability and seeking an optimal level of adaptive functioning in the community. Patients with personality disorders are believed to be good candidates for DTPs.

In contrast to day treatment, day hospital programs are concerned primarily with the treatment of acute illness. They focus on helping patients adjust to periodic crises. Day hospital is appropriate for individuals who would otherwise be treated as inpatients (e.g., a decompensated patient with borderline personality disorder). It is also used for the treatment or rehabilitation of patients who are in transition from inpatient to outpatient care. Also in contrast to day treatment, day care programs are concerned primarily with maintaining patients with chronic debilitating mental disorders. Expectations for rehabilitation and adjustment are modest. Treatment is likely to have only a minor role in day care programs. Patients with schizophrenia are major consumers of day care services.

DTPs differ from the other two forms of partial hospitalization in emphasizing intensive treatment and rehabilitation of patients. They involve an ambulatory approach that offers intensive and structured clinical services within a stable therapeutic milieu. Programs may or may not be time limited. They often use a treatment approach based on group psychotherapy, biological psychiatry, milieu principles, or a systems orientation. They may or may not incorporate individual psychotherapy. Patients typically participate in a variety of therapy groups several hours each weekday for several months. The therapy groups draw from different technical orientations. Family and couple interventions may also be used. DTPs share a number of goals that include reduction of problematic behaviors, modification of maladaptive character traits, symptom relief, and facilitation of psychological maturation.

Our patients suffer from personality disorders of significant severity. Our impression is that most of them function at a borderline level of personality organization, with recurrent relational difficulties, quite limited capacity for emotional intimacy, problems with work, periods of marked depression and anxiety, and vulnerability to substance abuse and other addictive behaviors, such as gambling, shoplifting, binge eating, compulsive sexual behaviors and paraphilias (sexual perversions), and addiction to video games and the internet. *Now, recognizing more profound personality disturbance more than I previously had, I believe that a significant portion of our patients function at a psychotic level of personality organization.* Our patients are also at high risk for self-harm via reckless behavior, including self-mutilation, sexual risk-taking, the acquisition of inordinate debt, and similar self-destructive activities (PDM Task Force, 2006:24).

Many of our patients have a history of suicide attempts and psychiatric hospitalization. Most of our patients have comorbid Axis I (symptomatic) conditions on admission, especially mood and anxiety disorders. At times of serious disturbance in DTP, we deal with threats of violence by patients to other members of the program (Steinberg & Duggal, 2004) or third parties (Steinberg, Duggal & Ogrodniczuk, 2008). Many of our patients, although they are not floridly psychotic, suffer from disturbances in their form or content of thinking, in their affect regulation, and/or in their capacity to contain their impulses significant enough to interfere with their progress in therapy and, for that matter, to interfere with the therapeutic work of other patients. These patients' therapy often benefits by the prescription of a low dose of neuroleptic medication (Steinberg, 2007). The findings described in this chapter are derived from therapists' clinical observations in groups rather than empirical research, although much research has been done on DTP (Piper et al., 1996).

There are a number of features of day treatment that tend to make it an effective treatment for personality disorders (Piper & Rosie, 1998). First, there is the intensity of the group experience. Patients spend a considerable amount of time participating in a number of different groups each day. Second, the structure of DTPs encourages patients to be responsible, engenders mutual respect between patients and staff, and facilitates patients' participation in the treatment of their peers. Third, patients benefit from working with multiple staff and a large number of other patients. Emotionally inhibited patients can benefit from observing emotionally expressive patients and vice versa. Fourth, the groups vary in size, structure, objectives, and processes. Such diversity provides a comprehensive approach to treatment. Finally, the system of groups is integrated and synergistic. Patients are expected to bring up important material and events that occurred in previous groups during current groups. In this way, they are encouraged to think in terms of the total system. This chapter describes the function and place of structured therapy groups within a psychodynamically oriented DTP (Steinberg et al., 2004). In psychodynamically oriented DTPs, the pervasive emphasis is on facilitating insight-oriented work. Such work is attempted in the unstructured, expressive psychotherapy groups. In our DTP, which has served as a model for several other programs abroad, there are two primary types of unstructured groups: the large psychotherapy group and small psychodynamic group.

The Large Group has an important role in reducing and resolving collective disturbances within the total treatment system. This daily meeting of all patients and staff is a crucial stimulus for open confrontation of conflicts

118   *Group Psychotherapy and Partial Hospitalization*

between group members. The Large Group has several other important functions. A primary one is the facilitation of personal insight of individual patients. The patients talk about deeply personal issues in the context of others sharing personal information. With the assistance of therapists and fellow patients, they develop insight about interpersonal conflict and painful feelings. Another function of Large Group is the opportunity for new patients to learn how to "do therapy" by observing their seasoned peers working in the group. It is also a meeting in which new patients are introduced to the group as a whole and departing patients may say goodbye. The group is characterized by intense, affectively laden, insight-oriented work by individual patients.

Throughout their treatment, patients are in one of a number of the unstructured small psychodynamic groups. Each group meets twice a week for 90-minute sessions. These groups are viewed as a central treatment group of DTP, the groups for which other groups are preparatory. Most of the patients attending DTP would not be treatable in a traditional, intensive, small weekly psychotherapy group in an outpatient setting. The structure and nature of DTP allows patients with profound difficulties in their interpersonal relationships to approach insight-oriented work while receiving sufficient support and containment to mitigate against destructive behavior. There is a strong emphasis on patients working to gain insight in the context of group support. Although the interpersonal aspects of group therapy, as emphasized by Yalom (1995), are valued, there is a strong emphasis on individual work. The work in the small groups inevitably reflects themes operating throughout the program. An advantage of the small groups, compared with Large Group, is the greater time available for several individuals to talk in depth on a given issue. The leaders have to ensure, however, that material raised in the small groups is actively integrated for discussion in Large Group.

Exclusive emphasis on expressive work can be counterproductive, especially with borderline and histrionic patients who need little encouragement to express themselves and can be difficult to contain. Such patients may restrict their therapeutic work to catharsis, with predictably limited beneficial results. They may make little effort to work at containing themselves, reflecting on the motivation for their behavior, determining what their intense affects are about, or clarifying what they need to change in themselves. To facilitate their capacity to think and to reflect about themselves and their motivations, as well as to promote the value of containing oneself, more structured exercises that do not emphasize expression of affect need to be incorporated into DTP.

The integration of the structured groups within a psychodynamically oriented DTP thus serves several purposes. First, they provide structure and containment for patients. Second, they teach specific skills. Third, they make day treatment less intimidating for patients who often find insight-oriented work frightening and overwhelming. Finally, such groups support the work of and provide material for discussion in the unstructured groups. We use the term "structure" to refer to groups whose activities are predetermined

Psychodynamic Group Psychotherapy 119

(i.e., the group works with an agenda to address certain topics or goals), as opposed to "unstructured" groups whose activities are not predetermined (i.e., the content flows from whatever the patients bring up in the group). The remainder of this article describes the different types of the structured groups within a psychodynamically oriented DTP and the role that each serves.

One quality that differentiates these structured groups from the structured groups in other types of programs, for example, cognitive behavioral therapy groups, is that these groups are conducted in the context of a psychodynamic group psychotherapy-oriented program whose aim is to help begin people deal with difficulties with their personality and their relationships through greater understanding of unconscious determinants of these difficulties, in addition to having transformational therapeutic experiences with therapists and other group members. This means that difficulties in these areas that inevitably arise in the structured groups can be brought back to the unstructured psychotherapy groups for psychodynamic psychotherapeutic work. When interpersonal difficulties arise within the structured groups, this provides information to staff about which patients need to work on what conflicts in the psychodynamic psychotherapy groups. Staff discuss what happens in the structured groups daily in morning staff meetings to provide each other with current aspects of the functioning of the groups and the individual patients. At times, it may be necessary to deal on the spot with a conflict in a structured group if it is interfering with the function of the group. The structured groups in other settings are not used in this way; their function is restricted to the specific skill or symptom they are addressing concretely.

The structured groups are important in psychodynamically oriented DTPs because patients attending such programs have significant difficulties not only in their relationships but also in the basic skills involved in establishing and maintaining educational pursuits and in securing and maintaining remunerative employment. Of course, difficulties in relationships are an important contributor to difficulties in employment. The structured groups are three-dimensional in addressing the concrete difficulties these patients face in securing employment and pursuing education, the intrapsychic/personality dimension and the interpersonal dimensions. By "intrapsychic/personality dimension," I am referring to factors such as lack of confidence, difficulties with authority, conflicts about success (including, for example, the wish, conscious or unconscious, to fail in order to foil the ambitions parents might have that do not coincide with the teenage or adult child's aspirations), irritability and other difficulties with affect regulation, and a sense of hopelessness or resignation about being able to attain a hoped-for achievement. By "interpersonal dimension," I am referring to difficulties in showing respect to others, insensitivity to others, and other behaviors (that admittedly have underlying "intrapsychic/personality" factors), which, taken together, can present a major obstacle for these patients in securing and maintaining employment or completing their education.

Projectives Group

In Projectives Group, patients are given pencils, crayons, and paper and are invited to illustrate their associations with a given theme, such as "At the

120   *Group Psychotherapy and Partial Hospitalization*

Dinner Table." The drawing may provide a glimpse of the patient's family dynamics and show the patient's role and level of involvement within the family. Usually, three patients sequentially circulate their pictures in any one group; all patients have an opportunity to associate with the pictures. The discussion may include the "nutrition" the family did or did not offer. The patients' associations can also be applied to their relationships in the DTP "family." How the patients interpret the instructions and process will reflect aspects of their psychological functioning. Thought processes, anxieties, and conflicts of the patient–artist are projected directly onto the drawing, whereas those of the other patients are made available through their associations.

Projectives Group may help to reduce some of the anxiety of patients who are starting DTP. When patients give feedback to each other, it is directed to some extent away from them and onto the drawing. The patients often become relaxed and less defensive. Once the artist shares that the drawing is, for example, a Thanksgiving turkey, he can go on to share what family gatherings were really like. This activity may provide an opportunity to provide access to information and interpretations that might be unavailable otherwise. A patient's drawing in Projectives Group also often is a catalyst to do work in other groups. Issues are raised in an informal way that facilitates deeper work later on.

Action Group

In Action Group, patients have the opportunity to reenact aspects of their life. They may explore scenes from their early environment or revisit past or current conflictual relationships. This allows patients to reexamine experiences from a different perspective with the support of the group. It can be a very powerful, emotionally charged process, not only for the patient who volunteers to direct the drama but also for all the group members. Patients are drawn into the drama by the content or by the shared emotional responses to the reenactment. Because patients with personality disorders can regress to a more primitive state under stress, therapists need to be vigilant about directing, containing, and controlling the activities in Action Group.

Action Group begins with a warm-up before engaging in the drama exercise. Examples of warm-up exercises are "Write a Mother's Day card and sign it," and using four cushions to represent a compass with the patients representing the needle, which patients use to discuss difficulties in finding a direction in life. Spontaneous responses in warm-ups are encouraged because they generate a great wealth of content to explore later in the group, which often can profitably be continued in the unstructured groups.

There are two formats possible in Action Group. In one format, after the warm-up, a patient volunteers to develop the warm-up theme further. The volunteer is invited to share more information pertaining to his or her response to the warm-up and decides on a direction for the drama. This usually lasts approximately 30–40 minutes. The volunteer chooses group members to represent significant individuals in her life. Often the roles have

Psychodynamic Group Psychotherapy   121

already been assigned unconsciously, based on previous interactions between patients in various groups. In the second format for Action Group, all the patients are involved in the drama exercise. Patients are divided into groups of four to five. Each group is asked to compose a meaningful drama related to the warm-up.

On Halloween, the theme was "Trick or Treat: Who would you trick or who would you treat?" A passive-aggressive patient enjoyed portraying her boss sitting in an outhouse. She tipped it over and delighted at watching her boss come screaming out of the outhouse with his pants around his knees. She was able to reflect on other people she may have liked to trick, and on her indirect but destructive methods of expressing her hostility, including toward therapists. Many patients' primary method of coping with uncomfortable affects has been through activity, which is often destructive in nature. Action Group offers the opportunity for verbalization of and reflection on hitherto unspoken difficulties. This process can promote group cohesion, strengthen the therapeutic alliance, and address avoided issues.

Once when patients were not confronting each other or the therapists, we constructed a paper ship. The patients were told to find their places on the ship quickly, without talking. When everyone had a spot, they were asked what their positions were. We had several captains at each end, some people in lifeboats, and others afraid to go too close to the water. Two patients chose to be in the water. After all the positions were identified, patients were told to assume their roles. Each captain unsuccessfully tried to direct his or her crew. Others were throwing out life preservers to the individuals in the water. One patient grabbed a life preserver, and the other kept yelling, "I can't reach it," making no efforts to swim toward it. Some patients complained of feeling seasick. The predominant theme was, "Don't rock the boat." This warm-up exercise fostered examination of several themes, including those of being an anti-leader, competition, rejecting help, and avoiding getting ones' feet wet in therapy.

In Action Group, as in other groups, it is important to integrate the content back into the unstructured groups to avoid creating a split among groups and to continue to deal with the considerable amount of material that this group can evoke.

Perspectives for Living Group and Life Skills Group

Perspectives for Living Group and Life Skills Group have similar functions. These groups permit examination of various aspects of patients' functioning and the appropriateness of their responses to a variety of situations. Many patients with personality disorders tend to act impulsively and to express their feelings in very strong terms. Although patients need to express their feelings, we highlight the importance of thinking and reflection in affective expression. Patients are encouraged to mitigate their tendencies to impulsivity and explosiveness and to try to reflect on and discuss their inner experience. Thus, the concept of critical thinking is a central theme for

122 *Group Psychotherapy and Partial Hospitalization*

the Perspectives for Living and Life Skills Groups. In the Perspectives for Living Group, patients are encouraged to reconsider their preconceptions and invited to reflect on how they tend to think, what they have tended to avoid thinking about, how their thinking is affected by conflict and deficit, and what impact on their lives their thinking patterns have.

After six weeks in the Perspectives for Living Group, patients move into the Life Skills Group. This group addresses topics related to maturity, realizing one's potential, success, intimacy, and guilt. In one exercise, patients pass around a small mirror and discuss, "Seeing myself as I actually am." It is a challenge for therapists to avoid turning these groups into psychoeducational experiences, in which they lecture patients on the theme of the group. Therapists must avoid colluding with patients' wishes for quick and easy answers. As well, they need to be committed to encouraging patients to be open-minded and tolerant of the anxiety associated with not being fed comfortable answers. *This is consistent with Bion's (1970) concept of negative capability, tolerating not knowing something, which can be very difficult at times. It is so tempting to hold strong convictions, to feel one is right, to brook no doubt, to feel certain, to not question oneself. Unfortunately, the price to pay for maintaining this type certainty is jettisoning the capacity to learn.* In the Perspectives for Living and Life Skills Groups, challenging patients' pathological beliefs raised alternatives that often are anxiety-provoking. When patients are supported in containing their anxiety, they are able to expand their capacity for thinking, in terms of the content about which they allow themselves to think, and in terms of the process of their thinking. This facilitates more reflective and abstract thought.

Problem-Solving Group

Day treatment includes a rehabilitative component geared toward integrating the practical side of life with the psychodynamic work of the program. Patients' strengths and weaknesses are respectfully capitalized on and accommodated for. The influences of patients' conflicts and deficits are considered. Problem-Solving Group accommodates those patients with lower psychological mindedness and limited capacity for insight by exposing them to a therapeutic experience that allows for some suggestions and practical support from other patients.

Often, patients' decisions are based on impulse rather than on a critical thinking process involving problem identification, goal setting, and planning. Problem-Solving Group introduces these tasks to help patients solve problems in their lives. Written worksheets are used to guide this process, which includes reflections on their accomplishments and identification of what they have learned by working on the problem. Problem identification is often a major stumbling block that hinders the process of problem-solving. Patients tend to state problems in terms of what needs to be done, rather than outlining what the problem is; for example, "I need to rake the leaves," rather than "I have an allergy to snow mould and my lawn is covered

Psychodynamic Group Psychotherapy   123

in leaves." A tendency to procrastinate often leads to an ambiguous presentation of the problem. For example, a patient may avoid budgeting to avoid taking responsibility for poor financial choices.

Patients are encouraged to formulate "SMART" goals: Specific, Measurable, Attainable, Realistic, and Time oriented. Feedback needs to be balanced and constructive. The therapist resists offering overt praise, which patients frequently attempt to elicit. It is felt to be more important for patients to recognize when their achievements are successful and constructive. Patients are asked to create a pie chart of their time in an average week. Considerable information may be revealed. For example, one patient didn't show time with her spouse anywhere on her chart. Patients become well acquainted with each other in DTP and are able to challenge or confirm each other's perceptions of their lives.

A patient who appeared limited in psychological mindedness had been unwilling to take responsibility for her abusive behaviors in relationships outside and within DTP. When she entered Problem-Solving Group, she chose to work on a problem regarding her need to identify and eliminate a bad smell in her apartment, a smell from the hall that her dog had picked up. She spoke with her landlady, found a way to remove the smell from the hall, and also washed her dog. Reflecting on what she had learned about herself while working on this problem, she observed that normally she would have just become very angry and abusive toward the landlady and would have demanded that something be done. She recognized that it was difficult to take responsibility for her own contribution to the problem. In the past, she had used her aggressiveness inappropriately in an attempt to get others to provide for her needs and wishes. On this occasion, she contained herself, worked through a difficult situation, took responsibility, and demonstrated some insight. She associated to the aggressive way in which her mother interacted with her, similar to how her parents treated each other. This patient was later confronted in an unstructured group with her ability to be insightful, of which she had limited awareness. Her awareness of this nascent strength enhanced her capacity to develop it. She was able to practice some of what she learned in Problem-Solving Group and to reflect on it in other groups. The therapists' perceptions of her changed as did their approach to her as they become aware of the faculties that she was developing.

Vocational Group

Patients in day treatment often fret about what they will do with regard to employment when they leave therapy: who will hire them, how they will get back into the workplace, and whether their pattern of failure in work or school will continue. These questions, which are accompanied by considerable anxiety, are addressed in Vocational Group. Practical issues are addressed as the patients prepare to return to the workforce, to school, or sometimes to retirement. All patients participate in Vocational Group, even those who

124　*Group Psychotherapy and Partial Hospitalization*

believe they don't need to because their problems are not work related. There is often much resistance in Vocational Group; patients are pushed to examine their weaknesses and focus on their strengths, a challenge for many of them. Improving patients' self-esteem and helping them set realistic goals regarding work opportunities and choices are important in Vocational Group.

Many patients see themselves as special, and have unrealistic expectations of themselves and of others. Much difficult work on their part is necessary to begin to perceive themselves and others in a more realistic manner. *This work, which addresses narcissistic defenses such as grandiosity and entitlement, which often are employed to avoid conscious awareness of feelings of helplessness, worthlessness, and low self-esteem, is developed further in the unstructured psychotherapy groups.* Patients are invited to evaluate themselves as employees. They frequently see themselves either as total failures or as outstanding, as opposed to realistically acknowledging their strengths and weaknesses. In this exercise, patients rate themselves on punctuality, reliability, and capacity to work well with others. One narcissistic patient used to come late to group at least twice a week. He believed that he was outstanding regarding punctuality, but received feedback from other group members that he was unsatisfactory at best. This helped him to become more realistic in his assessment of himself.

In examining their marketable skills, patients begin to recognize the strengths and positive qualities that they possess. For example, if they talk about a hobby with great enthusiasm, they are shown that the skills required to engage in the hobby are transferable. The patients are encouraged to look at what they can do, rather than focus on what they cannot do. Patients are required to prepare an updated resumé, which is shared and edited in the group. In preparation for presenting a resumé, patients learn how they can write a credible one when they have gone from job to job, been fired from many jobs, or have not been employed for a long time. Patients are given a resource book with examples of resumés to choose from, to find a format most suitable for their purposes.

The last exercise of the group is role-playing a job interview. Here the patients have an opportunity to practice answering difficult questions, such as whether they are currently working, how long they have worked, why they left their last job, and why the employer should hire them for the position advertised. Group members give each other feedback on how they answer these questions. They learn that there are ways they can answer questions without undermining themselves by offering more information than is judicious. By the end of Vocational Group, most patients gain confidence and begin realistically to believe that they are employable. There are many opportunities for patients to identify psychodynamic issues in Vocational Group, such as relationships with authority figures, tendencies to "workaholism," and dependency issues resulting in continuing failure, all of which can be explored in the unstructured psychotherapy groups. At the end of DTP, patients may be eager to return to work, but often also are anxious about how they will cope on the job. They are encouraged to utilize the Work Therapy program as an intermediate step before entering the workforce.

Work Therapy

Work Therapy involves 125 hours of voluntary work, to be completed within six weeks after discharge from DTP. Patients are encouraged to work in as full-time a capacity as possible. They choose the field of work they wish to work in while in Vocational Group. Each patient requesting Work Therapy is encouraged to assume some responsibility by researching potential work placements. Patient and therapist work together regarding placement; ultimately the therapist secures a suitable voluntary job. Participants must attend a weekly one-hour support group while in Work Therapy. Work Therapy enables patients to experiment in a new field of work, to gain confidence, to experience success on a job, to receive a current evaluation, and to network so as to be better able to find a job. In our DTP, our staff have been able to find suitable work therapy placements for nearly all patients requesting to participate in Work Therapy, even in times of high unemployment.

The Work Therapy program has proved valuable in terms of vocational rehabilitation of patients within the community. Although the goal of Work Therapy is to provide a volunteer work experience and not to attempt to secure employment for patients who have completed day treatment, several of our patients are hired by their placement employers after completion of Work Therapy and retain these positions for extensive periods of time.

Case Example

This vignette provides an example of the integration of issues explored in the structured groups further worked through in an unstructured group. James, a 49-year old postsecondary institution instructor, was admitted into DTP complaining of depression. Our primary diagnosis was narcissistic personality disorder. James felt discriminated against because of his superior intellect. He believed that a lot of his brilliant ideas and changes that he proposed were unappreciated, and felt unrewarded for the excellence of his work performance. In his frustration, he had written a critical letter to his administrators. He was angry that they had yet again failed to respond in an appreciative manner. In addition, he was fearful that he had jeopardized his position and reputation. James' first day in treatment was revealing. James is quite overweight; staff were aware that he would not fit into the regular chairs in the group rooms. A special chair therefore was placed for him in each of the group rooms. On his first day, he made a striking impression entering Large Group with a walking stick, which resembled a staff, with his long, graying hair and beard.

As the group commenced, he waited for the regular announcements to be over and wondered whom he should address about his concerns. He decided to speak to the whole staff collectively. He cordially thanked the staff for the consideration shown in providing a suitable chair for him. He indicated, however, that he had had an opportunity to observe the regular chairs and found that they were inadequate and uncomfortable. He sincerely hoped

126 *Group Psychotherapy and Partial Hospitalization*

that every effort would be made to provide more appropriate chairs for his fellow group members. He indicated that he would address these concerns at a later date. This message was delivered in a very benevolent manner that impressed some of the patients, shocked some, and amused others. All waited expectantly for some response or reaction from the staff. There was no doubt that this was a challenge to the group leaders.

The staff debated to themselves whether it was prudent to ignore the challenge and let the silence resonate. One of the coleaders of the group decided to respond to the challenge with an interpretation that the chairs were not reflective of the quality of treatment, and although not much could be done about the chairs, only the best was expected in terms of work and the quality of treatment that was offered. It was further hoped that James would be constructively critical of his own work. Patients who had been in group longer were invited to set an example for the newer patients in initiating some work themselves. Although this silenced James and got the group working, there was no doubt that it left him smoldering with anger, which he freely expressed in groups in which the coleader who had responded to him was absent. After some encouragement from staff, he addressed the coleader, stating that he felt enraged at the lack of consideration about a very legitimate concern that he had commented on. This only confirmed James' opinion that authority figures were "lofty" and unappreciative of others. He looked around for confirmation of this view but, apart from a couple of disgruntled group members, was unable to elicit much support.

To give James credit, he appeared to move past his anger and engaged in some meaningful work in the groups. In Large Group, he was less active but made his presence felt in other ways. He was often late, but his presence was nevertheless noticeable, as no one would dare to take his chair. James usually came in a few minutes late and offered neither an apology nor explanation, unlike other group members. After a stern warning from the coleader, he remained silent in Large Group but made it a point to voice his opinion about the pettiness of the staff. A change finally occurred once James moved into Vocational Group. In this group, patients deal with problems of a more practical nature and are encouraged to explore their strengths, capabilities, and conflicts in work-related relationships. The group climate could be equated to an administrative meeting where there is room for criticism of the work environment. James took great pleasure in pointing out to group members the various flaws in systems and rights of employees. The feedback that he received from other group members was contrary to his expectations. Most pointed out his blatant hostility and engaged in a constructive manner. There was much encouragement for James to explore the basis for his resentment of systems.

By the time patients complete Vocational Group, they are in the last stages of treatment, the Re-entry phase. There was a definite change in James's relationship with the coleader who had originally confronted him. This coleader had been cautious to not unnecessarily injure James' narcissism in group interactions. With gentle confrontation, James was able to begin to recognize that he had taken a rigid stance throughout his life and had been motivated since childhood to defeat the "maternal system." Introducing the term "maternal" was meaningful to James, who was raised by his mother. She was overwhelmed with her responsibilities as a single parent. James was the youngest of five boys with a seven-year gap between him and his next older brother. His father had died before he was born, and his mother was left to manage the farm with limited help from her sons. She was quite ineffective in her management of her children and strongly relied on her faith to instill the fear of God into her boisterous and unmanageable sons. God was used as the ultimate father who would bring upon them the punishment they so well deserved.

There is no doubt that James was very bright and well aware of his mother's limitations. Unlike his brothers, he invested a lot of time into reading about religion, and used to challenge his mother on her views. She was no match for him, and invariably resorted to screaming at him and stating that God would eventually take the Devil out of him. James recalled feeling powerful, in that he was going to be a challenge for God. There was a significant change in the quality of work James began to do. He began to talk about missing his father, and experienced the loss of not having a father. He realized that his hatred of systems was partly a defense against his longing for a parent whom he could respect. He stated in a group that he was shocked to find himself adopting some of the mannerisms that he had observed in the coleader with whom he had initially been in conflict.

Prior to discharge, James was starting to show a capacity and willingness to do some high-quality psychotherapeutic work. DTP offers an after-care program, a weekly psychotherapy group in which selected patients are offered to continue working after discharge. Patients are asked to make a commitment of a year if they wish to continue participating in DTP in this Follow-Up Group. James could not commit to attending this group, as he had to return to work too far away to make attending the group possible. A significant change was apparent in his willingness to consider negotiating with his administrators for some options for returning to work. His original plan had been to find ways of staying on disability until he was in a position to retire.

Conclusions

Personality disorders are serious long-term conditions that are resistant to change and difficult to treat. Day treatment, a form of partial hospitalization, may have unique advantages for the treatment of patients with personality disorders. It offers an optimal level of intensity and containment, thus facilitating treatment of the chronic emotional and behavioral difficulties experienced by these patients. Effective day treatment relies on the successful integration of its multiple components. We have described the role that structured therapy groups play within a psychodynamically oriented DTP for patients with personality disorders.

128 *Group Psychotherapy and Partial Hospitalization*

Important functions of the structured groups are reduction of resistance and modulation of anxiety. Exploring an assigned topic initially, in a more concrete way, is often perceived as less threatening than work in the unstructured groups. Patients often feel more comfortable revealing aspects of themselves in these groups than in the unstructured groups. This particularly applies early in treatment and with more anxious and disturbed patients. As a result, many patients are often more forthcoming about themselves and more open to self-examination initially in the structured groups. Projectives Group is a good example of a group in which patients enjoy themselves while actively analyzing the pictures and providing insights for each other. The rich material aroused in this group may be explored in more depth in some of the other, unstructured groups.

The Vocational, Work Therapy, and Problem-Solving groups are rehabilitative groups in DTP. In addressing practical problems, patients frequently identify psychodynamically understandable conflicts and deficits that contribute to their difficulties in work, love, and play (Steinberg, 1998). Being able to address underlying conflicts when discussing a nonthreatening structured topic enables patients to become comfortable with cognitive aspects of their difficulties before confronting themselves and engaging in more formal psychotherapeutic work in the unstructured groups. Being able to make some practical and concrete changes in one's life circumstances often provides an impetus toward initiating a psychotherapeutic process leading to internal changes.

It is imperative that the issues raised in the various structured groups be explored further in the unstructured groups, so patients can experience working through of issues, especially regarding interpersonal conflicts. To facilitate this process, effective communication among the staff group is critical. Staff members need to work together to maintain the boundaries of the structured groups, while being diligent in their efforts to refer back to the unstructured groups issues that need to be further addressed. Many dynamic issues often cannot be dealt with in the structured groups and usually require involvement of all patients and staff, especially when destructive interactions within DTP need to be confronted and resolved. Thus, the structured groups need to be psychodynamically oriented enough to be consistent with the overall approach of DTP, but structured enough to achieve their mandated goals. We have found the structured groups to have an important place in our psychodynamically oriented DTP, fulfilling functions complementary to our unstructured psychotherapy groups.

References

Bion WR (1961). *Experiences in Groups and Other Papers*. London and New York: Routledge.

Bion WR (1970). *Attention and Interpretation*. London: Karnac.

Ogrodniczuk JS & Piper WE (2001). Day treatment for personality disorders: A review of research findings. *Harvard Review of Psychiatry*, 9: 105–117.

Psychodynamic Group Psychotherapy   129

PDM Task Force (2006). *Psychodynamic Diagnostic Manual*. Silver Springs, MD: Alliance of Psychoanalytic Organizations.

Piper WE & Rosie JS (1998). Group treatment of personality disorder: The power of the group in the intensive treatment of personality disorders. *Session: Psychotherapy in Practice*, 4: 19–34.

Piper WE, Rosie JS, Joyce AS, & Azim HFA (1996). *Time-Limited Day Treatment for Personality Disorders*. Washington, DC: American Psychological Association.

Steinberg PI (1998). Attachment and object relations in formulation and psychotherapy. *Annals of the Royal College of Physicians and Surgeons of Canada*, 31: 19–22.

Steinberg PI (2007). The use of low-dose neuroleptics in the treatment of patients with severe personality disorder: An adjunct to psychotherapy. *BC Medical Journal*, 49(6): 306–310.

Steinberg PI & Duggal S (2004). Threats of violence in group-oriented day treatment. *International Journal of Group Psychotherapy*, 54(1): 5–22.

Steinberg PI, Duggal S, & Ogrodniczuk J (2008). Threats of violence to third parties in group psychotherapy. *Bulletin of the Menninger Clinic*, 72(1): 1–18.

Steinberg PI, Rosie J, Joyce AS, O'Kelly J, Piper WE, Bahrey F, & Duggal S (2004). The psychodynamic psychiatry service of the University of Alberta Hospital: A thirty year history. *International Journal of Group Psychotherapy*, 59(4): 521–538.

Yalom ID (1995). *The Theory and Practice of Group Psychotherapy*. 4th ed. New York: Basic Books.

8 Hatred and Fear

Projective Identification in Group Psychotherapy

Introduction

Severely disturbed patients suffering from personality disorders employ a variety of primitive defenses in interpersonal situations that, when unmodified, invariably perpetuate the chronic relational difficulties experienced by these patients. Among such primitive defenses used by personality disorder patients is projective identification (PI). Ogden (1979) defines PI as a group of fantasies and accompanying object relations having to do with the ridding of the self of unwanted aspects of the self; the depositing of those unwanted parts into another person; and finally, the recovery of a modified version of what was extruded. In the context of group psychotherapy, PI can have a significant negative impact of the emotional and interpersonal interactions among members of the group, including the therapist. Awareness of this potential can enable a group to convert what is a disturbing and potentially destructive experience into one involving learning and therapeutic benefit.

Familiarity with the concept of PI is useful for understanding regressive phenomena driven by intense affects such as rage. A therapist's awareness of how to identify, understand, and manage PI is crucial for overcoming what could otherwise become an impasse in group therapy. This article describes a psychodynamic group psychotherapy session illustrating an experience involving PI. I am considering PI both as a defense, that is, an intrapsychic experience, and an interpersonal process (Grotstein, 1985). The session occurred in an unstructured psychodynamic psychotherapy group that took place in the context of a group psychotherapy-based psychiatric day treatment program (described in previous chapters) for patients with severe personality disorders (Piper, Rosie, Joyce, & Azim, 1996). Pete, the primary subject of this session, is a middle-aged, unemployed individual diagnosed with self-defeating personality disorder and dysthymic disorder.

Some Ideas About Groups

Freud (1921) believes that emotional bonds between group members hold a group together, and members are prepared to give up their individuality and be open to the influence of other members on the basis of this attachment. He describes two "artificial"

DOI: 10.4324/9781003200581-11

groups, the church and the army, in which each member is bound by ties of love to the leader and to the other members of the group. Freud believes that not only love, but also hate, can bind members of the group together. He concludes that one can give up one's individuality, including one's standard of ethics, in a group, and follow the dictates of the group leader or the pressure of the mob. It is interesting to note that historically, Freud's work on groups was published one year before Mussolini's accession to power in Italy, and 12 years before Hitler's assumption of power in Germany. In spite of his trailblazing work on the analysis of groups, in 1936, Freud was still capable of commenting on how much civilization had progressed, in that 400 years ago they would have burned him, and at that time, they were just burning his books. In spite of his genius and understanding of groups, he lacked prescience of what was to come. Alternatively, what he was perceiving in Nazi Germany was too horrific for him to think about, and he denied the possibility that the Nazis could "progress" from burning books to burning people.

Summarizing my discussion in previous chapters, Bion (1961/2010) distinguishes between individual and group mentality. He describes a regression among members of groups based on group mentality. He described three "basic assumption groups" that function in opposition to the work for which the group originally was formed. These include dependency, in which the group members hope the leader will satisfy all of their wishes and needs, leaving them free to be passive and unthinking; fight-or-flight, in which the group is convinced there is an enemy who must be destroyed or avoided by fleeing; and pairing, in which the group awaits an event, messianic in nature, with the unconscious irrational expectation that a child will be born with the potential to be a savior of the group. Members of groups based on these basic assumptions are in a highly charged primitive emotional state, which expresses the group's unconscious fantasy. Bion concludes that groups always fluctuate between basic assumption and work functioning. He believes that basic assumptions are defensive and aggressive group reactions against psychotic anxieties reactivated in the group members (Vermote, 2019). Freud's and Bion's ideas about group irrationality and basic assumptions describe how groups can become irrational and destructive, showing the necessity for a leader to help the members of her group, be it a psychotherapy group, a working group in a health profession or any other profession, or the group of inhabitants of a country, to reflect on themselves rather than act in a chaotic or destructive fashion.

Narrative of the Session

(This session lasted 1½ hours. Pete's becoming more reflective actually occurred after more interactions and time than is represented in this narrative, which was reconstructed some hours after the session occurred, on the same day. The narrative as written suggests that Pete abruptly and quickly became more capable of reflecting on his own experience, which was not the case. Several interventions by different group members, which the writer could not recall exactly, preceded Pete's change of attitude.)

PETE: Fred followed me out of the group to the cafeteria. He watched me eat my toast and coffee for lunch. That was all I could afford. When

132   *Group Psychotherapy and Partial Hospitalization*

I finished one piece of toast, he asked me if I was going to finish the second piece. Why the hell did you follow me and ask me for food! I was really angry with Fred. I wouldn't give him any food. That lunch was meagre enough already.

FRED: (rather meekly) I just wanted to eat his toast because I didn't have any money for lunch. I thought it would be better for me to eat the toast than for him to waste it.

PETE: I wasn't going to waste it! You made me very uncomfortable, asking for my toast. You give me the creeps. I wish you wouldn't hang around me like that. It's like you're stalking me.

THERAPIST: Pete, it was positive for you to manage to maintain your boundaries and not let Fred intrude. You were able to contain him and not allow him to infringe on you. So I wonder what made you so angry about his behaviour? What bothered you most about his "stalking" you and begging?

PETE: (loudly, becoming enraged at the therapist.) Begging?! Fred was stalking and hounding me, and now you're harassing me with questions! It should be clear why I was angry with Fred. I don't know why I should have to put up with this. I was the one being bothered in the first place.

THERAPIST: You seemed to get furious with me immediately when I used the word "begging." What made you so angry?

PETE: (After a pause, much more quietly and reflectively. This is the point where some interventions by other group members are omitted.) When I was young, my three brothers and sisters and I used to go hungry a lot of the time. I was the oldest. My parents used to drink, and often we didn't have enough food in the house. I used to go begging for food from the neighbours when my parents weren't home, so we could have something to eat. I wouldn't dare go to the neighbours when my parents were home. My father would've been furious. I also used to scavenge in the neighbours' garbage cans to find some food for myself and the kids. It was so humiliating, asking the neighbours for food.

THERAPIST: You know, in a family where there was so much neglect, it wouldn't be surprising to hear that there was some abuse as well.

PETE: (still more quietly) My uncle used to babysit us a lot. When the younger kids went to bed, he used to take me to the attic and have sex with me. He used to rape me on the old sofa up there. I was pretty sure my mother must have known what my uncle was doing. She must have wondered why I looked so upset after my uncle babysat. But she never asked me about it, and did nothing about it.

GROUP: (very moved) Ohhh. (Significant pause.)

PETE: I was very frightened of Fred. I felt he was following me and threatening me.

THERAPIST: Did Fred say anything to threaten you, or behave in a threatening manner?

PETE: No, he never said nothing like that. But his physical appearance reminds me of my father. My father was very critical.

Discussion

In this session, the therapist was aware of a strong countertransference reaction when Pete became enraged at him. The therapist initially felt quite intimidated and then angry at what he experienced as an unprovoked attack. He needed to contain these feelings and focus on what Pete was experiencing. When the therapist was able to collect himself, and managed to ask Pete about what is bothering him, Pete replied much more reflectively (after some supportive comments by other patients, including one patient describing his tendency to become enraged when he feels threatened). The therapist's feelings of anger and intimidation melted away; he became interested in what Pete was describing of his early experience and felt much empathy for Pete.

One can try to understand Pete's anger at Fred and the therapist using object relations theory. Pete appeared, in a defensive maneuver, to displace his hatred and fear of his neglectful parents and abusive uncle onto Fred, attacking Fred instead of being aware of his intense, painful feelings about his parents and uncle. In doing so, he projected his unconscious internal images of hated parents and uncle onto Fred. Pete also appeared to project a helpless, attacked self-image onto both the therapist and Fred, inducing in them the fear and hatred that he once felt toward his parents and uncle. Pete also appeared to project an image of a hated, abusive, neglectful parent onto the therapist, experiencing the latter as mistreating him. He thus elicited in the therapist the fear he experienced in his relationship with his parents and uncle, and also provoked in the therapist hateful feelings toward him, recapitulating his early experience with his uncle.

Pete experienced Fred, and perhaps the therapist, as dangerous. This appeared to help him defend against remembering both how dangerous his uncle was and how dangerous he felt his own hatred of his uncle and parents was. This also helped keep out of Pete's conscious awareness how much Fred reminded Pete of himself, in trying to beg for food from Pete, the way Pete had to beg for food from the neighbors and scavenge in their garbage cans. Transference can be seen here, in part, as a displacement. This is not to deny Fred's and the therapist's roles in co-creating Pete's experience of them (Aron, 1996). *The relational movement in psychoanalysis has highlighted contributions of both analyst/therapist and patient to the patient's experience of the analyst/therapist, rather than understanding transference solely as a distortion of the patient's perception of the analyst based on the patient's earlier relational experience. This concept, however, also developed in other psychoanalytic schools, for example, with Sandler's (1976) concept of role-responsiveness. This is an example of the evolution of psychoanalytic thought, often along several parallel lines using different theories, coming to consistent conclusions.*

The therapist's anxiety about Pete's turning on him in anger was important information. The therapist's awareness of this countertransference experience enabled him to understand Pete's reaction as communicating to him a little about how Pete felt as a child with his parents and uncle. At the same time,

134 Group Psychotherapy and Partial Hospitalization

Pete defended against conscious awareness of these feelings by projecting them into the therapist.

The subject of shame did not arise explicitly during this group. However, it appears very likely that Pete felt much shame based on his experience of abuse, and likely also felt it in the group when he brought up his having been abused. One may interpret his rage, in part, as a defense against feelings of shame. It would have been potentially beneficial to invite the patients in this session to talk about experiences involving shame, including experiences in which they had little or no control over what happened, and how they dealt with it.

Why did the therapist seemingly change the subject from neglect to abuse? Perhaps in his anxiety, he unconsciously felt abused himself, in reacting to Pete's rage at him. This might be considered an unconscious understanding of Pete's reaction, operating at a more profound level than the therapist's conscious awareness permitted. On the other hand, it might also have represented a manifestation of the therapist's defense against his own countertransference anger at Pete, projecting his aggression into Pete's family, accusing them of abuse.

The therapist tried to center himself in the midst of this barrage from Pete, which provoked considerable fear and guilt in the therapist. The fear was about being attacked by Pete. The guilt was related to the therapist's feeling that he must have somehow mistreated Pete. The therapist thought that Pete must have learned from someone how to treat people in this manner. Openness to one's feelings during a psychotherapy session—anger, fear, hatred, anxiety, boredom, joy, sexual excitement—is essential for therapists. This helps them to become aware of the feelings that patients are struggling not to feel. This can be emotionally exhausting and anxiety-provoking for therapists, no matter how experienced they are. However, one of the most important sources of satisfaction in therapeutic work is when the therapist can observe what is going on between her and her patient(s) and convey this to the patient(s) in a manner that is helpful. This can help relieve the therapist of the burden of the affective toxins that patients sometimes inject into the therapist. This can occur only if the therapist eschews trying to talk the patient out of his feelings or taking revenge on the patient for the way the patient unburdens himself by stimulating the same feelings in the therapist that he is trying to not feel.

Rather, the therapist needs to try to help patients understand their role in what is going on between them and the therapist, and needs to help patients to explore the origins of their interacting this way, based on repeated similar experiences in early relationships. The patients then may be able to accept their roles in the interaction. It is easier for the patients to consider this if the therapist is open to considering her contribution to these types of interactions, which often are enactments of experiences familiar to the patients in many of their relationships (Hoffman, 1998). The example of a different style of relating (compared to the patient's early and current relationships) that the therapist offers also can help patients learn a more

Hatred and Fear   135

adaptive way of relating. *Now I would put more focus on the interactions between therapist and patient or between group members, including the therapist, both being the prime mutative (Strachey, 1934) factor in helping the patient or members of the group grow, and what needs to be focused on most in the mutual exploration of therapeutic dyad's, or group's, experience. A related technical factor is the contemporary focus on what is happening at any given moment in a psychoanalytic or psychotherapeutic session, an intense attention to the current experience between therapist and patient, which proponents of the analytic field have given emphasis (Ferro, 2005).*

Elaborating on the 'toxin' analogy, one might suggest that the therapist absorbs the toxins from the patients, but rather than projecting them back in the same toxic form, the therapist metabolizes the toxins and offers them back to the patient in a form that the patient may be able to absorb, so the patient doesn't need to continue projecting his experience in the same toxic way, but can contain it within himself. This notion is based on Bion's theory of alpha function, in which a mothering figure uses her reverie to experience her infant's distress, is able to contain it within herself, and "returns" it to the infant by expressing it (usually in a high-pitched voice with a characteristic use of words and "baby talk", in a manner that soothes the baby. Similarly, therapists can use their reverie to help patients contain previously unbearable feelings and unthinkable thoughts, allowing themselves to experience something of what the patient is experiencing and "returning" it to the patient with an intervention that helps make the experience more bearable for the patient (Bion, 1962).

Conclusion

To conclude, object relations theory can be useful in conceptualizing potentially destructive interpersonal events occurring within psychotherapy groups in terms of the projection of self-representations and internal objects. Early traumatic relationships may be recapitulated with accompanying painful affects by means of PI. The latter can be conceptualized in both intrapsychic (as a mechanism of defense) and interpersonal terms. The therapist's awareness of his countertransference experience is crucial in his understanding of what is transpiring and in his finding a way to enable patients to put into words and explore in a therapeutic way what up to that point is a potentially retraumatizing enactment.

In this case, the patient's feelings about his early abuse and neglect appeared to become more accessible to his conscious awareness and were therefore less likely to overwhelm him in future experiences reminiscent of the traumata he experienced in childhood. The patient can become better able to differentiate between his early experience of helplessness in the face of trauma and his present situation as an adult and to recognize resources in himself and in the environment that were unavailable to him as a child. *With the support of the therapist and other group members, he will become able to better contain his feelings about his early traumatic experiences.* Consequently, it should be less necessary for him to defend against conscious awareness of both his

136 *Group Psychotherapy and Partial Hospitalization*

fear and his hatred by projecting his self-representation and internal objects onto the environment. In turn, this should result in the patient developing more adaptive ways of interacting and maintaining a more realistic perspective of present-day reality.

Of course, what applies to psychotherapy groups applies to group functioning in many other venues. The types of interaction described above, both potentially destructive and potentially growth-enhancing, can occur in individual psychotherapy and psychoanalysis (which involve very small groups), and in all sorts of nontherapeutic settings, such as staff meetings (of health-care providers or anyone else), clinical units (see Chapter 15, Freud on the ward: Integration of psychoanalytic concepts in the formulation and management of hospitalized psychiatric patients, in Psychoanalysis in Medicine *[Steinberg, 2021]), as well as in non-health-care settings, including committees, business meetings, meetings of professional groups, and, naturally, family meetings. Whether the outcome is destructive or growth-enhancing depends on whether one or more members of the group involved (hopefully including the formal leader or leaders if the group has one/them) are able to foster reflection and thinking about the situation at hand in the other group members, rather than impulsive and potentially destructive action in an effort to evacuate unbearable anxieties that have been stimulated in the members of the group. There is always the possibility of a destructive member of a group attaining "power" in the group by preying on the anxieties of the other group members, often engaging the group in a fight-or-flight basic assumption, and finding a scapegoat. This results in the hatred and fear that the new "leader" has elicited becomes directed toward one or more members of the group, potentially with catastrophic consequences, if other group members are not able to contain the toxic affects aroused and help the group to think. That is one way of understanding the rise of the Nazis in Germany, as well as more contemporary destructive political developments.*

References

Aron L (1996). *A Meeting of Minds: Mutuality in Psychoanalysis*. Hillsdale, NJ: The Analytic Press.

Bion WR (1961/2010). *Experiences in Groups and Other Papers*. Hove, East Sussex and New York: Routledge.

Bion WR (1962). *Learning from Experience*. London: Tavistock.

Ferro A (2005). Which reality in the psychoanalytic session? *Psychoanalytic Quarterly*, 74(2): 421–442.

Freud S (1921). Group psychology and the analysis of the ego. In Strachey J (ed.). *The Standard Edition of the Complete Psychological Works of Sigmund Freud*. Vol. XVIII, pp. 65–143. London: The Hogarth Press and the Institute of Psychoanalysis.

Grotstein JS (1985). *Splitting and Projective Identification*. New York: Jason Aronson.

Hoffman AZ (1998). *Ritual and Spontaneity in the Psychoanalytic Process: A Dialectical-Constructivist View*. Hillsdale, NJ: The Analytic Press.

Ogden TH (1979). On projective identification. *International Journal of Psychoanalysis*, 60: 357–373.

Piper WE, Rosie JS, Joyce AS, & Azim HFA (1996). *Time Limited Day Treatment for Personality Disorders*. Washington, DC: American Psychological Association.

Sandler J (1976). Countertransference and role-responsiveness. *International Review of Psychoanalysis*, 3: 43–47.

Steinberg PI (2021). *Psychoanalysis in Medicine: Applying Psychoanalytic Thought to Contemporary Medical Care*. New York and London: Routledge.

Strachey J (1934). The nature of the therapeutic action of psycho-analysis. *International Journal of Psychoanalysis*, 15: 127–159.

Vermote R (2019). *Reading Bion*. Abingdon, Oxon. and New York: Routledge.

Part C

Individual Psychoanalytic/ Psychodynamic Psychotherapy

9 Clarification and Confrontation

Two Techniques of Supportive Psychotherapy

In this chapter, I propose to define what supportive psychotherapy is and what it is not, to describe two techniques of supportive psychotherapy with clinical illustrations, and to elaborate on the defense of splitting and its handling, on a supportive approach to understanding and treating patients who have difficulty in thinking, and to deal with projective identification in the form of provocativeness. This chapter ends with a table of what to do and what to avoid in supportive psychotherapy.

Supportive psychotherapy, in my experience, may be the most thoughtlessly (if most commonly) performed form of psychotherapy. In Kernberg's (1984) opinion, supportive psychotherapy is more difficult to perform than expressive (insight-oriented) psychoanalytic psychotherapy and should be taught only after the student therapist has mastered the latter. Whether or not Kernberg is correct, most mental health (MH) clinicians will never be trained to do expressive psychotherapy. Nevertheless, they are frequently called on to provide supportive psychotherapy for their clients. None of these clinicians acquired their professional training merely in order to provide a shoulder to lean on, dispense "common sense,"" be a friend," or to serve as "someone to listen." In fact, no program of professional training is intended to, or could, teach people to perform these functions, even if they wanted to learn, although some professional training does involve enhancing one's ability to listen. The motivation (mostly unconscious) and the capability to become a member of a helping profession develop along with the rest of the individual's personality, and cannot be learned at school any more than can other personality traits (Sussman, 1992). Although the clinical examples in this chapter are drawn from family medical experiences, the patients are the same types of individuals who often consult nonmedical MH clinicians. I believe the conclusions I draw about these experience are very pertinent to MH practice.

What Supportive Psychotherapy Is Not

The above indicates what supportive psychotherapy is not. It is not the giving of advice; it is not the wholesale dispensing of friendliness; and it is not automatic encouragement and reassurance. Personal advice, which many

DOI: 10.4324/9781003200581-13

142 Psychoanalytic/Psychodynamic Psychotherapy

clinicians are tempted to give, may be based on the advisor's wishes, fantasies, aspirations, and conflicts, and thus cannot be trusted to correspond to the patient's real needs. In addition, the motive for giving advice must be suspect. Is this advice being given for the benefit of the patient, or to reduce the anxiety of the clinician, who reacts personally on hearing the patient's dilemma?

For the purpose of this discussion, I am excluding, of course, professional advice that the caregiver has been trained to give and for which she is being consulted, for example, a psychologist's recommendation that neuropsychological testing is indicated. Otherwise, a request for advice, however framed, can usually be met with an attempt to investigate the basis for the patient's inability to come to an appropriate decision on his own. When necessary, the clinician might confront the patient with the potentially dangerous effects of a decision or of not making a decision, rather than simply telling the patient what to do. This approach prevents fostering a dependent unthinking attitude on the patient's part, which would amount to the opposite of real support; instead, it helps the patient to function at his or her optimum *(which I would call real support)* rather than in the way the caregiver thinks he ought to function. *(In Jewish tradition, the highest form of charity is helping someone to help herself.)* This also avoids the real possibility that the clinician may give unhelpful advice and consequently be blamed or even sued.

It is unnecessary to elaborate on the wholesale dispensing of friendliness. This cannot be done sincerely, and when it is attempted, I believe it is generally motivated by feelings relating to the "dispenser's," not the patient's, emotional needs. It follows that the clinician or therapist who is full of love for her patient must be fooling the patient or herself or both, often, again, for her own reasons. On the other hand, a certain basic friendliness in the clinician and the therapist is a necessary condition to any psychotherapy— necessary but not sufficient. Some theoretical understanding and application of technique, whether supportive, behavioral, interpretive, or other, is also required.

It is unnecessary to belabor the notion that the essence of patient support is encouragement and reassurance. It is difficult to reassure one's patients when unable to predict the future oneself. Moreover, reassurance can have the same infantilizing effect on the patient that inappropriate advice can have. *Providing reassurance can actually result in the opposite of what is intended; the patient whom the clinician is attempting to reassure may interpret the reassurance as an indication of the clinician's inability to stay with the painful, perhaps terrifying thoughts and feelings the patient has just shared with her. I believe it is more reassuring to give the patient some acknowledgment about what one has heard, possibly with an indication of how the patient appears to be experiencing what they have described, without the (unrealistic) need to suggest that things will work out in the end. We really don't know, do we? If we can tolerate not knowing, our patients may be better able to do so as well. This is very relevant when the prognosis of a serious condition is unknown or unknowable. At least the patient may feel that his clinician will be able to stay the course with him, however difficult it turns out to be, if the latter doesn't need to resort to unrealistic reassurance.*

Clarification and Confrontation   143

I experienced an egregious example of how an attempt at reassurance backfired as a first year psychiatry resident. I had assessed a man in the emergency department as having acute mania and arranged for his admission to hospital. We were in an old hospital built on a large property that was horizontal, and it was close to a quarter mile walk to the psychiatric unit. It was part of my job to accompany him there. I very lightly touched his forearm with two of my fingers, hoping to calm him down him a little and make him more comfortable for the trip to the ward. In a completely deadpan tone of voice, with absolutely no expression on his face, this six-foot five tower of muscle slowly and quietly said, "If you don't take your hand off my arm, I'll knock your block off." That taught me something about the wisdom of not touching patients, especially ones I had just met. In retrospect, it seems that I was so anxious about being with this person that I was the one who needed soothing and reassurance. I was just looking for it in the wrong place. This patient also taught me something important about boundaries.

Regarding the possibility of providing reassurance by touching a patient, one should remember when crossing this boundary to think of the possible consequences. How will the patient interpret this behavior of the therapist? Could it be seen as a sexual advance? Obviously, one would be very careful with a patient who had experienced any form of abuse in the past. Whenever we are tempted to do something uncharacteristic with a patient, we need to think about our motivation for doing so. Is this for the patient's benefit, or is part of us not wishing to be aware of being gratified by this. Having noted this, Little (1985) describes feeling adequately held by Winnicott, who held her hand during a session of extreme emotional pain. Perhaps, there rarely is an exception that proves the rule.

In one course, I was the only one of six psychoanalytic therapists who didn't regularly hug their patients. The other participants seemed mildly judgmental of me about this; I had the impression that they thought I was rather stiff and unnecessarily formal. The teacher of the course, an internationally renowned clinician, indicated that he regularly hugged his patients, and saw nothing wrong with this.

I thought that it was not clear to what extent this hugging was being done to gratify the patients and to what extent it gratified the therapists. Now I interpret my colleagues' mildly judgmental tone to be defensive in nature. On some level, I think they knew that a habit of hugging patients would not benefit their patients in the long term but had some other motivation. Also, to what extent might their hugging their patients be motivated by their feeling that they were not otherwise providing enough for their patients? To the extent that the therapists felt this way, some self-analysis was called for. To the extent that the therapists were experiencing a feeling of the patient not getting enough, that needed to be put in the words and explored. How many of their patients really needed hugging? How would they know which patients needed hugging? What psychotherapeutic explorations of unmet needs, for example, were not being made but were being replaced with hugs? Who was motivated to avoid undertaking these explorations?

If the patient feels the therapist is motivated to hug him for his own reasons, he may feel betrayed, that the therapist is indulging his own wishes rather than the patient's therapeutic needs. Also, some patients may be eager to comply with what they feel are the therapists' wishes, which probably involves the reenacting a familiar scenario

144   *Psychoanalytic/Psychodynamic Psychotherapy*

for the patient, of gratifying a caregiver's wishes and/or needs at the expense of the patient. This should be discussed in the therapy rather than recapitulated with the therapist. For more egregious examples of boundary crossings that become boundary violations that definitely are harmful to the patient, see Psychoanalysis in Medicine *chapter 19.*

Perhaps giving advice, reassurance, and encouragement and behaving in a friendly manner have been considered important aspects of supportive psychotherapy because these behaviors are important in other relationships. In particular, they constitute the nurturing that parents quite legitimately provide to their children. It does not follow, however, that these same behaviors, when performed by clinicians, will help their patients, even if this nurturing was exactly what the patients were deprived of in their early years, and is what they want now. I do not wish to deprecate appropriate encouragement and reassurance that are based on the clinician's knowledge of the patient and of his situation, but I believe that such reassurance should be given as part of a supportive psychotherapy. That is, in order to enhance the patient's awareness of reality, when there are positive factors that the patient is ignoring, in the event, for example, that a patient could take action to help himself and is not doing so. I disagree with providing encouragement without taking into consideration the individual patient's personality and circumstances, factors which may dispose a patient to assume that "it will all work out in the end," without his doing any further thinking or taking appropriate action.

The Literature

Werman (1984); Kernberg (1984); and Winston, Pinsker, and McCullough (1986) offer cogent reviews of the supportive psychotherapy literature. They comment on the paucity of that literature, despite its wide use among psychotherapists. Winston and colleagues indicate the confusion between "supportive psychotherapy" and the supportive aspects of any therapy. They discuss the mechanical misapplication of psychoanalytic techniques in some therapists' handling of supportive psychotherapy.

Kemberg believes that in supportive psychotherapy, primitive ego defenses, such as denial and projection, ought not be left undisturbed, as has been suggested by many earlier authors. He proposes that primitive defensive operations themselves weaken the patient's ability to deal constructively with the problems he faces, and that these defenses should be tactfully confronted. This is consistent with work of the British psychoanalysts Bion (2018), Segal (1950), and Rosenfeld (1987), who treated psychotic patients with psychoanalysis.

Arnold and Chapman (1984), in a comprehensive review, describe different forms of psychotherapy and what those psychotherapies have in common. They discuss the appropriate provision of psychotherapy and seek to define its effectiveness. Goldberg and Green (1985) attempt to outline "medical psychotherapy" as a specific approach using reassurance, suggestion,

Clarification and Confrontation 145

and manipulation. They discuss the value of catharsis, of initiating changes in the patient's environment, and of clarifying the patient's problems. Abrahams (1985) describes the work of a Balint-trained family clinician who conducted an independent psychotherapy practice.

MacDonald and Brown (1986) describe brief psychotherapy, enlarging on characteristics of the therapist and patient, and the use of a specific developmental model and a process of therapy. Pelton (1985) emphasizes the need for the clinician to change if he is to become a psychotherapist. Hazzard (1983) describes a series of general practice patients who received brief psychotherapy, and indicates the importance of helping the patient to discover the connections between his present symptoms, recent relationship events, and past relationship events.

Zigmond (1981) surveys the principles of psychopathology and outlines aspects of the self known and unknown to self and others. He suggests that the therapist must first support the patient's present *modus vivendi* and cautions that interpretations may appear "correct" to the therapist without helping the patient. Zigmond defines confrontation and outlines the importance of transference. He also outlines criteria for accepting patients into psychotherapy.

Andrews and Brodaty (1980) document the high proportion of patients who present with psychological symptoms, and discuss the cost-effectiveness of psychotherapy. They advocate a better organized approach to education in psychotherapy for family clinicians. Eleff and Prosen (1983) differentiate indications for short-term and long-term therapy, and compare three forms of short-term therapy. Lieberman and Stuart (1986) describe an approach to psychosocial assessment that focuses on the patient's feelings and suggest the establishment of a contract with the patient. Walker (1981) describes specific therapeutic techniques for different conditions, rather than outlining a general approach to patients.

Two Techniques of Supportive Psychotherapy

The technique of clarification involves exploring, with the patient, the implications of his statements, and questioning what is contradictory, unclear, or incomplete. Clarification is an attempt to bring out additional facts, while making more obvious what questions are implied but left unexplained, in the patient's information. The limits of the patient's understanding of the problem in question are thereby made more clear (Kernberg, 1984).

Mr. A., for example, a minor executive in a large corporation, presented to his MH clinician with vague complaints of anxiety and depressive mood. He complained about management's unfair coercion of the employees, taking advantage of them, and dismissing them when they did not meet management's unreasonable expectations. He alluded vaguely to fear that he would suffer a similar fate, although he was part of management, but was evasive when asked why or in what way. Clarification led to a hesitant revelation that Mr. A. strongly supported the employees behind management's

146 *Psychoanalytic/Psychodynamic Psychotherapy*

back, meeting with them, and even coaching them on how to combat most effectively the management he was expected to represent. Mr. A., although anxious about his activity, believed that management would have no way of finding out about it.

The technique of confrontation, despite the connotations of the term, does not involve an aggressive forcing of unpleasant facts down the patient's throat. Rather, it consists of pointing out to the patient that certain aspects of what he has said appear contradictory or confusing to the interviewer and limit the interviewer's understanding (Kernberg, 1984). What the interviewer is questioning, the patient has previously accepted as natural, whereas to the interviewer, this acceptance is evidence of defensive non-thinking, resulting in a decreased awareness of reality. The patient's attention is brought to the incongruity in his thinking and is asked to consider in combination material previously kept separate in his mind. The defensive "non-thinking" has provided the patient with some relief from anxiety about the implications of the material, but only at the expense of limiting his awareness of reality and his capacity to think of ways to solve the problem. As well, Mr. A still complained of anxiety in spite of employing this defense. *Keeping things separate in one's mind involves the defense of splitting. This is considered a relatively primitive defense.*

Splitting is compared to repression, in which some aspects of one's thoughts, feelings, impulses, or other psychic contents are pushed out of conscious awareness. By definition, psychic contents that have been pushed out of mental awareness at some point had been articulated consciously. If these psychic contents are too threatening to the individual, raising his anxiety to too high a level, various unconscious defense mechanisms of the ego are employed to render them unconscious. Repression is felt to be at the basis of all defense mechanisms and also is considered a defense mechanism in itself. Repression may be reversed, either by the individual being confronted with something in himself, for example, that he cannot deny; by some helpful friend or relative who provides support that makes what was unbearable become bearable, or in a psychoanalytic form of treatment. In the case of splitting, what is maintained out of conscious awareness may never have been in conscious awareness. Splitting is felt to originate in the first months of life, when the infant, who at this point does not even recognize himself as a separate entity from his mother (who essentially consists of his entire world) gradually divides his experience of the Other, as it develops, into positive and negative experiences, so that the negative ones do not overwhelm the positive ones. This experience of the positive and negative is gradually internalized, taken into his mind, so there develops little by little positive and negative unconscious images of the other.

In relative health, these two images, called part-objects, gradually coalesce into one internal object that in the best circumstances has positive and negative qualities and is an experienced ambivalently. That enables the individual to accept mixed feelings in relationships and to perceive others in a more or less realistic manner. Based on the child's temperamental sensitivity and his early experience with his caregivers, as well as other factors that may intervene, such as maternal depression, the child's need for surgery in the first months or years of life (which may be experienced as very traumatic) and other factors that may cause suffering or interfere with a positive parent–child attachment, the development of this ambivalent internal object, or even the development of the positive and negative part-objects, may be interfered with, which results in a persistence of splitting.

Heavy reliance on splitting makes it difficult for individuals to be realistic about themselves and other people. Devaluation and idealization both of the self and the other are more predominant, making it difficult to be realistic about oneself and others, which complicates one's adaptation in life. To the extent that one idealizes oneself, one may not recognize one's realistic limitations, which can involve one in imprudent and even dangerous activities. To the extent that one devalues oneself, one is predisposed to depression and to not utilizing one's capacity for personal agency in a constructive way. To the extent that one idealizes someone else, one may have unrealistic expectations of them and at the same time feel relatively devalued and helpless, not able to do even one what one could do to take care of oneself. To the extent that one devalues the other, one feels impoverished in his relationships, discourages the other from having a relationship with him, and fosters a negative attitude toward the other that again may interfere with a relationship, such as condescension or contempt.

One example of splitting involves patients who are described as having a borderline level of personality functioning and who may initially idealize and then devalue the other. In the idealization, there is the projection onto the other person of an all-good part-object, until the other person disappoints the individual, whereupon an all-bad part-object is projected onto him, leading to devaluation. Idealization and devaluation lead to caricatures in one's perception of others, so that one cannot realistically perceive what is the other's real strengths and weaknesses, and how they can be worked with and worked around. The same, of course, is true of idealization and devaluation of the self. Splitting is heavily relied on in individuals with post-traumatic stress disorder. The experience of trauma with the associated intense feelings of terror can be split off and inaccessible to the individual, being unbearable, unless the individual finds a relationship, such as a therapeutic relationship, in which they can feel contained.

To continue Mr. A's story, confrontation of the potentially self-destructive nature of his behavior, combined with confrontation of his denial that management might discover it, led to an open discussion of Mr. A's sympathy for the "downtrodden workers," with whom Mr. A strongly identified in their struggles with management. Mr. A was determined to help them win against management, ignoring the fact that he was exposing himself to the very danger of being fired from which he hoped to protect the employees. Further discussion discovered that this situation reflected a life-long pattern of sympathy for the underdog, resulting in Mr. A's often missing promotions or being reprimanded for involving himself inappropriately in other people's problems. *A more ambitious interpretive psychotherapy would involve exploration of the unconscious bases for this identification, likely originating in experiences of feeling helpless and vulnerable in early relationships. This would involve interpretation as a central technique.*

A third technique of psychotherapy, interpretation, is defined in such a way as to distinguish it from confrontation and clarification. Interpretation is used mainly in expressive psychoanalytic therapy rather than in supportive

148   *Psychoanalytic/Psychodynamic Psychotherapy*

therapy. It is used in attempts to explore the patient's unconscious motivation for thoughts, feelings, impulses, and behavior that distress the patient and/or involve the patient in difficulties in his relationship with his environment. Where confrontation may expose the self-destructive nature of a patient's behavior, interpretation attempts to explain it on the basis of a short-term gain for the patient, usually involving reduction of anxiety about an unconscious conflict. *However, the short-term reduction of anxiety usually comes at the cost of long-term interference with optimal functioning because of unconscious limitations in what the patient allows himself to think or feel consciously.*

Mr. A described his parents as overbearing and punitive. It was not difficult for the psychotherapist he saw in consultation to infer that Mr. A's sympathy for the underdog was based on forgotten memories of being the underdog in his own family. The psychotherapist thought Mr. A's self-destructive behavior was unconsciously motivated by feelings about his parents that were influencing his current reactions at work, and that it would be in Mr. A's interest to react to the present reality on its own merits, rather than being influenced unconsciously by previous experiences. In fact, the psychotherapist had the impression that Mr. A was not only reliving his unconscious resentment toward his parents by helping the employees fight the corporate "parents," but that this resentment inhibited Mr. A from achieving promotion, which he consciously wanted, because promotion would involve his becoming one of the hated "parents," that is, a member of upper management. Both the mistreatment of the employees and the prospect of being a "parent" made Mr. A intensely anxious.

The psychotherapist suggested that Mr. A engage in some psychoanalytic psychotherapy to continue to examine the kinds of situations that he got himself into, in order to learn more adaptive ways of dealing with this conflict. One outcome was that Mr. A decided that he would more effectively be able to see to it that justice was done if he were promoted to a more responsible position. He eventually obtained a promotion. Mr. A's increased awareness of his tendency to overreact on the employees' behalf helped him to deal with these situations more constructively.

What Supportive Psychotherapy Is

It is important to distinguish between telling the patient what is wrong and what to do and helping him to understand how certain automatic ways of functioning are detrimental to his interests. That is, there is a difference between giving advice and employing the techniques of clarification and confrontation. These techniques encourage the patient to raise questions and find solutions for problems he may never have considered. Giving advice does nothing to encourage the patient to improve his ability to deal with the external world. I would like to emphasize how a supportive therapeutic approach, in supporting the patient's optimal ego functioning, fosters the patient's perceiving, remembering, thinking, judging, deciding, and then taking appropriate action, in dealing with a problem in external reality.

Clarification and Confrontation   149

Admittedly, some advice to the patient is inherent in this approach. This advice, which often is provided more by the therapist's attitude rather than explicitly, is to think first and act afterward. This involves the internalization in the patient of a set of attitudes toward himself and a set of attitudes toward the world as a result of his interaction with the therapist. This occurs to some extent in all psychotherapies and, to some extent, in all relationships. Some believe that this internalization is among the most powerful factors promoting change in psychotherapy, especially in supportive psychotherapy.

A Non-Thinking Patient

Ms. Q complained of depression. She had recently left her alcoholic, physically abusive, unfaithful husband for the third time. She related that she had known during her engagement that her husband (then her fiancé) had broken another woman's arm. Her reaction then was, "It wasn't my arm." Although Ms. Q appeared to be of average intelligence, she seemed unaware that she could have used this knowledge to help predict her fiancé's future behavior. After attempting to clarify the circumstances under which the violence had occurred, Ms. Q's family physician gently confronted her with her not having asked herself what kind of relationship her fiancé might have had with this other woman, that he would be in a position to break her arm. It turned out that Ms. Q knew that the incident had taken place in a hotel but was unsure whether it was in the bar or a hotel room. The family physician further pointed out that Ms. Q drew no conclusions from the violence that she knew her fiancé was capable of, as if, because it had not been inflicted on her at that time, she had no reason to worry.

In other words, the physician tried to clarify how much Ms. Q consciously knew about what had happened and to confront her defense of denial, her "not knowing," which led to her experiencing, over a period of years, the same type of abuse, the significance of which she originally denied when it had been inflicted on someone else. Further interviews disclosed that this "not knowing" was a pattern that invariably involved Ms. Q's suffering abuse which, given her observations, could have been avoided. This nonpsychotic patient exemplified a serious deficit in remembering, judging, deciding, and acting. Without going into the motivation for this deficit, the family physician, meeting her weekly over a period of months, was able to help her to see more clearly the kinds of situations that spelled danger to her. She gradually acquired a repertoire of coping mechanisms that helped her to avoid the dangers once she saw them, rather than ignoring them, which had been her former response.

One can consider what might be the unconscious motivation for the style of avoidance of thinking that Ms. Q displayed. One would be that the individual as a child suffered from abuse either inflicted by her caregiver(s), and so had no one to turn to, or inflicted by someone else, but found her caregivers to be obtuse, disinterested, terrified of hearing about the abuse, or even punitive, blaming the child for the abuse. All of these experiences would tend to discourage the child from thinking about the

150   *Psychoanalytic/Psychodynamic Psychotherapy*

abuse. Also, a very traumatic aspect of childhood abuse is not having an adult to help the child cope with their feelings about the abuse. This is a crucial aspect of to what extent a potentially traumatic situation results in an ongoing experience of trauma, and, in the worst circumstances, symptoms of chronic post-traumatic stress disorder, which can affect an individual for their entire life if it is not adequately treated. A child's very painful and sometimes terrifying feelings about abusive experiences can be mitigated with the comfort of an understanding adult who helps the child contain the pain and terror, while the adult lets himself experience his own pain and terror, among other feelings, reacting to hearing about the child's abuse. This kind of containment is what may enable a child to emotionally survive an experience that otherwise might be traumatizing on an ongoing basis. The child is able to internalize the containment of the adult. Abused children often grow up without this containment, which can be provided to the adult in a psychoanalytic psychotherapy or psychoanalysis. A supportive psychotherapeutic approach is ineffective in these cases; what is required is a psychoanalytically informed exploration in depth of the experience of trauma and how it has affected the individual. Often the style of avoiding thinking described above is a main presenting feature of a traumatized patient. The therapy would involve reexperiencing the painful feelings and, with the support of the therapist, being helped to think about them and the traumatic experience. A successful outcome would involve the patient no longer being as dominated by their feelings about the traumatic experience, and better able to think, as the inhibition to thinking related to the trauma has been relieved. (See Chapter 3 for more about understanding and managing traumatized patients.)

Another possible motivation for such a disturbance in thinking is if a child is overtly encouraged by her parents not to think. When this happens, it is likely that the parents, possibly having been traumatized themselves, cannot bear to hear about the child's thoughts and feelings, which might remind them too much of their own painful and terrifying thoughts and unbearable feelings.

Individuals with histrionic personality traits frequently exhibit a superficiality of thinking, with an impressionistic cognitive style, not looking "too closely at details for fear of seeing too much and being overwhelmed" (PDM Task Force, 2006:60).

There is not an absolute boundary between supportive psychotherapy and psychoanalysis and interpretive psychoanalytic psychotherapy. Being seen four times a week, for example, in psychoanalysis can be a very supportive experience, although overtly supportive techniques generally are not relied on. Similarly, supportive psychotherapy, even though it generally does not utilize interpretations as a technique, can involve patients in considerable learning about themselves. Rather than an absolute boundary, there is a spectrum of psychotherapies from the most interpretive, psychoanalysis, which also provides the opportunity to explore the patient's internal experience, including unbearable feelings and unthinkable thoughts, in the greatest depth, to the most supportive.

A Provocative Patient

This is an example of a family physician working in consultation with a psychiatrist who recommends that he employs some techniques of supportive psychotherapy with his patient. Ms. Z, an 18-year-old student living

Clarification and Confrontation   151

with her parents, believed that she was pregnant; her belief was confirmed by her physician. Her boyfriend initially planned to marry her after the baby's birth but, instead, left her without warning. Ms. Z had hoped to keep the fact of the pregnancy from her parents, despite expecting to live with them during the full term of pregnancy. Eventually, she agreed to having the baby adopted away, which was done shortly after birth. Ms. Z was subsequently seen by a social worker at a community agency, to whom she complained of insomnia and difficulty with her studies. She was then assessed by a psychiatrist, certified for involuntary admission, and taken to a provincial psychiatric hospital.

Shortly after discharge, Ms. Z consulted her family physician, asking whether her sleeping pill could cause apathy, depression, and decreased appetite. She indicated that she just wanted the doctor to answer her questions. She was afraid to talk about anything personal, for fear she would be recertified to the psychiatric hospital. During this interview, she also informed her physician that she knew the lethal dosage of several medications, including over-the-counter preparations. This revelation was immediately followed by a request for "something for my nerves."

By this time, the family physician was quite suspicious of Ms. Z's real goals in the interview, and refused to prescribe any medication. He was left feeling very anxious when Ms. Z abruptly terminated the interview, complaining that doctors "didn't care," and that her doctor was impersonal and gave only textbook answers. The physician was aware of growing frustration and even resentment in himself toward this patient, who complained of the doctor's lack of involvement, although Ms. Z herself was unwilling to provide a proper history. The physician knew from previous interviews that Ms. Z was reluctant to discuss her pregnancy with her parents because she "knew they wouldn't understand," Ms. Z, in previous interviews, had indicated how uncaring, critical, and hostile she considered her parents to be. She also stated that she began feeling more depressed on the anniversary of having been coerced into sexual intimacy some years before, by another boyfriend who also had subsequently left her.

Ms. Z refused regular follow-up appointments that her physician, by now anxious, several times offered. Nevertheless, she requested frequent unscheduled "emergency" appointments, expecting to be seen the same day, on weekends, or in the evenings. The physician considered it was important to stay in touch with this patient, whom he believed was potentially suicidal, but was frustrated by her lack of cooperation and unreasonable expectations.

The danger of suicide in this kind of patient, combined with her complaints about the physician's level of interest and competence and her lack of consistent follow-up, inevitably raises feelings in the physician that affect the management of the patient. The danger is that the physician may respond on a personal basis, that is, according to experiences, for example, frustrations, in his present or past relationships. Insofar as this occurs, the physician is reacting based on unconscious motivations in order to reduce

152 *Psychoanalytic/Psychodynamic Psychotherapy*

his own anxiety and not necessarily in the patient's interest. Although this reaction is provoked by the patient, it is the physician's job to be vigilant and reflect on it rather than merely acting on it.

The physician must continue trying to understand the patient's problem without succumbing to the patient's unconscious invitation to become part of her inner world of neglect, abandonment, and hostility. He must be sure not to justify the patient's accusations, which themselves may be irritating enough to provoke the physician to do just what he is being accused of doing. In brief, the patient must not be allowed to succeed in projecting her internal world onto the physician, manipulating him into living out with her a stereotyped frustrating relationship, reminiscent of the patient's experiences with her parents. *This would be an example of projective identification in which the clinician assumes a role of someone in the patient's internal world, and enacts in external reality a relationship in the patient's internal world that likely recapitulates in some way the patient's experience with early caregivers. It is preferable to catch oneself in such an enactment and provide an opportunity for clinician and patient to think together about what is happening in the interaction. Now I would not say "manipulating," as the physician plays an active role in accepting the patient's projection and enacting the old relationship with the patient, rather than providing the opportunity for a different type of experience, which involves more thinking, including thinking about feelings, than mere acting.* Instead, the physician must continue eliciting a history, controlling *(now I would say "containing")* his own reaction, confronting the patient in a neutral manner with inconsistencies in the history, and showing the patient how her behavior is self-destructive.

The doctor may consider some questions raised by this history: How and why did the patient allow herself to become pregnant? What is her motivation for not telling her parents? What motivates her interest in this boyfriend, and how did she fail to see that he was not trustworthy? The doctor should also consider his relationship with the patient, and the possibility of an unconscious communication in the latter's demand for pills. The patient acts as if she wants something to make her temporarily feel better and can expect nothing more. To have a friendly relationship where problems can be worked on seems to be more than she can hope for. This leads to another question: Why does the patient return despite her complaints? What does she really want?

The physician could try to involve the patient in observing with him what is going on in the patient's life, and even in their relationship, instead of the patient passively receiving the physician's "gift" (pills, which she may use to poison herself), or being the victim of the physician's "attack," which she provokes. The physician's reaction of frustration, or anger, is the diagnostic clue that he can use to warn himself that he may be involved in a reliving, with the patient, of problems in the patient's ways of relating to others, rather than understanding the situation and helping the patient to look at it objectively.

The physician could avoid either complying with or refusing Ms. Z's demand. Instead, he could look with Ms. Z at what she is hoping for and

Clarification and Confrontation   153

Table 9.1 Supportive Psychotherapy

What to Avoid
Freely give personal advice
Dispense wholesale friendliness
Automatically encourage and reassure

What to Do
Clarify what the problems are
Support the patient's best functioning, by supporting his capacity to think
Confront the patient with what he is not considering, to help him think about it,
   particularly about his feelings about it

Winston, Rosenthal, and Roberts (2020) and Sharpless (2019) are recommended
   for those wishing to read more about contemporary psychoanalytic approaches
   to supportive psychotherapy.

---

at how she expects what she is asking for will help. This approach at least demonstrates interest in what the patient wants, without engaging her in a fantasy that the physician can satisfy her demands or rejecting the patient for what she wants. It may lead to discussions of frustrations in other relationships and, eventually, to considering how the patient contributes to these difficulties, which are already manifest in her hints about suicide and her unconstructive use of "emergency" appointments. This resistant patient responded at first with the comment, "Talking won't change the past." The physician was able to reply that the patient was correct; the past can't be changed, but learning about the past may help the patient make better decisions for herself in the future and avoid similar frustrating situations.

Conclusions

Supportive psychotherapy is a distinct treatment with definite goals and techniques, rather than a friendly chat with a clinician who is "flying by the seat of her pants." Clarification and confrontation can be used to improve the patient's ego functions of perceiving, remembering, judging, deciding, and acting, which can result in the patient's improved interpersonal functioning. The clinician's emotional reaction to the patient's behavior can be put to use in observing the patient's interpersonal difficulties. Table 9.1 summarizes this supportive psychotherapy approach.

References

Abrahams S (1985). Psychotherapy in general practice: An early experiment. *The Practitioner,* 229: 1117–1120.
Andrews G & Brodaty H (1980). General practitioner as psychotherapist. *Medical Journal of Australia,* 2: 655–659.
Arnold JF & Chapman RJ (1984). Primary care clinician and psychotherapy. In Rakel RE (ed.). *Textbook of Family Practice,* 3rd ed. Toronto: Saunders.

154 Psychoanalytic/Psychodynamic Psychotherapy

Bion WR (2018) *Second Thoughts*. Routledge: New York & London.

Eleff MK & Prosen H (1983). Short-term psychotherapies. *Medical Clinics of North America*, 35(1): 3275–3279.

Goldberg RL & Green S (1985). Medical psychotherapy. *American Family Clinician*, 31: 173–178.

Hazzard AJ (1983). Brief psychotherapeutic sessions in general practice. *The Practitioner*, 227: 107–109.

Kernberg O (1984). *Severe Personality Disorders*. New Haven, CT: Yale University Press, 153: 147–164.

Lieberman III JA & Stuart MR (1986). The 15-minute hour. *Patient Care*, 20: 87–94.

Little MI (1985). Winnicott working in areas where psychotic anxieties predominate: A personal record. *Free Associations*, 1(3): 9–42.

MacDonald PJ & Brown A (1986). Brief psychotherapy in family practice. *Canadian Family Clinician*, 32: 1333–1338.

PDM Task Force (2006). *Psychodynamic Diagnostic Manual*. Silver Spring, MD: Alliance of Psychoanalytic Organizations.

Pelton CL (1985). Family clinician as psychotherapist. *Postgraduate Medicine*, 78(2): 227–230.

Rosenfeld H (1987). *Impasse and Interpretation: Therapeutic and Anti-Therapeutic Factors in the Psychoanalytic Treatment of Psychotic, Borderline, and Neurotic Patients*. London: Tavistock, New Library of Psychoanalysis.

Segal H (1950). Some aspects of the analysis of a schizophrenic. *International Journal of Psychoanalysis*, 31: 268–278.

Sharpless BA (2019). *Psychodynamic Psychotherapy Techniques: A Guide to Expressive and Supportive Interventions*. New York: Oxford University Press.

Sussman MB (1992). *A Curious Calling: Unconscious Motivations for Practising Psychotherapy*. Northvale, NJ: Jason Aronson.

Walker JI (1981). Office psychotherapy: Supportive techniques and indications for referral. *Postgraduate Medicine*, 70(4): 34–43.

Werman DS (1984). *Practice of Supportive Psychotherapy*. New York: Brunner/ Mazel.

Winston A, Pinsker H, & McCullough L (1986). Review of supportive psychotherapy. *Hospital Community Psychiatry*, 37(11): 1105–1114.

Winston A, Rosenthal RN, & Roberts LW (2020) *Learning Supportive Psychotherapy*. Washington, DC: American Psychiatric Association Publishing.

Zigmond D (1981). Elements of psychotherapy. *The Practitioner*, 225: 1280–1291.

10 Coping with Catastrophic Feelings

Supportive Therapeutic Relationship
with Patients Suffering from Chronic,
Serious or Life-Threatening Illness—
Lessons from HIV-AIDS-Related Illness[1]

Introduction

The paper on which this article was based was published over 20 years ago. In that time, there fortunately has been excellent progress in the treatment of HIV-related illness and AIDS. As well, there is more social support and less social stigma for these patients. However, the issues raised in herein remain valid and are relevant in the management of much chronic serious or life-threatening illness. Patients living with HIV-AIDS present clinicians with different types of problems. For example, patients may demonstrate psychiatric symptoms and signs that reflect an underlying medical complication such as dementia. Patients with any serious illness may have an adverse psychological reaction to its symptoms or its medical complications. Other patients may have an adverse psychological reaction to having serious illness, to the diagnosis that is made, or to management of the condition (Steinberg, 1987). A case vignette will raise important considerations in the psychological management of an HIV-AIDS patient. What is dealt with here is applicable to the mental health aspects of management of many patients with chronic, potentially life-threatening, debilitating diseases, especially those whose sufferers bear a stigma for having them. The case history describes a physician–patient relationship, but the principles of management to be derived from it apply to all mental health professional (MHP)–patient/client relationships.

Literature Review

Evidence that there is a link between social support and the psychological well-being of people with HIV (Gree, 1993) is not surprising. In North America, the extent to which gay men with HIV infection have access to social support and informal care at times of illness has been investigated; the demands of long-term or serious illness are such that adequate support services should be available in the community (Hart et al., 1990). Persons with HIV infection and AIDS have complex psychosocial needs, although they lack crucial social support (Hedge & Glover, 1990). Health-care personnel

DOI: 10.4324/9781003200581-14

156 Psychoanalytic/Psychodynamic Psychotherapy

are encouraged to address the grief and dysphoric affect that are common responses to HIV spectrum illness, to strengthen the patient's coping skills and maximize interpersonal comfort (Lippmann, James & Frierson, 1993). Adults infected with HIV who experience a greater sense of derived meaning and purpose from the situations and those with more social support report higher self-esteem and lower anxiety than other HIV-infected adults (Line et al., 1993). Mental health clinicians are in an excellent position to provide much of the support that AIDS–HIV patients need.

Forms of support and counseling that are available to HIV–AIDS patients include informal "carers" (McCann & Wadsworth, 1992), cognitive behavioral couples therapy (Ussher, 1990), structured psychoeducational support groups (Levy et al., 1990), brief cognitive behavioral group therapies (Kelly et al., 1993), social support group therapy, psychoeducational support cognitive group therapy (Levine et al., 1991), support workshops (Wong-Rieger, 1993), interpersonal psychotherapy (Markowitz, Klerman & Perry, 1992), group psychotherapy (Beckett & Rutan, 1990), support group (Daniolos, 1994), group intervention by nurses through computer networks (Ripich, Moore & Brennan, 1992), and rural community psychoeducational telephone groups (Rounds, Galinsky & Stevens, 1991). Complications in group therapy with AIDS patients include the threat of early death, a variable course of illness, and stigma related to the illness and to the preexisting lifestyles of most patients (Funnell, 1991).

Health professionals have been encouraged to promote more adaptive coping strategies and to help patients use existing sources of positive social support (Leserman, Perkins & Evans, 1992). Satisfaction with one's social support networks is related to more healthy coping strategies and asymptomatic HIV-positive men. Satisfaction with emotional, practical, and informational types of social support has been inversely correlated with depression in a sample of gay men (Hayes, Turner & Coates, 1992). Subjective social support has been associated with lower depression and lower distress in a sample of gay men at risk for AIDS (Lackner, et al., 1993a). Individuals in this group reported a subjective sense of isolation and subsequently experienced more adverse mental health, suggesting that certain types of social support influence mental health in this group (Lackner et al., 1993b). Assessment of social support for the person with AIDS has been described as important because of its devastating psychosocial consequences (Feingold & Slammon, 1993). A model integrating mental health and primary care services for families with HIV has been described in which primary care team members are empowered to management of problems whenever possible (McGough, 1990). This hospital-based program is an example of early integration of mental health and primary care services at the community level.

Family systems theory has been used to provide physicians with a comprehensive paradigm to investigate the social and interpersonal contexts of life-threatening and chronic illness, which profoundly affects the patient's family life. The changes in family circumstances, in turn, have an impact on the physically ill patient. Knowledge of family systems theory has been

Coping with Catastrophic Feelings   157

suggested to enhance the therapeutic reach of physicians (Sholevar & Perkel, 1990). Psychotherapists working with patients with HIV infections must be willing to confront psychodynamic issues in the past and realistic medical and social concerns of the present and future. The therapy must not be driven by the disease but must be informed by the evolving needs of the individual patient for self-understanding and a sense of enhancing competence (Zegans, Gehard & Coates, 1994).

The value to mental health professionals of this literature is limited by several factors. A few of the articles contain general conclusions, while other articles describe specific psychological approaches that have been found to be effective without outlining in detail what measures clinicians can take in trying to manage these patients optimally. Reference is made to a need to explore psychodynamic issues and the need for self-understanding without indicating how this may be done. Chapter 9 offers an approach to this question.

Case History

Mr. A, a 29-year-old patient new to Dr. C's family practice, gave a history of sexual involvement with many female partners without protection. There is no other significant medical history. Testing for HIV infection was positive. Mr. A reacted with feelings of shock and depression, but was not suicidal. No history of neurovegetative signs of depression was elicited. Dr. C initially encouraged Mr. A to be "upbeat" and found him to alternate between feeling up and down. Mr. A consulted Dr. C regularly for support for three months. Then, he made an unexpected suicide attempt by overdosing on aspirin. He was admitted briefly to the psychiatric unit of the local general hospital. After discharge, Dr. C asked the psychiatric consultant who liaised with the family medicine clinic (Steinberg & Morrissey, 1995) how Dr. C might help keep Mr. A "in a good mood," and how to deal with his preference to kill himself, as opposed to "shrinking away" with AIDS.

Mr. A's father was described as a demanding, harsh, and physically violent man who beat his wife and threatened his children. His mother was described as affectionate but ineffectual in protecting the children from the father. Mr. A has supportive relationships with his younger brother and his girlfriend of one year. She has stayed with him in spite of the diagnosis of HIV infection and the fact that she has to be tested for it herself. Dr. C was especially concerned about Mr. A's ongoing suicide risk. His history was presented by the family physician to the consulting psychiatrist in a liaison psychiatry format (Steinberg & Morrissey, 1995).

Discussion

This case, in spite of the limited history available to the psychiatric consultant, presents the attending clinician with several challenges. *(The clinician happened to be a physician in this case, but I am calling him a clinician because we*

158 *Psychoanalytic/Psychodynamic Psychotherapy*

are concerned now with the psychodynamically informed management of the patient, which any health professional might undertake.) Who is the patient in whom this disease occurring? What assets does he have to help him adapt to his chronic disease? What difficulties will compromise his adaptation? What limitations in the patient does the clinician have to recognize? Consequently, what are realistic therapeutic goals for the clinician? The clinician's need to "cheer up" the patient and to maintain a "positive attitude" in the patient has to be explored. Whose need is this, the patient's or the clinician's?

In cases such as these, unconscious communications and countertransference considerations are important. The clinician must be aware of her reaction to the patient (for example, despair, clinical nihilism, or a value judgment about the patient's lifestyle), although this usually is better not expressed to the patient. The more aware the clinician is of her own reaction, the more she is able to set it aside, deal with it, and attend to the patient, treating the patient in a way that is most in the patient's interest. The clinician's reaction to the patient may also indicate how other people may react to the patient, and may suggest the type of reaction that the patient may elicit from others (Slakter, 1987:19).

Antidepressants are generally indicated in individuals who have sustained symptoms suggesting major depressive disorder or (sometimes) persistent depressive disorder. Mr. A's history did not suggest that he was suffering from a clinical depression, and antidepressants did not seem to be indicated. This should be a consideration, however, if his depressive symptoms were to increase. One may tend to prescribe antidepressants more freely in a case like this, where there are obvious limitations to what can be done to help the patient, than in a patient where there is more hope that psychotherapeutic treatment will result in a definitive and long-standing improvement (Steinberg, 1989a). One would have to consider which antidepressant would be safest if taken in overdose, given the suicide risk.

Supportive psychotherapy involves more than the provision of support (Steinberg, 1989b) (see also Chapter 9). Techniques of supportive psychotherapy include clarification of the patient's problem and confrontation of the patient with what he is not considering. These techniques encourage the patient to raise questions and find solutions for problems that he may never have thought about. In contrast, the definitive technique of insight-oriented (psychoanalytic) psychotherapy is interpretation, which involves an attempt to help the patient understand the unconscious motivation for his behavior. Interpretation may show how a patient reduces anxiety about an unmet need or an unconscious conflict in a manner for which he pays a high price, psychologically, concretely, or both. A supportive therapeutic relationship might involve the clinician seeing the patient regularly, perhaps initially for 30–60 minutes weekly, and being available on an ongoing basis for emergencies. This relationship could focus on what is in the patient's interest, on enhancing the patient's quality of life, and on exploring with the patient can do to give meaning to life. The clinician can function as a positive attachment, permitting internalization of a more benign object than was

Coping with Catastrophic Feelings 159

possible in Mr. A's relationship with his parents and, in doing so, may mitigate the punitive and threatening internalized image of his father. This is one way of explaining how a positive attachment reduces risk of suicide. *One can also consider to what extent a life-threatening illness might reinforce an internal persecutory object, for example, by representing an unconscious punishment for some imagined or real transgression.*

The description of Mr. A's family life suggests that his unconscious self-image is characterized by feelings of helplessness and victimization. His internal object seems to be demanding, harsh, and threatening. Important affects related to the self-image and internal object appear to be fear and hostility, both on the basis of his father's threats and violence and of his mother's ineffectiveness in protecting the children. One would expect a longing for a friendlier father and a stronger, more protective mother. One's self-image and internal objects and related affects influence one's relationships in adult life. One could expect Mr. A to be afraid of harsh, demanding, and threatening treatment from his clinician, or to fear that the latter will be ineffective in caring for him. One would similarly anticipate that Mr. A would wish for a friendly yet strong and effective clinician. These longings will be accompanied by a tendency to experience fear and hostility that is not explainable by what transpires between clinician and patient. The clinician who keeps the patient's history of early relationships in mind, and observes how they may be affecting the clinician–patient relationship, will be in an advantageous position to deal with difficulties in their relationship when they arise. The clinician will not look at problems in her relationship with a patient such as Mr. A as an unpleasant mishap, but rather as an inevitable part of the work, which offers an opportunity to help the patient grow and learn more constructive ways to relate.

The description of Mr. A's relationship with his parents suggests that he had a negative internalized object characterized by a demanding and threatening attitude toward himself. This internal object, especially when it is associated with a violent parent, makes Mr. A's reaction to his diagnosis with the suicide attempt more understandable. An "unexpected" suicide attempt very often is associated with a threat to or disruption in an important relationship. This underlines the importance to Mr. A of supportive relationships to mitigate against the neglect and hostility that he seems to have internalized. One interpretation of the sexual contact with multiple partners is it may represent a search for the close personal contact that otherwise feels is unavailable and a defense against an awareness of feeling unloved and neglected. *I am not suggesting that such an interpretation be made to Mr. A; that is not within the purview of a mainly supportive psychotherapy. The clinician's understanding of Mr. A's unconscious motivations can assist her in their work together. The clinician should never underestimate her importance to the patient. One possible precipitant for a suicide attempt, or for a patient becoming suicidal, is the patient's feeling that the clinician's support has been or may be withdrawn. This may be on the basis of the patient perceiving, accurately or not, a negative attitude in the clinician toward him; the clinician's absence, planned or not; the clinician planning to discharge the patient*

160 *Psychoanalytic/Psychodynamic Psychotherapy*

when the patient doesn't feel ready for this; or the clinician being transferred to another workplace, with the patient being transferred to the care of another clinician.

The most hopeful prognostic sign regarding Mr. A's suicide risk seems to be the two positive ongoing relationships with his brother and his girlfriend. The risk appears to be heightened by the harsh and punitive image of his father. To the extent that Mr. A identifies with his father's attitude toward him, he is likely to be at a higher suicide risk. One may try to quantify his suicide risk by comparing the influence of the negative image of his father, "the bad introject" with the influence of what seems to be an ambivalently positive interject of his mother and of the supportive, positive ongoing relationships. An important role for Dr. C is to try to tip the balance away from suicide by offering a positive relationship and help Mr. A cope constructively with his illness. Dr. C's anxious attitude seems to reflect the need to "cure" Mr. A, in spite of his knowing that there is no cure for HIV infection.

Bion warns about therapeutic zeal and the misguided wish to "cure" a patient. "Curing" a patient of emotional disturbance is a tall order for any clinician–patient dyad. The patient may be intimidated by the clinician's unrealistic or idealized expectations of him. The result may be a regression, motivated by the fear that the clinician is ambitious for the patient to get better according to the clinician's timetable, and so be discharged before the patient is ready. Alternatively, the patient may feel hopeless about meeting the clinician's (perceived or real) expectations. The patient will feel poorly understood. The clinicians' ambitions may at times involve an enactment, in which the clinician has unconsciously accepted the patient's unconscious invitation to enact a scene from the patient's internal world of self-image and internal objects. This may be a replay of actual untoward experiences the patient had with early caretakers, whom he experienced as not understanding his suffering. The outcome may be as grave as a suicide attempt, the patient's attempt to put the brakes on the clinician's ambition and clarify for the clinician how unwell and far from "cure" the patient feels. This is a good example of the clinician being preoccupied by his own feelings and wishes, at the expense of focusing on the patient's experience.

The psychiatric consultant emphasized the importance of not expecting to cure her patient with a chronic or incurable condition, but rather to take the best possible care of the patient. The clinician's excessive demand on himself to cure the patient may be a clue not only to an aspect of the same demanding attitude that Mr. A experienced from his father. Mr. A may have unconsciously influenced the clinician to feel like Mr. A felt in his relationship with his father (Cashdan, 1988:96–118). Such concordant counter-transference experiences are a valuable indication of patient's experiences in relationships, including the therapeutic relationship (Racker, 1968).

Maintaining or establishing a supportive relationship with an individual who has difficulties with his parents poses challenges. Mr. A likely may begin treatment with a negative transference toward the clinician, experiencing him as similar to his punitive, harsh, and demanding father. The clinician should observe any sign that Mr. A feels that way and explore it with him when Mr. A appears comfortable enough to look at this. The interest that the clinician shows in exploring in this will go a long way toward dispelling Mr. A's apprehensions. It also makes possible for them to

Coping with Catastrophic Feelings 161

have a candid discussion regarding Mr. A's beliefs about the clinician's attitude toward Mr. A, comparing it with what Mr. A expected, and indicating the ways that the clinician is willing to be available. There is no point in offering more than what can be realistically provided or in declaring feelings that are more intense than a patient realistically can expect from an MHP (Racker, 1968).

Many patients like Mr. A would likely respond to the attitude of respect, reasonable limit-setting, interest, concern, and friendliness on the clinician's part. *(See following paragraph for the exceptions to this.)* This attitude, when conveyed on an ongoing basis, will do much to mitigate the effects of a bad internalized object. The clinician can also function as an auxiliary ego when necessary, confronting the patient with what is in his best interest. This does not imply a paternalistic attitude toward the patient, but acknowledges that, at times, patients, especially when overwhelmed with anxiety about serious illness, and its social effects, may not adequately consider realistic problems. Nor does this suggest that the clinician should make decisions for the patient, but that she should confront the patient about not making the decisions that should be made, or making decisions that are not in the patient's interest. The clinician must intervene when Mr. A is suicidal and, when necessary, arrange for his hospitalization. Deciding upon hospitalization can be a challenge, because patients with chronic and potentially life-threatening illnesses may become chronically suicidal. When Mr. A is acutely suicidal, the clinician must take the responsibility of admitting him to hospital, involuntarily if necessary, during the period of increased risk. When Mr. A is not acutely suicidal, the clinician may need to accept what may feel like a risk, to foster Mr. A's best adaptation outside the hospital. If Mr. A's course is complicated by an organic mental disorder as a sequela of AIDS, Dr. C may be obliged to assume responsibility for making decisions in areas in which or at times when Mr. A cannot make decisions in his own best interest. In most circumstances, family or close friends are available to share or assume this role. The availability of psychiatric consultation when needed is an important support to the clinician who is managing such a patient.

However, some patients cannot accept positive treatment. Some of them cannot believe in it and are suspicious that the clinician has another hidden motive or agenda for appearing friendly. Some individuals are painfully reminded of what was lacking in their early relationships if an MHP merely treats him in her usuall courteous, respectful way. It may be too painful for them to recognize this and accept it. Some individuals are determined to prove that the clinician is not what she seems to be and may provoke the clinician and unconsciously attempt to elicit the negative reaction that they are expecting. These people are very difficult to manage and appear to be impossible to please. The clinician who is determined to prove that she is "good" has fallen into a trap and cannot win with these patients. Also, the "better" the clinician tries to show herself to be, the worse the patient will feel by comparison; sometimes, the patient is made so desperate and feels so "bad" compared to the clinician's "goodness" that he may resort to a suicide attempt. Another situation where this is a

162 *Psychoanalytic/Psychodynamic Psychotherapy*

danger is if the clinician is so overwhelmed by her countertransference need to succeed that she attempts to provide all the patient's needs. When she inevitably fails, or gives up, often with considerable resentment, the patient may feel he has no recourse but suicide. One needs to be able to let the patient hate you, without trying to force him to seeing your goodness, which he emotionally may not be able to afford to see. He won't feel as bad about his hatred if you don't portray yourself as Mother Teresa (Sherby, 1989).

In my opinion, individuals like this frequently consult MHPs and are called "difficult" or "impossible." They elicit very strong negative countertransference reactions, including countertransference hate. Sometimes clinicians are so adversely affected by these patients that they treat them in a destructive way that they would never do with someone else. Although it may be necessary for an MHP to manage these patients, in my opinion, the only treatment likely to affect a definitive change in their adaptation is psychoanalysis or psychoanalytic psychotherapy. An important consideration in managing these patients when one cannot offer this type of treatment is to pay special attention to containing one's countertransference, have a colleague with whom to talk about the patient, limit the patient's destructive behavior, and try to see what you might be able to do that might be helpful to the patient, although the last thing this type of patient might do is acknowledge that you have helped them.

Conclusion

Effective provision of supportive psychotherapy for patients with chronic potentially life-threatening illness requires a consideration of the patient's personality and circumstances, including the assets and liabilities in his character and his social environment, and of the limitations of treatment. The setting of realistic therapeutic goals that are mutually agreeable to therapist and patient is important, as is the clinician's awareness of countertransference reactions. An important aspect of the psychotherapeutic relationship is the positive attachment it provides to the patient, with the opportunity for internalization of a more positive internal object. The therapist–patient relationship should be a factor favoring a more constructive way of coping with the patient's illness. Suicide risk must be assessed on an ongoing basis as required. Intervention may be needed when a patient is inadequately coping with realistic problems, becomes suicidal, or suffers from a cognitive deficit. In managing patients with chronic life-threatening conditions, the clinician must not only attempt to take the best care of the patient possible but also accept whatever limitations, psychotherapeutic or medical, there may be in management of the patient.

Note

1 This chapter was adapted from Steinberg PI (1998). Supportive therapeutic relationships with an HIV-AIDS patient. *Annals of the Royal College of Physicians and Surgeons of Canada*, 31(1): 23–26. Adapted with permission.

Coping with Catastrophic Feelings   163

References

Beckett A & Rutan JS (1990). Treating persons with ARC and AIDS in group psychotherapy. *International Journal of Group Psychotherapy*, 40: 19–29.

Cashdan S (1988). *Object Relations Therapy: Using the Relationship*. New York: Norton.

Daniolos PT (1994). House calls: A support group for individuals with AIDS in a community residential setting. *International Journal of Group Psychotherapy*, 44: 133–152.

Feingold A & Slammon WR (1993). A model integrating mental health and primary-care services for families with HIV. *General Hospital Psychiatry*, 15: 290–300.

Funnel G (1991). Complications in group psychotherapy with AIDS patients. *International Journal of Group Psychotherapy*, 41: 481–498.

Gree G (1993). Social support and HIV (editorial) (review). *AIDS Care*, 5: 87–104.

Hart G, Fitzpatrick R, McLean J, Dawson J, & Boulton M (1990). Gay men, social support, and HIV disease: A study of social integration in the gay community. *AIDS Care*, 2: 163–170.

Hayes RB, Turner H, & Coates TJ (1992). Social support, AIDS-related symptoms, and depression among gay men. *Journal of Consulting and Clinical Psychology*, 60: 463–469.

Hedge B & Glover OF (1990). Group intervention with HIV-seropositive patients and their partners. *AIDS Care*, 2: 147–154.

Kelly JA, Murphy DA, Bahr GR, Kalichman SC, Morgan MG, Stevenson LY, Koob JJ, Brasfield TL, & Bernstein BM (1993). Outcome of cognitive-behavioral and support group brief therapies for depressed HIV-infected persons. *American Journal of Psychiatry*, 150: 1679–1686.

Lackner JB, Joseph JG, Ostrow DG, & Eshleman S (1993a). The effects of social support on Hopkins symptom checklist-assessed depression and distress in a cohort of human immunodeficiency virus-positive and -negative gay men: A longitudinal study at six time points. *Journal of Nervous and Mental Disease*, 632–638.

Lackner JB, Joseph JG, Ostrow DG, Kessler RC, Eshleman S, Wortman CB, O'Brien K, Phair JP, & Chmiel J (1993b). A longitudinal study of psychological distress in a cohort of gay men: Effects of social support and coping strategies. *Journal of Nervous and Mental Disease*, 18: 4–12.

Levine SH, Bystritsky A, Baron D, & Jones LD (1991). Group psychotherapy for HIV-seropositive patients with major depression. *American Journal of Psychotherapy*, 45: 413–424.

Leserman J, Perkins DO, & Evans DL (1992). Coping with the threat of AIDS: The role of the social support. *American Journal of Psychiatry*, 149: 1514–1520.

Levy RS, Tendler C, VanDevanter N, & Cleary PD (1990). A group intervention model for individuals testing positive for HIV antibody. *American Journal of Orthopsychiatry*, 60: 452–459.

Line VG, Lewis FM, Cain VA, & Kimbrough GA (1993). HIV illness, social support, sense of coherence, and psychosocial well- being in a sample of help-seeking adults. *AIDS Education Prevention*, 5: 254–262.

Lippmann SB, James WA, & Frierson RL (1993). AIDS and the family: Implications for counselling. *AIDS Care*, 5: 71–78.

Markowitz JC, Klerman GL, & Perry SW (1992). Interpersonal psychotherapy of depressed HIV-positive outpatients. *Hospital and Community Psychiatry*, 43: 885–890.

164　*Psychoanalytic/Psychodynamic Psychotherapy*

McCann K & Wadsworth E (1992). The role of informal carers in supporting gay men who have HIV-related illness: What do they do and what are their needs? *AIDS Care,* 4: 25–34.

McGough KN (1990). Assessing social support of people with AIDS. *Oncology Nursing Forum,* 17: 31–35.

Racker H (1968). *Transference and Countertransference.* Madison, WI: International Universities Press.

Ripich S, Moore SM, & Brennan PF (1992). A new nursing medium: Computer networks for group intervention. *Journal of Psychosocial Nursing and Mental Health Services,* 30: 15–20.

Rounds KA, Galinsky, MJ, & Stevens LS (1991). Linking people with AIDS in rural communities: The telephone group. *Social Work,* 36: 13–18.

Sherby LB (1989). Love and hate in the treatment of borderline patients. *Contemporary Psychoanalysis,* 25: 574–591.

Sholevar GP & Perkel R (1990). Family systems intervention and physical illness. *General Hospital Psychiatry,* 12: 363–372.

Slakter E (1987). *Countertransference.* Northgate: Jason Aronson.

Steinberg P (1987). Broader indications for psychiatric consultation. *Canadian Family Physician,* 33: 437–440.

Steinberg P (1989a). The misdiagnosis of depression. *Canadian Family Physician,* 135: 1105–1107.

Steinberg P (1989b). Two techniques of supportive psychotherapy. *Canadian Family Physician,* 135: 1139–1143.

Steinberg PI & Morrissey J (1995). Psychiatric liaison to family medicine. *Canadian Family Physician,* 41: 97–104.

Ussher JM (1990). Cognitive behavioral couples therapy with gay men referred for counselling in an AIDS setting: A pilot study. *AIDS Care,* 2: 43–51.

Wong-Rieger DL (1993). Causal evaluation of impact of support workshop for HIV+ men. *Canadian Journal of Public Health,* 84(suppl 1): 566–570.

Zegans LS, Gehard AL, & Coates TJ (1994). Psychotherapies for the person with HIV disease. *Psychiatric Clinics of North America,* 17: 149–162.

11 Whipped Cream and Other Delights

A Reverie and Its Aftermath

Introduction

In this chapter, I refer to "psychoanalysis" and "psychoanalyst," as the original article was written from a psychoanalytic point of view for psychoanalysts. However, the therapy described is a psychodynamic (or psychoanalytic—the two are interchangeable, in my opinion) one, and all that follows refers to both psychodynamic psychotherapy and psychotherapists as much as it does to psychoanalysis and psychoanalysts. The term "psychoanalysis," of course, refers not only to an approach to treatment but also to a body (or bodies, more accurately) of theory, on which both psychoanalysis the treatment and psychodynamic psychotherapy are based.

As outlined in Bion (1962b), "The mother's capacity for reverie is the receptor organ for the infant's harvest of self-sensation gained by its conscious." This chapter has grown out of reflection on a reverie I shared with a patient whom I treated for four years some years ago. The reverie involved a vivid and unexpected image of a record album cover that I had not seen or thought about in 40 years. At first, it seemed to come from nowhere—an example of what Stern (2013) has called the "unbidden." However, once viewed in the context of the intersubjective dynamic with this patient, and the uncanny resonances and dreams that ensued in the patient's response, I believe that this event was part of a larger process of unconscious communication and reverie that had been developing for months between us. My impulse to share the sense of inspiration packed into the conscious image that came to mind had also been foreshadowed through a difficult period of struggle with my countertransference alienation from my patient.

This experience remained vivid in my memory for all the years after the treatment concluded and during subsequent years of psychoanalytic training. The following reflections on the material encapsulate for me the importance of imaginative retrospection as a fundamental element of learning in the process of becoming an analyst. Just as memory is subject to revision as we grow (or fail to grow) emotionally, so our previous clinical work, with its inevitable blind spots and evasions, always awaits us as material for learning from experience. As we mourn the losses and imperfections of our previous work, whether in a session we had yesterday, or with a patient we treated years ago, we also celebrate the value of psychoanalysis as a gift we

DOI: 10.4324/9781003200581-15

166 *Psychoanalytic/Psychodynamic Psychotherapy*

are constantly receiving, and that we try in turn to offer others. *Perhaps this is part of what attracts psychotherapists and psychoanalysts to working past the conventional age of retirement, the combination of grief and frustration at what we have been unable to do, the joy of what we have been able to accomplish with our patients and how meaningful it is to us, and the ongoing hope of learning more, both for its own sake in terms of our personal growth and to be able to apply it to our work in ever more fruitful ways.*

My reflections on my work with Mr. D revolve around the significance of one spontaneous associative imagistic experience during a session, which I subsequently shared and discussed with him. In retrospect, I believe that this "enactment," involving an intuitive impulse to disclose an associated personal memory, was an attempt on my part to break out of a mutual impasse in the treatment. Mr. D's complete lack of satisfaction in any area of his life was tediously reflected in his relationship with me, which soon led me to feel a matching sense of paralysis in my work with him. One might say that I had deadened myself defensively in response to Mr. D's having deadened himself over the previous decades of his life.

Retroactively applying what I have since learned about projective identification, reverie, and the container–contained relationship, I can now see how the turning point in our work involved a complex exchange of unconscious communications between us, in which my reverie, and my disclosure of it, constituted the beginning of a more adequate response to his urgent but inarticulate emotional plea, leading us gradually to create something new and alive in the relationship.

History

When Mr. D was referred to me, he had already undertaken individual and group psychotherapy for years, with no sense of progress. In his mid-50s and still single, he had succeeded as the administrator of a nonprofit governmental agency, but felt lost, disconnected, and insecure. He believed simultaneously that he was not living up to his potential, and that he was not worthy of his position. His social life was stagnant and uneventful, dominated by the feeling that he would never get around to what he wanted to do, and that he belonged nowhere.

Mr. D was nine when his father died suddenly of a heart attack. He initially reported that he was very close to his father, looked up to him, and remembered that he wanted to be special in his father's eyes. But as details of their relationship emerged, Mr. D was evasive about the actual quality of their relationship. He remembered that his father had once offered to take him out in a boat, but took a sibling instead, which left him feeling very hurt. *One might call this a screen memory (LaFarge, 2012), which may represent a combination of memories and defenses against remembering a traumatic event.* After his father's death, Mr. D always looked for a man to guide him through life, but never found one, and became an island unto himself. This is a very typical description of what Herzog (2001) has described as "father hunger."

Whipped Cream and Other Delights 167

Mr. D's mother decided it would be better for the children not to attend their father's funeral. *One wonders in such circumstances if this is really intended to be in the children's interest, or whether it is motivated, consciously or not, to help the individual making the decision to avoid being confronted with painful feelings.* For a long time, Mr. D believed that his father had gone away and had not died. *In this case, his mother's decision appears to have interfered with Mr. D's capacity to start grieving, by permitting him to deny his father's death.* Mr. D and his mother were always distant. He never felt close to her; little affection was shown in the family. Mr. D described his mother as unsupportive and quite critical. Their relationship was always strained. He felt she could never be pleased. After his father's death, his mother said that he was the man in the family, which Mr. D took literally. As the eldest sibling, Mr. D did his best to fill in for his father, becoming responsible for his father's chores, trying to do what was beyond him. *This would have interfered with age-appropriate developmental tasks, such as cultivating closer relationships with male friends, eventually becoming interested in girls, considering career possibilities, and devoting time and energy to rewarding recreational pursuits; that is, becoming a pre-teen and teenage boy. He and his mother did not appear to focus on his inner experience after his father died, but rather on his behavior, in terms of his filling father's role doing chores. This attitude toward his mind probably obtained long before his father's death and would tend to interfere with the optimal development of his mind, in terms of imaging what he wanted to do with his life, cultivating interests and pursuing desires.*

Mr. D felt he had been emotionally frozen since his father's death. He had limited closeness with his younger brother and sister. He wanted to study his father's profession, but his mother discouraged him from pursuing this. He subsequently wanted to learn a trade, but his family disapproved of blue-collar work. His mother would not let him take a part-time job in high school. *Mr. D's wanting to follow professionally in his father's footsteps, apart from representing a potentially healthy adaptation, could be interpreted as a form of mourning, characterized by identification. Another interpretation would be that he was trying to revive his father in himself, potentially denying his father's death, whether to console himself for the latter, or trying to replace his father in his mother's eye, and become more fully her partner, in a form of oedipal triumph. His mother's influence appears to be in the direction of discouraging personal agency, activity and initiative. This appears related to the description of his work and relationships below.*

As an adult, Mr. D felt he never had any direction in life, and was never committed to anything. He never planned for the future. He decided not to get very involved in relationships, as they become too painful. Mr. D couldn't make decisions about relationships. In his 30s, he dated a girl for four years. They both wanted to marry, but he was "petrified" of making a commitment, although he loved her. He both was afraid of growing up and becoming responsible and of losing his girlfriend, who eventually married someone else. He usually was the one who left his girlfriends, but his last girlfriend ended their relationship.

Mr. D said he spent his life playing the clown, trying to put on an amusing act, which kept him emotionally distanced from others. Now he wanted

168 *Psychoanalytic/Psychodynamic Psychotherapy*

to show some of his feelings. He used to feel very responsible when he was young; he observed that afterward, he didn't want to be responsible for anything. Mr. D gradually withdrew from the few male friends he had. He described himself as essentially going through the motions of his job, not taking the necessary initiatives, and allowing his subordinates, whom he described as very loyal, to do so, within the limits of their capabilities and positions, "taking care" of him this way. This seemed to involve the projection into his employees of a precociously pseudo-mature child-self attempting to fill his father's shoes. *That is, he experienced his employees as if they were he as a child, trying to perform father's duties for mother. Insofar as they responded by behaving in this manner, assuming the responsibilities of his position, one could describe this as an example of projective identification. That is, he unconsciously influenced them in the direction of behaving toward him in a way analogous to how he behaved toward his mother and siblings after his father's death, to which they conformed. To expand on this, one could say that he projected a self-image into them, inviting them to assume his role in the family after his father's death, filling in for his father, while he assumed the role of his family, benefitting from their initiatives, which were in reality his responsibility to undertake.*

Overview of the Treatment

Mr. D and I began psychoanalytic psychotherapy once a week and increased the frequency to twice a week after six months. Not surprisingly, I found Mr. D pleasant and polite, but somewhat distant in our relationship. His covert general attitude toward life appeared characterized by "Screw you, I won't do it," and "You can't make me do it." He felt this was his message to his mother. It also seemed to be his response to any initiative from his environment. This attitude was prominent in the transference, though nearly always displaced and disguised. Through his frequent criticism of previous therapists, for example, Mr. D tacitly communicated that he saw me as ineffective and incapable of changing him. This inhibited aggressive side of his personality was also expressed in his fastidious caution against committing any "*faux pas*," his concern that he would hurt anyone who got too close, and his constant anxiety that something bad would come out of him.

Mr. D talked about feeling guilty about killing his father with his anger, but could not describe what he was angry about. Subsequently, he talked about not marrying because he was concerned that he would have to subordinate his needs and wishes to those of his girlfriend. *He seemed to feel (perhaps with some justice) that he inevitably would recapitulate with a girlfriend his relationship with his mother, establishing a relationship in which the girlfriend's wishes and needs would prevail over his.* He still felt he owed "service" to his mother. Apparently, there had been some fun and liveliness in the house before his father died, but afterward, he had given up trying to get his share of what pleasure was available. He felt he had lost all contact with the world when his father died. *This leaves the impression that he experienced his father as a lifeline to the world outside of his family, while feeling he was imprisoned in his*

Whipped Cream and Other Delights 169

family, specifically in his relationship with his mother. However, the limitations that I suspected obtained in his relationship with his father raised a question regarding to what extent his father actually provided a gateway to the outside world. His father's influence, while he was alive, did not appear strong enough to counterbalance his mother's influence on him after his father's death.

Mr. D's passivity and passive-aggressive manner quickly came to dominate our sessions, as they already dominated his life. He was quick to give up on a prospective girlfriend. He stopped himself from thinking and then called himself stupid. He dealt with his anger about being interrupted in a meeting at work by clamming up, as opposed to continuing to develop his thoughts with his colleagues. A dream suggested that Mr. D found me unhelpful, sleepy, unavailable, and critical. As our work continued, he came to see me as a sadistic torturer who had the answers but wouldn't tell him. In retaliation, he would come late for appointments. He seemed to take pleasure in defeating me by not understanding what I said.

Some months before my reverie experience of the album cover image, Mr. D recounted a dream. He was in South Africa or Australia with a group of people. He chose a woman to sit with, but the chairs were moved, and other people took his place. He did not protest. Two sessions later, Mr. D recounted dreaming of punching a man who put his hand down his shirt and actually hit the wall in his sleep. In a previous dream, he had kicked someone. He associated to when he was 12, and a 14-year-old boy forced him to show his penis, and showed him his. He had no one to tell about this experience. His responses to my asking about the anger implied in the dreams (involving his kicking and punching) were lifeless, as was his response to my observations about his responses. I suggested that he seemed to feel that he would be equally trapped and coerced by a woman he went on a date with as he was by the boy who made him show him his penis, as if a second date would be a commitment to marriage. I said he might feel similarly with me, as if he had no agency over how long we met or whether we would meet once or twice a week.

These sessions and dreams involve violence and feelings of helplessness in the face of loss, a memory of coercion, and experiencing a lack of personal agency in Mr. D's relations with others. The material in the sessions certainly was not dull or dead, although the interactions between us felt that way. I thought the dream of punching the man who put his hand down his shirt, combined with the association of the older boy forcing him to show him his penis, was very likely a reference to his experience of our relationship, with overt homoerotic overtones. At the time, I felt that Mr. D would not be receptive to any comments about this. Now, I think that should not have prevented me from being more adventurous; I at least would have asked whether Mr. D found me too intrusive (or even penetrating) at times. So in retrospect, some of the deadness seems to have been mine, likely, however, influenced by Mr. D.

The relational turn in psychoanalysis of the last several decades has emphasized the role of the contribution of the therapist's personality to the therapeutic relationship. This

170 *Psychoanalytic/Psychodynamic Psychotherapy*

has been expressed by the term "transference-countertransference," demonstrating how dependent on each other the patient's and therapist's experiences of each other are. So the patient's transference to the therapist is understood not just to involve a displacement from previous important relationships, as Freud discovered, but also to include reactions to realistic perceptions of the therapist, often unconscious on the patient's part, including aspects of the therapist that are outside of her conscious awareness. This makes a side benefit of being a therapist or analyst, that of having the opportunity while doing our work to grow and learn more about ourselves, understandable. Our patients, sometimes uncomfortably (for us), can put their fingers on our tender spots.

The Unbidden: A Pivotal Session

By the time of my reverie, after two years of work, I wished I could stop meeting Mr. D, but felt guilty for feeling this way, and for feeling that I was not helping him. I wondered how much these feelings also represented Mr. D's feelings, frustrated with my passivity and unhelpfulness. This also might have represented a complementary countertransference (Racker, 1968), giving me some indication of how someone else in Mr. D's life might have not wanted to be with him. Of course, in this, I may also have been connecting with a part of Mr. D who felt bored and hopeless with himself. *That does not preclude my experience representing a dead part of me that Mr. D had brought to life, if you can accept this seeming oxymoron.*

Mr. D told me, for the first time, that when he was younger, he had performed in a good deal of minor acting jobs, until he relocated to a different city. He gave this up, lacking confidence, feeling that he had given everything else up too. He used to feel most at home in front of a camera since enjoying it as a child with his relatives. This and his reference to playing the clown suggest an individual playing a part rather than interacting with others. He thought of taking acting classes to give him confidence. He conveyed a sense of passion; I restrained myself from urging him to go out and get right back into it. I had a fantasy (a reverie, really,) of Sleeping Beauty being woken up with a kiss and decided to disclose this to Mr. D. He replied that he would like Beyoncé to wake him with a kiss. When I asked if he thought of anyone else waking him up, he thought of me, agreeing that he had already thought of me but did not want to say it. He agreed with my suggestion that the homoerotic connotations of me waking him up with a kiss made him uncomfortable. Mr. D thought of waking up from a sleep. His fantasy was that he would wake up like a jack-in-the-box and spring open. I suggested that having such an explosive opening up might be a little frightening, adding that imagining opening up like a flower in the sun might be more comfortable. It seems to me now that I too was frightened by the image of him as a jack-in-the box. *I offered a milder less threatening substitute, rather than exploring his fantasy of what it would be like to open as a jack-in-the-box, which would have been my usual approach.*

At this point, to my puzzlement, I thought of the album cover of the 1960s trumpeter Herb Alpert, *Whipped Cream and Other Delights* (1965).[1]

Whipped Cream and Other Delights 171

It portrays an alluring picture of an attractive young woman, covered in nothing but whipped cream. After a few minutes, I gave in to a strong urge to describe this to Mr. D, suggesting that he would not have to "come out" in that dramatic a manner. The image of the album cover was unexpected and, given my mental torpor, seemed outrageous; I was in danger of dismissing it out of hand. I should have paid more attention to my torpor, but my capacity to do that was impaired by the torpor. Perhaps an alive part of Mr. D threw me a life preserver. I might have kept the reverie to myself and reflected on what it might be representing about Mr. D, our relationship, and me. I think I longed to enliven what didn't seem like a going concern and wanted to share something exciting and a little risqué, so I succumbed, after only a few minutes, to describing the image to Mr. D. Perhaps my willingness to share my reverie with Mr. D was influenced by my feelings of desperation in our work and by a hope that he might respond to my disclosure. During the session, it just felt right to tell him. I think I was also motivated by a wish to do *something.* Mr. D may have experienced my disclosure as a welcome change from what he may have experienced as my characteristic glum, unenthusiastic silence. *I believe, reading this again, that my perseverance in and dedication to being helpful to Mr. D, even by "breaking the rules" (that is, by making a disclosure that would have been frowned on by many analysts in years gone by), may have been a factor in enlivening Mr. D. My intention to be helpful, I think, may have been unconsciously conveyed to him, and may have touched him, especially after my apparent deadness. I believe I also was encouraged to do something lively by Mr. D's example, telling me about his acting work.*

Mr. D surprised me by responding that he had had a dream the night before in which he had his uncle's trumpet, minus the mouthpiece, so he had to go to a grave and open a box to get it so he could play. He associated to a picture of his father and uncle as young children, resembling him and his brother. He recently had mentioned to a friend that he used to play the cornet. The dream came up at the very end of the session, as Mr. D's association to my reverie of the album. My association with the grave was to his father's premature death. My first reaction regarding the dream was that Mr. D needed something from his father to find his voice or to be able to play.

During the session after my reverie, Mr. D said that he was complying less with what he believed were the expectations of others—for example, his sister's wish that he be more refined. He looked at photos that reminded him of the pain of his father's death. He remembered that afterward he used to dream of a black cloud enveloping him. He showed his employees some of his acting videos. He felt that he was changing. He described not showing much of himself to a woman he was dating, not sure where the relationship was going. I suggested that he was depriving himself of seeing her reaction to a livelier part of him. He thought of the album cover, saying he was afraid of the "way out" side of him. I suggested that the only possibilities he envisioned were either of being locked up inside himself or of being a jack-in-the-box, as opposed to a spectrum of ways of interacting with others

172 *Psychoanalytic/Psychodynamic Psychotherapy*

and experiencing himself. Not wanting to be hurt, he had not had sexual relations since his last girlfriend left him several years ago. He still had sexual fantasies, which he refused to describe, "moving slowly, like tectonic plates." I suggested that he might be afraid of volcanoes or earthquakes.

I initially employ this type of metaphor without explaining it, hoping to elicit some symbolic thinking, especially in patients who find this difficult. If a patient asks me what I mean, I invite him to see what comes to his mind. I am prepared eventually to let him know what I was thinking, in this case that Mr. D might be afraid of the volcanic or tectonic power of his feelings and desires, hoping to "infect" him with metaphoric thinking little by little. I don't think it works to be too mysterious or to refuse on theoretical grounds to say what I am thinking. It is a matter of judgment how disclosing one should be. The more primitive, disturbed, concrete, and/or distressed a patient is, the more generous I am inclined to be with my thoughts. I tend to be less generous when I think the patient has the capacity to stretch himself a bit and find an association or is able with encouragement to attempt his own interpretation. That is, I think the most important consideration is to help the patient, in particular, to help him grow his mind and his capacity to think, including thinking about his feelings, and am prepared to be flexible regarding technique, without violating my or the patient's boundaries.

Below I will recount a little about what there was about the Herb Alpert album cover that led the 15-year-old future psychoanalyst to lay it down in his memory so carefully as to be able to retrieve it effortlessly some 40 years later, in spite of the fact that I never had listened to much of the music in that album. A psychoanalyst isn't needed to observe that the cover's image is sexually alluring in a way that would appeal to teenage boys. This is an example of something unconsciously meaningful to the analyst that eventually, with the help of the patient, becomes more accessible to conscious reflection and therefore potentially useful in analytic and self-analytic work. Vapenstad's (2014) reverie consisted of an aria from a Bach cantata, as opposed to mine, which is associated with popular music. The content of my reverie may have been aesthetically less exalted than a Bach cantata, but no less meaningful to me, I suspect, than Vapenstad's was to him.

We need to embrace what we think of when with a patient, however exalted it may or may not seem. That is what we have to offer our patient at any given time. (Of course, there is always the possibility that what we think of may refer to an unconscious conflict or unmet psychological need of our own and represent countertransference in the narrow meaning of the term, indicating that the patient has stirred something up in us that needs our attention. Even if that is the case, however, it does not preclude the possibility that what we think of also can help us understand our patient better.) Ogden (1994) describes his thinking of what seem to be irrelevant, quotidian, banal aspects of his life while with his patients, that he is able to show convincingly represent useful and at times fascinating and revealing unconscious communications to him from his patients.

Perhaps my reverie and the discussion that followed its disclosure represented Milner's (1952) "aesthetic moment." It felt like a beautiful experience, like seeing a cactus flower after a long trudge in the desert.

Whipped Cream and Other Delights   173

The excitement associated with the album cover's sensuality contrasted with the dullness I had felt in Mr. D, my corresponding dullness, and the lack of sensual experience in Mr. D's life. I had succumbed to a psychic deadness (Eigen, 1996) where no reverie appeared possible. Perhaps I had identified with a dead self that Mr. D had projected into me, and was paralyzed. This could be interpreted as Mr. D's early experience in his relationship with his mother after his father's death. Mr. D's description of his mother's being critical, unsupportive, unaffectionate, unable to be pleased, and discouraging him from his own initiatives suggests that Mr. D's deadness may have had its origins much earlier than the time of his father's death, as I suggested earlier. His description of his mother suggests she may have been limited in her capacity for reverie and in her sensitivity to his inner states, unable to keep Mr. D in her mind when he was an infant.

Bion (1962b), in the quotation at the beginning of this chapter, expresses the infant's need for a mothering figure ("mother") attentively observing and experiencing in themselves the baby's sensory and proto-emotional experiences (that is, what will become emotional experiences when the baby is able to separate her experience of emotions from physical sensations, a capacity that is not present at birth), emotional experiences that may be more than the baby can bear herself. The mother needs to tolerate feeling the baby's painful experience and to express it in a way that soothes the baby and makes the pain more bearable for the baby. This is typically done by identifying what is bothering the baby and saying it, often in a high-pitched voice, in soothing and understanding tones. This not only helps the baby to bear what might otherwise be unbearable but is an invitation to the baby along the road that will lead to the development of thinking; as the baby's experience is put into words, the baby will gradually learn to identify and eventually articulate it. Thomas Ogden, a prolific, profound and lucid contemporary psychoanalytic author, has usefully expanded Bion's notion of reverie (1997a). I warmly recommend the reader to Ogden's work, which covers many important areas of psychoanalysis.

Mr. D's experience of his mother expecting him to do her bidding and not follow his own inclinations may have interfered with his developing capacity for play and creativity. *The capacity to play is an important developmental achievement involving the development and use of fantasy, the ability to share and play with others, and ultimately to become involved in cultural experiences involving creativity. This capacity is fostered by parents who recognize that their child has an internal world and do not intrude on the child's natural inclination to manipulate objects in the environment as a way of expressing their internal experience, including attempting to resolve what is disturbing to them (Winnicott, 1971).* Mr. D's mother may have been preoccupied with what she thought he needed and would be best for him. This may have contributed to Mr. D's deadness in his early years. Perhaps Mr. D's father's death was only the final blow to his capacity for liveliness and agency. It is unclear how much Mr. D's father kept him in mind, but he could inspire him with a sense of fun and liveliness.

About six weeks after my reverie, Mr. D said he had been having chest pains for several months. He did not discuss this symptom with his family physician or me until he finally felt he had to get it investigated and had

174 *Psychoanalytic/Psychodynamic Psychotherapy*

an electrocardiogram (ECG) stress test. Dying of a heart attack had always been "a snake slithering in the grass" for Mr. D. He initially experienced my inquiring why he had not discussed this with me or his family physician as intruding on him and telling him what to do. It became clear that he was uncomfortable with experiencing my caring about him and wanting him to be properly taken care of. His motto had always been "Why bother?" This relieved him of the responsibility of taking care of himself, advancing himself at work, or having close relationships. *In my opinion, this neglectful attitude toward himself represents an internal object, that is, an unconscious image of the Other, in Mr. D's mind, based to some extent on his experience of others, beginning with his parents, that he has internalized. His finally telling me about his chest pain could be interpreted as an invitation to me to be the caring one, in the absence of his willingness/ability to assume this role on his own behalf. Perhaps he only felt he safely could issue this invitation after the meaningful experience we had shared around my reverie.*

Mr. D laughed off any expression of concern from family or friends regarding his health, uncomfortable with their caring. I suggested that he was not prepared to experience the pain he would have to experience regarding disappointments in his life and his feelings about people like me caring. I said that he was not prepared to live, and told himself he would not die, but rather would inhabit an in-between state of being alive but not living and not dying. My association was with the Norse myth of Valhalla, in Wagner's Ring cycle, where the gods know they are doomed to perish. When Mr. D's girlfriend used to be unavailable on the weekend, he was reminded of his father's death. He felt that no one would ever love him again. All of his relationships involved his fear of the woman never returning. He felt the same pain when he decided not to marry the woman he loved. *One sees here an example of Freud's "return of the repressed" (1919/1955:242). That is, just what Mr. D fears most, his behavior makes inevitable. By avoiding women because he fears they will abandon him, he ends up alone, a self-fulfilling prophecy.* When his last girlfriend left him, he closed himself off from his feelings. He claimed to be open to an intimate relationship, but was unwilling to talk about positive feelings in our relationship. He had difficulty in expressing tender feelings regarding appreciating my help.

Coming Alive in the Process

In the two years of therapy following my reverie, Mr. D gradually changed. Our work continued to be arduous. It was difficult to help Mr. D stay in touch with his pain and reflect on how his adaptation to disappointments in life was to withdraw angrily in a way that perpetuated his sadness and isolation. In the last year of therapy, Mr. D noticed that as he became more active and less depressed, people reacted differently to him. He could imagine making himself the center of his life without being self-centered. He wanted to help his employees to realize their potential, even if it meant their leaving his employ. He thought of becoming a Big Brother. He wanted

Whipped Cream and Other Delights   175

to see more of his family and to travel. He was recognizing the limitations of age more, and the fact that he had not done what he could have done in the past, but was considering what he could do in the future. He appeared to try to avoid mourning the loss of our relationship, which he connected to his father's death, not letting himself be aware of how close he had gotten to me. Mr. D remembered many positive memories of his father and became aware that, as a child, his only thought about his father being dead was his having to be sad, feeling that he mustn't enjoy himself, which interfered with his having fun, as if he had had only a dead father, and had not also had a lively father who had offered him a lot and wanted him to have fun. He had left the woman he loved because he couldn't stand the intensity of his love for her, and had kept his brother at arm's length for the same reason. *Now I would add that although Mr. D's father had been dead since he was nine, Mr. D had an internal father that would accompany him throughout his life. After his external father's death, he had lost touch with the liveliness of this internal father that could help him live his life rather than merely exist. Our work in part was aimed at finding that liveliness and cultivating it. That is, finding precious lost parts of a patient that they need to live their life. Perhaps experiencing his lively internal father was too painful a reminder of losing his father for Mr. D. Alternatively, it may have been a reminder of Mr. D's anger at his father for abandoning him by dying. Of course, both possibilities may apply.*

Mr. D complained that in our work there was never a light bulb that went off when he would understand everything, so he wouldn't have to keep on working on himself. *Of course, that is not the aim of psychoanalytic psychotherapy; quite the opposite. We cannot know everything, and if we could it would make for a very boring life, having nothing to learn. Bion's "negative capability," the capacity to tolerate not knowing, not jumping to a quick conclusion because we can't stand uncertainty, is an important concept. This allows us to keep trying to learn. This involves a tolerance of ambiguity, uncertainty, not knowing. The person who has to know everything immediately is incapable of learning anything. Rather, the goal of psychoanalytic psychotherapy and psychoanalysis is to set in motion a process, the capacity to think, including containing previously unthinkable thoughts and unbearable feelings, which the patient can continue for the rest of his life. That makes these therapies different from other psychological and medical treatments, where the best possible result usually is a restituo ad integrum, that is, a return to the patient's previous level of functioning or wellness. In psychoanalysis and psychoanalytic psychotherapy, the goal actually is to help the patient grow to a level of functioning that is more advanced than prior to their "falling ill." One price of this is recognizing that the work of thinking, which at least frequently should be a pleasure, is never complete.*

However, Mr. D also felt that he had the opportunity to think about his own mind, similar to how I thought about it. He began talking more openly about how much he would miss me. He realized that he would have to take the risk of being hurt in a relationship in order to have one. He saw the extent to which he repeatedly had given up on himself, and how that had led to failure and low self-esteem. He realized that he never had allowed himself to think, always asking others for advice, although he found what

176 *Psychoanalytic/Psychodynamic Psychotherapy*

they offered to be unreliable. He now could think abstractly and interpret proverbs himself, although he never gave himself credit for that. He had been too afraid of rejection to be true to himself, and therefore had given people little opportunity to respond to him in a genuine way. He was more confident, and stood up for his point of view in work situations. He rarely felt depressed, handled upsetting experiences more adaptively, and, was more active in interpersonal situations. His family relationships were much better; he stood up to his mother when necessary. He accepted that his sister would not change, and protected himself against her. He enjoyed work more now that he was functioning as a leader.

Mr. D's interactions with me became livelier. He became more willing to confront and disagree with me. His conversation became wittier and more pointed. I felt our discussion after my reverie marked some kind of turning point in our work and our relationship, leaving Mr. D feeling freer to be himself with me. My countertransference during this period also changed, from languishing in the doldrums of boredom and impatience to intense interest and considerable empathy.

Discussion

When the father of a young boy dies, one can question to what extent this might be experienced as an Oedipal victory, the fulfillment in reality of the boy's wishes that his father die and that he displace his father in his mother's affections. If Mr. D experienced conscious death wishes or excessive aggression toward his father, his father's death might have convinced him of how powerful his destructive wishes were, which might have made him terrified of his aggression, resulting in its being massively repressed. I do not think the evidence favors this interpretation. Mr. D experienced his father as offering him more than his mother. I had the impression that after Mr. D's father's death, he experienced his mother as straitjacketing him into meeting her expectations and living according to her standards and values, as opposed to encouraging him to grow. Perhaps this represented Mr. D's and his mother's way of coping with his father's death. This seemed reenacted in the transference–countertransference matrix, where I felt straitjacketed and constrained from performing my analytic function, a concordant countertransference (Racker, 1968), with my identifying with the projection of Mr. D's self-representation, while Mr. D identified with an internal mother. I am aware of a passive tendency in myself, which Mr. D's projective identification may have found as a suitable target. I suggest that my state of mind, in which my analytic function was compromised, and my reverie and our use of it, were co-creations of Mr. D and me.

This is another example of a relational way of conceiving of the therapist–patient relationship. I am suggesting that what went through my mind was influenced by Mr. D and was not my thought alone. That is, we influence each other's thinking, outside of our conscious awareness. This raises the question of to what extent is the therapeutic function of psychoanalysis and psychotherapy (of all kinds) unconscious.

Whipped Cream and Other Delights 177

A lot, in my opinion. It may not be so much the specific techniques, whether psycho-analytic, cognitive behavioral or whatever, that effect therapeutic change, as much as unconscious processes going on between patient and therapist. Of course, part of the work of psychoanalysis and psychoanalytic psychotherapy involves exploring just these processes, enabling therapist and patient to be more conscious of what is transpiring between them.

One might interpret Mr. D's involvement in acting as an escape from his experiencing his mother straitjacketing him. Perhaps my reverie represented his projecting this dramatic side of himself into me in an attempt to revive me, to convey that he had a livelier side that I was not perceiving in him, and to "cure" me of my paralysis/deadness, like Searles' (1979) description of patients treating their analyst. I suggest that the creative aspect of my analytic functioning had been marginalized, or I had fled into a retreat (Steiner, 1993) or claustrum (Meltzer, 1992), or joined Mr. D in his. I think I resorted to the exciting album cover in an effort to escape from my deadness. The cover likely represented a liveliness, free expression of sexuality, and *jouissance* that I yearned for and felt excluded from in my early teenage years. I recall back then my attraction to an alluring girl who seemed unavailable. This might have been my unconscious experience with Mr. D, or his with me. I think revealing my reverie encouraged him to become more active in disclosing more about himself and to become more active in the world. His dream could be interpreted as his feeling closer to experiencing his feelings about his father's death.

I also would interpret my reverie to represent a communication from Mr. D of similar longings to mine that he had experienced throughout much of his life, when conforming to his mother's expectations, not going to university, remaining single after being disappointed in a relationship, remaining in a dead-end job, and giving up acting. My psychic deadness involved difficulties in thinking about and making interpretations to Mr. D, and wanting to escape from him and from my deadness, rather than helping him to contain his pain and emptiness. My feelings of desperation, representing in part Mr. D's projective identification conveying his desperation to me, related to his empty life and what felt like an empty therapy to us both. This also contributed to my decision to share my reverie with Mr. D, perhaps finding a lively place in myself to share with Mr. D. One might also interpret my reverie as Mr. D's trying to help me by showing me there was some life left in him that I was blind to, unconsciously attempting to reengage me.

The album cover is a product of its time and seems to categorize women, with whipped cream, as objects to be consumed and enjoyed. One might relate this to Mr. D's relationship with women. He might have been avoiding women as a defense against an awareness of a tendency to use women, although his history does not suggest this. He still may have fantasized about women that way. Given Mr. D's description of his relationship with his mother, it is likely that it was *he* who had been afraid of being consumed by women. He also may have had fantasies of enjoying women like whipped cream as a way of not getting close enough to get hurt.

178   *Psychoanalytic/Psychodynamic Psychotherapy*

I also believe that Mr. D was hungering for a man, specifically for his father, who died without warning. I think I was the father he was hungering for (Herzog, 2001) by that time in our work, retreating from his depression and emptiness, longing to get away from him. So my reverie might represent my defense against an awareness of Mr. D's longing for me, with my displacing his longing for me and his father onto a woman clothed in whipped cream. This also might represent a similar defense in Mr. D, although it was my reverie. Along these lines, my feeling of deadness may have been in part a reaction to Mr. D's consuming hunger, which might have made me feel that he would swallow me up. Mr. D also may have feared this, deadening himself to protect me from being consumed by him. Herzog (2001) describes the experience of the young boy's loss of his father, whose presence is needed to integrate and modulate aggression. Mr. D appears to have adapted to his father's death and his mother's tendency to dominate him by constricting appropriate outlets for aggression, not attending university, not pursuing his chosen career, not leading his employees, and not pursuing the life partner he longed for. This constriction is another way of understanding his deadness.

Literature Review

Giustino (2009) notes that according to Bion (1962a), it is the mother's reverie—her capacity to understand the child's anxieties and wishes and to return them to him transformed—that enables the child to internalize the function of understanding his own states of mind. It is therefore the analyst, through his capacity for intuitive understanding, who must facilitate establishment of the function of recognition that will enable the patient to gain access to an emotional truth, helping him to become aware of his internal world, personal history, and emotional perceptions.

Ogden (1997a) views reverie as both a personal/private event and an intersubjective one. He does not often speak directly to his patient about such personal experiences. He describes responding to his patient's dream by drawing upon the imagery of his reverie. My patient responded to my disclosing my reverie with the memory of a dream that heralded a change in our work. Moreover, my reverie may have been an uncanny response to this dream, which had occurred the night before.

After his reverie, Ogden experienced a change, feeling the intensity of his love for his dying friend, as well as the depth of his feelings of sadness and loss. Following the disclosure of my reverie, the feelings of inner deadness I had experienced with my patient diminished. Vapenstad (2014) notes that Ogden tries to speak from the personal experience he arrived at in his reverie. Frayn (1987) reports patient and analyst both experiencing dreamlike states during the same session. He agrees with Ogden that their somnolent states had dyadic significance, but contrary to Ogden's usual approach, Frayn disclosed the content of his reverie to his patient, as did I. I agree with Christopher Bollas (personal communication, 2007) that the choice of

Whipped Cream and Other Delights 179

whether to disclose one's reverie to one's patient is based partly on personal predilection.

Ogden (1997b) uses reveries to experience the unconscious intersubjective constructions being generated in the analytic relationship. He views reveries as metaphorical expressions of what the unconscious experience is like. Ogden feels the analyst must possess the capacity to sustain a state of receptivity to the patient's undreamt and interrupted dreams as lived out in the transference–countertransference. He believes that the analyst's reveries constitute a critical avenue through which the analyst dreams dreams that the patient cannot dream on his own (Ogden, 2004). Ogden (2001) suggests that the analyst's reverie initially seems to represent his own mundane idiosyncratic concerns. However, the example I offer is not mundane.

Thomson (1980) describes the subjective experience of the analyst, which constitutes his receptive function. He indicates that a neutral, observing stance toward one's own subjective experience is as necessary for the analyst as his neutral stance toward the patient's material. The analyst utilizes his receptive function to experience the patient's unconscious and to help the patient find language for phenomena and experience therein for which the patient had not previously any verbal symbols.

Ferro (2011) describes two forms of reverie: the flash or "short-film" type and the "feature-length." For Ferro and Foresti (2013), "Reverie phenomena … are observed where there is a capacity … to come into contact with the pictogram inside one's mind. The work done on this pictogram … a countertransference microdream" often permits contact with something hitherto unknown (p. 369). In my reverie, the trumpet of the bandleader might represent a pictogram of the cornet my patient played as a child, connecting him to his feelings about his deceased father. Ferro and Foresti believe that reveries "involve direct contact with the pictograms that make up waking dream thought" (p. 381). One could interpret my reverie as a manifestation of the dream my patient and I shared during the session.

Vapenstad (2014) describes a reverie in the form of a Bach cantata aria, and concludes that impressions in art can help the analyst to understand the patient. He describes reverie as a mental state in which the mother is both completely absorbed in her own mind and fully concentrated on every psychic signal from her child, adding that this is the ideal state of mind of the analyst. Vapenstad believes, "The best way to capture the emotional truth that we are looking for is through artistic inspiration … the dream-work … created in the analyst's reverie" (2014:163).

Brown (2013) suggests that the analyst may acknowledge her unconscious fantasy, not the actual reverie, but a more general description of the analytic couple's experience as illustrated in the reverie. He adds that the analyst might consider making direct reference to her reverie, as Ferro and Foresti (2013) described. Brown sometimes does this, especially with patients who are afraid to "dream" in the session, enabling their capacity to indulge more freely in the waking dream thought of the field. My experience with Mr. D is similar.

180   *Psychoanalytic/Psychodynamic Psychotherapy*

Eshel (2019) describes telepathic dreams that "embody an enigmatic 'impossible' extreme of patient-analyst deep interconnectedness or analytic oneness, and unconscious communication in the analytic process" (p. 117). Perhaps my reverie that appeared connected to a dream I hadn't yet heard involved a similar process. If I had been familiar with the work of Eshel and of Henry Markman (2017), much of which hadn't been published when I was treating Mr. D, I would have focused much more on experiencing with him the depths of his depressed mood in an effort to help him contain it more thoroughly and help him internalize a containing analytic relationship that would help enable him to experience and think about his feelings in a creative way and continue to support ongoing emotional growth.

A Note on Disclosure

During my career as a psychiatrist and subsequently a psychoanalyst, my attitude toward self-disclosure has fluctuated. I first adhered to the principle of abstinence (of abstaining from behavior intended to gratify patient and/or analyst) rather rigidly and unnaturally, attempting to "follow the rule." My initial psychoanalytic training was relational. I became more self-disclosing with my patients and felt this helped my work with them. More recently, I interpret the concept of anonymity as a relative starting position from which to deviate according to each patient's therapeutic needs and the circumstances of the moment. I am comfortable disclosing little, in a way that feels natural, believing that I am in a better position to explore my patients' minds when disclosing less, and feeling I can do so in a non-depriving way.

Ehrenberg (1992, 1995) suggests that sharing our own reactions, especially when we do not grasp their meaning, gives the patient data to reflect on that they might not otherwise have access to, thereby helpfully expanding the field. This may apply to the disclosure of a psychoanalyst's reverie. Meissner (2002) charts "a course between unconstrained self-disclosure and absolute anonymity" (p. 827), both of which he feels foster misalliances. He concludes that the decision whether to self-disclose involves the analyst's assessing what may contribute to the analytic process and the patient's therapeutic benefit.

Bergstein (2013) described to his patient a picture he recalled from a movie. He experienced a faceless object—which could not keep an emotional impression within it—as very present in the session but jumped out of the two-dimensional picture and became a three-dimensional figure after he disclosed his reverie. He believes that the frenzy of thoughts which his patient described were beta elements that his patient could not dream, that overwhelmed his patient. *(The term "beta elements" was coined by Bion [1962c] in describing sensorial and emotional experience that could not be thought of, whether that of the baby who requires the mother's "digesting" the experience to make it bearable for the baby, or that of the patient who requires the analyst's reverie to help the patient think what hitherto had been unthinkable or feel what had been unbearable to feel.)* Bergstein emphasizes the need for an object who can dream what

Whipped Cream and Other Delights 181

the patient cannot yet dream. Cooper (2008) describes his use of privacy and reverie, which may result in direct statements of affects, ideas, or behavior, which the patient would not have a way of knowing without what he refers to as the analyst's disclosure, rather than self-disclosure, because it relates to the use of his privacy.

A distinction can be made between self-disclosures that spontaneously express and reveal an underlying intersubjective or "field" process, and self-disclosures that are calculated by the analyst to create a certain effect. Some experience suggests that the former tend to be workable in a productive way, whereas the latter are often met with distrust (Charles Levin, personal communication, 2017). Stern (2013) suggests that therapeutic action depends on our allowing ourselves novel, unbidden experience, "courting surprise" (Stern, 1990). He believes that the formulation of experience depends on conscious and unconscious events of the interpersonal field, which facilitate some formulations of experience and prevents others. He favors fostering the free evolution of the analytic relationship, to encourage the freedom to experience, the willingness to allow our minds their freedom, as "relational freedom [which] underpins therapeutic action" (2013:227). In my experience of reverie and my spontaneously disclosing it to Mr. D, I believe I was associating myself both with Levin's and Stern's viewpoints. I also believe they would agree with my opinion that it is the analytic couple who together create the interpersonal field in which a novel experience like a reverie can occur.

Was my disclosure of my reverie an unconscious enactment on my part, as opposed to the disciplined use of reverie? *That is, was it based on my personal reaction to what was transpiring, motivated by my need to reduce my anxiety, as opposed to a decision, albeit partly unconscious, based on what might further our therapeutic aims?* I felt under some pressure to do something to enliven what felt like a dead therapy. I was having difficulty in containing the sense of deadness in a way that could be therapeutic. I believe that I may not have disclosed my reverie so quickly were I treating Mr. D today. I feel better able to contain painful affects now. Perhaps if I had not disclosed the reverie, eventually an interpretation or other intervention would have occurred to me as a reaction to my reverie. However, I am not Ogden or Bollas, and this might not have happened. I am aware of sometimes feeling I need my patient's help. I believe that Mr. D responded in a constructive way. I think this raises a question of how one makes use of reverie with different patients and at different stages of one's career. I believe that there are some reveries that probably never ought to be disclosed, such as having a sexual fantasy about one's patient. However, Jody Davies (1994) describes disclosing her erotic countertransference, which could represent a reverie.

Perhaps Mr. D needed me to be a father with access to my own internal world, including an internal object like a mother so abundant with milk that she is covered in cream (Rose Vasta, personal communication, 2016). He could access such a wish through me. Maybe my reverie was what he needed, for me to be whole and a dad who is being richly fed. My term "come out,"

182   *Psychoanalytic/Psychodynamic Psychotherapy*

referring to Mr. D's opening like a flower as opposed to popping out like a jack-in-the-box, after the reference to homoerotic feelings regarding my waking Mr. D up with a kiss, together with the early dream of punching the man who put his hand down his shirt, with the association of the older boy forcing him to show him his penis, is suggestive. One might interpret this as the only measure of increased closeness between us. I don't think either of us was open to exploring the homoerotic aspect further at the time, and, to my awareness, it did not come up again subsequently in the therapy.

Some conflicts in my relationship with my father likely interfered with my awareness of Mr. D's longing for his father and for me. My reverie and Mr. D's revelation of his dream led to his being more open to discussing his grief. Mr. D and I seemed more ready to deal with this then, making possible the reverie and the dream. Would Mr. D have remembered his dream if I had not disclosed my reverie? Or, if he had recounted his dream without my disclosing my reverie, how would we have worked with the dream? I believe the absence of the intimate feeling between us that was engendered by his dream's being an association with my reverie would have affected the outcome.

Envoi

I do not think it is unusual to look back on work one has done years ago and feel that, with the experience one has acquired, one could have treated patients more effectively than one had. As I have suggested, that is both one of the painful aspects of practicing psychoanalysis and one of its great attractions; we can keep learning and growing throughout our careers. My reflecting on this while thinking about Mr. D might say something about him too. He appeared focused on avoiding pain, at the expense of giving up on the joys of experiencing and learning in life. *His attempts to avoid pain led to much pain, as well, regarding his loneliness and frustrated ambitions. In my experience, this very frequently is the price individuals pay for attempting to avoid pain.* Could my feeling that I could have done better with Mr. D also partly represent a feeling of Mr. D's, that he could have done better with his father, or with me? Might Mr. D have regretted not using the limited time he had with his father more advantageously and felt the same about his time with me?

I have tried to share a few thoughts about a psychotherapy from years ago in which reverie played a significant role, which increased my interest in reverie and my respect for my reveries. I think this experience demonstrates how many possibilities there are for understanding a reverie and the circumstances that engender it. I believe that at times it can be appropriate and helpful for an analyst to disclose his reverie to his patient. One can eschew the dichotomy of self-disclosure as opposed to attempted anonymity *(which relational psychoanalysis has demonstrated is a fruitless endeavor; our patients perceive and know an awful lot about us, even if much of it does not reach their conscious awareness)* and consider a spectrum of possibilities regarding what, if anything, to disclose, including a reverie, based on what is happening in the interaction between psychotherapist and patient at any given time.

Note

1 It can be viewed at www.allmusic.com/album/whipped-cream-other-delights-mw0000201513.

References

Alpert H (1965). Whipped cream & other delights. A&M Records. www.allmusic.com/album/whipped-cream-other-delights-mw0000201513.

Bergstein A (2013). Transcending the caesura: Reverie, dreaming and counter-dreaming. *International Journal of Psycho-Analysis,* 94: 621–644.

Bion WR (1962a). *Learning from Experience.* London: Karnac.

Bion WR (1962b). The psycho-analytic study of thinking. *International Journal of Psycho-Analysis*, 43: 306–310.

Bion WR (1962c). A theory of thinking. In Bion WR (ed.). *Second Thoughts.* New York: Aronson, 1967, pp. 110–119.

Brown LJ (2013). Bion at a threshold: Discussion of papers by Britton, Casorla, Ferro & Foresti, and Zimmer. *Psychoanalytic Quarterly*, 82(2): 413–433.

Cooper SH (2008). Privacy, reverie, and the analyst's ethical imagination. *Psychoanalytic Quarterly,* 77: 1045–1073.

Davies JM (1994). Love in the afternoon: A relational reconsideration of desire and dread in the countertransference. *Psychoanalytic Dialogues*, 4: 153–170.

Ehrenberg DB (1992). *The Intimate Edge.* New York: Norton.

Ehrenberg DB (1995). Self-disclosure: Therapeutic tool or indulgence? – Countertransference disclosure. *Contemporary Psychoanalysis*, 31: 213–228.

Eigen M (1996). *Psychic Deadness.* Northvale, NJ: Jason Aronson.

Eshel O (2019). *Emergence of Analytic Oneness: Into the Heart of Psychoanalysis.* Abingdon, Oxon. and New York: Routledge.

Ferro A (2011). Shuttles to and from the unconscious: Reveries, transformations in dreaming, and dreams. *Italian Psychoanalytic Annual,* 5: 89–106.

Ferro A & Foresti G (2013). Bion and thinking. *Psychoanalytic Quarterly*, 82(2): 361–391.

Frayn DH (1987). An analyst's regressive reverie: A response to the analysand's illness. *International Journal of Psycho-Analysis*, 68: 271–277.

Freud S (1919/1955). The uncanny. In Strachey J (ed.). *The Standard Edition of the Complete Psychological Works of Sigmund Freud.* Vol. XVII. London: The Hogarth Press and the Institute of Psychoanalysis.

Giustino G (2009). Memory in dreams. *International Journal of Psycho-Analysis*, 90: 1057–1073.

Herzog J (2001). *Father Hunger: Explorations with Adults and Children.* Hillsdale, NJ: Analytic Press.

LaFarge L (2012). The screen memory and the act of remembering. *International Journal of Psycho-Analysis*, 93(5): 1249–1265.

Markman H (2017). Presence, mourning and beauty: Elements of the analytic process. *Journal of the American Psychoanalytic Association,* 65(6): 979–1004.

Meissner WW (2002). The problem of self-disclosure in psychoanalysis. *Journal of the American Psychoanalytic Association*, 50: 827–867.

Meltzer D (1992). *The Claustrum: An Investigation of Claustrophobic Phenomena.* Perthshire: Clunie Press.

Milner M (1952). The role of illusion in symbol formation. In *The Suppressed Madness of Sane Men* (pp. 83–113). London: Routledge.

184 *Psychoanalytic/Psychodynamic Psychotherapy*

Ogden TH (1994). The analytic third: Working with intersubjective clinical facts. *International Journal of Psycho-Analysis*, 75: 3–19.

Ogden TH (1997a). Reverie and interpretation. *Psychoanalytic Quarterly*, 66: 567–595.

Ogden TH (1997b). Reverie and metaphor: Some thoughts on how I work as a psychoanalyst. *International Journal of Psycho-Analysis*, 78: 719–732.

Ogden TH (2001). *Conversations at the Frontier of Dreaming*. London: Karnac.

Ogden TH (2004). This art of psychoanalysis: Dreaming undreamt dreams and interrupted cries. *International Journal of Psycho-Analysis*, 85: 857–877.

Racker H (1968). *Transference and Countertransference*. Madison, CT: International Universities Press.

Searles HF (1979). The patient as therapist to his analyst. In *Countertransference and Related Subjects*. pp. 380–459. New York: International Universities Press.

Steiner J (1993). *Psychic Retreats: Pathological Organizations of the Personality in Psychotic, Borderline and Neurotic Patients*. London: Routledge.

Stern DB (1990). Courting surprise: Unbidden perceptions in clinical practice. *Contemporary Psychoanalysis*, 26: 425–478.

Stern DB (2013). Relational freedom and therapeutic action. *Journal of the American Psychoanalytic Association*, 61(2): 227–255.

Thomson P (1980). On the receptive function of the analyst. *International Review of Psychoanalysis*, 7: 183–205.

Vapenstad EV (2014). On the analyst's reverie: From Bion to Bach. *International Forum of Psychoanalysis*, 23: 161–170.

Winnicott DW (1971). *Playing and Reality*. London: Tavistock.

Conclusion

I believe that if a reader responds to an author by reading their book, then the author owes the reader a type of farewell for their dedication in reading the book. I am suggesting that there is some form of interpersonal relationship between author and reader, and that they do meet in the reading of the book, although of course they never meet in any physical sense. I like Thomas Ogden's notion of a reader re-creating a book in reading it and being active in creating meaning from the book.

I will not attempt to summarize the contents of this book, but rather just offer a few parting thoughts. Our patients, at some level, understand that we cannot make them new people or "cure" them of being who they are. I think the best we can do is to help them be themselves in a more authentic way. However, they do appreciate being understood. Part of this is understanding some things that our patients themselves don't understand, that is, what is not in their conscious awareness. It is a matter of judgment how much of our understanding, which of course may be imprecise, or even completely off the mark, should be disclosed to a patient. The patient senses the clinician's understanding, expressed by tact, empathy, tone of voice, and body posture, when making clarifications, confrontations, or interpretations, in addition to the unconscious communications between therapist and patient that are inevitable and more or less continuous when a clinician and a patient have an ongoing relationship. This may be conveyed by projective identification, reverie, and a patient's or therapist's fantasies, among other means.

The history of psychoanalysis started with Freud's exploration of the unconscious mind. Contemporary mental health care often neglects consideration of this very important and vast expanse of thoughts, feelings, fantasies, impulses, hopes, and fears. To the extent that we neglect this, we may be trying to relieve symptoms, but are not treating people. Our patients and clients perceive this at some level, often unconsciously. This does not help in their recovery. It can contribute to deepening their despair. This is understandable to the extent that a clinician accepts that part of the patient's difficulties may derive from the experience of not feeling understood in their earliest relationships. It stands to reason that the patient then would want the clinician, the current caregiver, to understand something unseen in him, and help him to experience it.

DOI: 10.4324/9781003200581-16

186 *Conclusion*

I have found that writing is like teaching: a very good way to learn, including to learn what you did not know that you knew. (One could say that this is also a goal of psychoanalysis and psychoanalytic psychotherapy.) I believe that many more people are capable of writing interesting and worthwhile books than actually do write them. I hope that reading this book might encourage some clinicians, of whatever discipline, to consider whether a distillation of their experience in book form would be of interest and use to fellow clinicians.

As I noted in the introduction, this book and its predecessor, *Psychoanalysis in Medicine*, although both have health professionals as their target readership, contain much that could help people who are not clinicians choose a physician, psychotherapist, or other health professional who would keep them in mind as individuals with their own unique difficulties and needs, and treat them as a whole person, rather than as a target with a symptom or condition that needs to be eradicated. I hope that my readers experience the same satisfaction as I have in growing and learning while treating our patients and clients.

Glossary

Alpha-function is a mental function that transforms sensuously apprehensible stimuli into elements useful for thinking, dreaming, and laying down for memory. This is a model for how we deal with the apprehension of reality. The analyst receives projections from the patient, metabolizing or digesting them through alpha function and returning them to the patient in a more bearable form. This is analogous to a mother's central role in helping her infant manage emotional pain. This has been described as the ability of the patient to put unbearably painful feelings in the analyst and leave them there long enough for them to be modified by their sojourn in the analyst's mind.

Conflict, unconscious mental Conflict refers to the unresolved tension between different agencies of the mind. For example, a young man might find a female classmate to be very sexually attractive. One could describe this as an id impulse. However, he may have been raised on a very strict religious basis such that sexual feelings, to say nothing of sexual relations, are totally unacceptable outside of marriage. One could describe this as a superego prohibition when this parental attitude has been internalized by the young man. One solution to this conflict between id and superego is to render the conflict and the sexual feelings unconscious. In this situation, the tension between id and superego continues. The purpose of rendering the conflicts and the unacceptable impulse unconscious, involving the defense of repression, is to reduce anxiety about an aspect of mental contents, in this case, a sexual impulse not acceptable to the individual. If the feelings associated with the conflict are too strong, a psychiatric symptom may result.

Countertransference in the broad sense refers to the analyst's total experience of the patient, including the analyst's reveries and fantasies about and emotional reactions to the patient, which can provide information about the patient. In the original, narrow sense, countertransference refers to unresolved psychological disturbance in the analyst stirred up by his exposure to the patient; that is, the analyst's transference to his patient.

188   *Glossary*

Defenses are unconscious mental mechanisms designed to reduce anxiety and other uncomfortable feelings about unconscious conflict and unmet emotional needs usually originating in childhood.

Displacement is a defense in which thoughts, feelings, impulses, or attitudes concerning one individual are redirected toward another individual. For example, if it is dangerous for a child to express anger at a potentially violent father, the anger may be displaced toward mother if she characteristically responds in a more understanding and gentle way. Displacement is a central feature of transference, in which thoughts, feelings, impulses, and other mental contents related to important individuals in the patient's life are reexperienced in the relationship with the analyst or with a physician.

The **Ego** is the executive function of the mind that balances the demands of the superego and id and external reality

Ego functions include judgment, relation to reality, capacity to think, relations with important others, regulation of emotion, impulse control, frustration tolerance, motility, and unconscious defenses required to contain painful feelings to bearable levels of intensity.

Enactments are experiences that occur between analyst and patient in which, rather than thinking about or discussing an experience between the two, these are expressed in some form of action. These are potentially destructive if, for example, they involve abusive or exploitive behavior on the part of the analyst, such as sexual relations with a patient. Enactments also can involve a playful way of working through difficult aspects of the patient's relationships or experiences of himself that analyst and patient are not able to talk about in a productive way.

Fit in psychotherapy or psychoanalysis refers to how well analyst and patient are suited to work with each other. This largely depends on the personalities of patient and analyst, in particular how flexible they are. It is the analyst's responsibility to know if the fit of the therapeutic dyad is too poor for them to work together, although sometimes the patient will have this sense.

The **Id** refers to the repository of instinctual impulses, such as sexuality and the capacity for aggression, as well as a capacity for imagination, playfulness, and creativity.

Internal objects are unconscious internal representations of others in one's mind. They largely are based on one's early experiences with caretakers, especially parents, but do not correspond exactly to the parents' characteristics, depending on how the child perceives the parents, which partly depends on the child's temperament.

Narcissistic personality features popularly refer to excessively self-centered people. However, a wide range of characteristics may be considered narcissistic. Narcissistic individuals often use grandiosity as a defense against low self-esteem. Central affects of narcissistic individuals include shame, envy, and contempt. Idealization and devaluation are often employed to manage painful feelings. Some narcissistic individuals behave with

Glossary 189

an overt sense of entitlement, devaluing others, and appearing vain and manipulative or charismatic and commanding. Others behave ingratiatingly, seeking people to idealize, are easily wounded, and envy others seen as superior. Narcissistic features are evident in everyone to some extent.

Neurotic refers to unconscious conflicts between the agencies of the mind, the ego, superego, and id. When conflicts become closer to conscious awareness, one becomes anxious. Unconscious mental mechanisms of defense are utilized to keep conflicts outside of conscious awareness. The term "neurosis" refers to conditions such as anxiety disorder, obsessive-compulsive disorder, and conversion disorder, in which these conflicts are identifiable in the individual. Each neurosis has characteristic anxieties, conflicts, and defenses that are usually found in individuals suffering from that neurosis.

The **Oedipus complex** originally referred to the combination of loving and hostile wishes that children experience toward parents, classically wishing for the death of the same-sex parent, perceived as the rival, with sexual desire for the opposite-sex parent. Contemporary psychoanalytic thought has expanded this concept to include development of the mind and personality. One's experience of the transition between the original mother–infant dyad to the triadic experience of mother, father, and infant has implications regarding children's introduction to the world outside of the infant's original world of their mother, and being able to recognize that other people have relationships excluding them. This leads to children becoming able to think about their own minds and to be aware of and be able to think about the minds of others. It also helps to develop a capacity for mourning, as children recognize that mother has a relationship with someone else, and the parental couple enjoys experiences with each other, from which children are excluded. This also may increase the children's envy.

"Primitive" can refer to thoughts, feelings and impulses related to mental functioning of early life, representing feelings of infancy, such as terrifying, violent thoughts, experiences of falling endlessly into an abyss, experiencing oneself as not existing, thinking in illogical or unrealistic ways, experiencing overwhelmingly painful or frightening feelings, or having violent or unwanted sexual impulses.

Projective identification is a mental mechanism involving relations between unconscious images of the self and others, having to do with the ridding of the self of unwanted aspects of the self. Originally, unwanted fantasies and images of oneself, another, and/or one's relationship with others were, in fantasy, thought to be deposited into another person. A contemporary understanding of this mechanism involves an interpersonal aspect in which one individual influences another to feel, think, and/or act in a way that the projecting individual cannot tolerate to experience in himself. Recent history provides an evocative example of projective identification. Once during a meeting of the Supreme Soviet, Khrushchev was enumerating Stalin's errors. Someone in the audience

190 *Glossary*

of several thousand called out, "Why didn't you confront Stalin about this at the time?" Khrushchev screamed, "Who said that!" This was followed by dead silence. Khrushchev then replied, "Now you know why." Rather than providing a logical explanation, Khrushchev induced in the audience members the emotions he and others felt at the time of Stalin's violent misuse of power, communicating his terrifying experience directly to them. An individual similarly uses projective identification to induce in another an emotional experience, evacuating the feeling into the other, rather than having to continue to experience it himself (the projective aspect), while still remaining in touch with the experience (the identification aspect).

Projection involves the experiencing in someone else of a personal quality, such as a thought, feeling, or impulse, that an individual finds unbearable to recognize in himself. For example, an envious person, rather than experience envy in himself, may feel that someone envies him and may even accuse her of doing so. In projective identification, by contrast, the envious person might actually incite envy in another person, rather than just believe that she is envious.

Proto–mental emotions are the precursors of emotions in infants not yet able to experience emotions *per se*. Infants initially don't distinguish between proto-emotions and sensory experience; somatic and psychological experiences have not been differentiated at this point. Individuals with psychosomatic conditions often are thought to have deficiencies in this differentiation and limitations in the capacity to experience emotions, with consequent transduction of the emotions into somatic symptoms.

Psychodynamic refers to a type of psychotherapy based on psychoanalytic concepts with some differences in the therapeutic frame and more limited therapeutic goals. Typically, patients in psychodynamic psychotherapists meet on a weekly or perhaps twice weekly basis, and usually do not use lie on a couch. The therapist is often more active and perhaps more overtly supportive than in a psychoanalysis. The terms "psychoanalytic psychotherapy" and "psychodynamic psychotherapy" usually are used interchangeably. Psychodynamic formulation refers to the use of psychoanalytic principles to understand how a patient has developed, including attempting to explain the basis for the patient's symptoms and personality style.

Psychosis refers to psychiatric conditions in which the capacity for experiencing reality as it is consensually agreed upon (reality testing) is lost. These conditions are frequently characterized by hallucinations and delusions. In psychoanalytic parlance, the term "psychotic" is used in various ways. One can describe psychotic and nonpsychotic parts of one's personality. Some defenses, such as projective identification, splitting, projection, and denial, when heavily relied upon, are considered characteristic of psychotic thinking. Anxieties that usually occur in more primitive mental states involving concerns about one disappearing, falling endlessly, ceasing to exist, losing one's identity as an individual, merging into

Glossary 191

another person, becoming mentally fragmented, or losing one's mind are described as psychotic anxieties.

Repetition compulsion is a tendency to repeat situations one has experienced in the past, despite the fact that they are painful and/or result in disadvantageous outcomes for the individual. The motivation for this is unconscious and may involve unconscious guilt or hostility. For example, an individual may choose a partner who resembles aspects of his parents with which he consciously would not wish to be associated. A person with domineering parents who demanded compliance might choose a wife with those qualities. Alternatively, such an individual might treat his children in a similar domineering way, in spite of consciously not intending to do so.

Splitting is considered a primitive defense in which aspects of mental contents, such as one's view of oneself or another person, are unconsciously divided and kept apart. For example, an individual may split his positive feelings about a friend from his negative feelings and experience only positive or only negative feelings toward the friend, as opposed to the ambivalent experience of being aware of both positive and negative feelings simultaneously. This might result in alternating between idealizing and devaluing the friend, depending on whether the positive or negative feelings are being experienced, such that the friend is experienced in one of two opposite ways, rather than the individual having a more consistent attitude ambivalent toward the friend.

The **Superego** refers to the internalization of attitudes of early caregivers, parents in particular. This develops into one's conscience and moral standards for oneself, as well as one's unconscious ideal version of oneself, the person one aims to become (the "ego ideal").

The **Transference** originally referred to distortions in the patient's perception of the analyst based on feelings, thoughts, impulses, and attitudes toward other important people in the patient's life that become displaced onto the analyst. In the broader contemporary sense, transference is taken to include all of the patient's experience of the analyst, including her accurate perceptions of him.

The **Unconscious** originally referred to a mental space where sexual and aggressive drives are located, a repository for childhood relational schemas (unconscious understanding of current relationships based on early relationships), where mental contents unacceptable to conscious awareness are repressed, and the location of defense mechanisms by which these mental contents are kept out of conscious awareness. A more contemporary view of the unconscious includes it being a source of energy, pleasure, and passion, creating experiences and meaning, a generative system with the capacity for creativity and an evolving sense of aliveness and the capacity to make a passionate commitment to life.

Index

Abrahams, S. 145
Action Groups 120–121
actual neurosis 43
actual trauma 50
addiction 51
addictive behaviour 63–65
Adult Attachment Interview 15–16
advice giving 148–149
affect regulation difficulties 109
Aisenstein, M. 43–47
Alpert, H. 170
alpha function 12, 44, 135
anamnesis 27
Andrews, G. 145
anorexia nervosa 59–62
anxiety 11; autistic-contiguous 56–57;
    castration 54
Appelbaum, R. 85
Arnold, J. F. 144
Aron, L. 33
attachment theory 13–17; internal
    objects and 19
auditory hallucinations 18
autistic-contiguous mode 56–57
autistic disturbance 55–57
autistic shapes 56
autistoid anorexics 61–62
autonomy 54
Azim, H. F. A. 101–102

basic assumption groups 12, 110–112,
    115, 136
Bergstein, A. 41, 180–181
beta elements 180
binocular vision 12
Bion, W. R. 1, 11–13, 23, 42, 57, 144;
    on beta elements 180; on capacity for
    reverie and alpha function 44, 135,
    165, 173, 178; on group functioning
    110–112; on individual versus group

mentality 131; on negative capability
    122, 175; study of groups in military
    psychiatric rehabilitation unit 115;
    theory of containment 43
Black, M. 11
Bollas, C. 12, 58, 178–179
borderline personality 20, 21–23, 89;
    splitting in 147
Bowlby, J. 15, 16
Britton, R. 13
Brodaty, H. 145
Bronstein, C. 44
Brown, A. 145
Brown, L. J. 179
Bruch, H. 59–61

Caldwell, L. 12
Carveth, D. 51–52
Cassidy, J. 17
castration anxiety 54
catastrophic feelings, coping with:
    case history on 157; challenges of
    treating patient 157–162; conclusions
    on supportive therapy in 162;
    introduction to 155; literature review
    on 155–157
Chapman, R. J. 144
child analysis 12
children: eating disorders and 60; sexual
    abuse of 49; terrorism of suffering
    in 49–50; unable to express
    opposition 46
chronic, serious or life-threatening
    illness See catastrophic feelings,
    coping with
Civitarese, G. 13
clarification technique in supportive
    psychotherapy 145–147
confrontation technique in supportive
    psychotherapy 146–147

Index   193

Cooper, S. H. 181
coping *See* catastrophic feelings, coping with
countertransference 30–31, 52, 133

day treatment programs (DTPs) 69, 71; Action Group 120–121; case examples from 72–76, 88–94, 125–127; introduction to 115–119; Large Groups 117–118; management of 80–83, 88–89, 95–97; Perspectives for Living Group and Life Skills Group 121–122; Problem-Solving Group 122–123; Projectives Groups 119–120; psychodynamic psychiatry service (PPS), University of Alberta Hospital 103; source of threats in 77–80; threats of violence in 72–76; Vocational Group 123–124; Work Therapy 125
defense mechanisms 18–19, 21
delusional states 58
denial 21
dependency 12
Diamond, D. 16
disclosure by mental health professionals (MHPs) 180–182
drug-dependent individuals 63–65
duty to protect laws 85–86
dysthymic disorder 91

eating disorders 59–62
Ego and the Id, The 11
Ehrenberg, D. B. 180
Eleff, M. K. 145
Ellman, S. J. 11
epistemophilia 12
Eshel, O. 42, 54, 180
Etchegoyen, H. 13
Experiences in Groups 112
external reality 20
external world 21

father hunger 166
feature-length reverie 179
Feldman, M. 13
felt shapes 56
Ferenczi, S. 47–49
Ferro, A. 13, 17, 179
field theory 13
fight-or-flight 12, 111, 115, 136
flash reverie 179
Fonagy, P. 16
Foresti, G. 179
Frayn, D. H. 178

Freud, S. 3, 11, 20, 24, 42, 185; on emotional bonds between group members 130–131; on return of the repressed 174; on sexual abuse 49

Giustino, G. 178
Goldberg, R. L. 144
good-enough fathers 16
good-enough mothering 12
Green, S. 144
group functioning 110–112; emotional bonds in 130–131
group psychotherapy: clinical ramifications of threats in 86–87; cohesive coleaders of 87; decision for individual versus 69–70; Follow-Up Groups (FUG) 89–91; for personality disorders (*See* personality disorders, day treatment program (DTP) for); projective identification (PI) in (*See* projective identification (PI)); temporary ruptures in 87; threats of violence in 71–83; threats of violence to third parties in 85–97; *See also* day treatment programs (DTPs); individual psychotherapy

Handbook of Attachment 17
Hazzard, A. J. 145
Herzog, J. 166, 178
Hirsch, I. 33
history-taking proficiency 27–28
histrionic personality disorder 91
HIV-AIDS-related illness *See* catastrophic feelings, coping with
Holmes, J. 15–16
hypochondriacal symptoms 43
hypothalamic-pituitary-adrenal axis 50

idealization 147
individual psychotherapy: clarification and confrontation in 141–153; for coping with catastrophic feelings 155–162; *See also* group psychotherapy
Inhibitions, Symptoms and Anxiety 11
insecure attachment 16
internal objects 17–20, 34, 146–147
internal reality 20
internal world 21
interpretation in supportive psychotherapy 147–148
Interpretation of Dreams, The 11
irrational thinking 12
itching 44

194 *Index*

Joseph, B. 13
Joyce, A. 12

Kadish, Y. 61–62
Kalinich, L. J. 45
Keats, J. 1
Kernberg, O. 141, 144
Klein, M. 11, 12, 57; paranoid-schizoid
   position (PS) and depressive position
   (D) 51–52
Knapp, S. 85
Koopman, C. 72
Krystal, H. 63–64

Large Groups 117–118
Levin, C. 181
Levine, H. B. 13
Lieberman, J. A., III 145
Life Skills Groups 121–122
Little, M. 58, 143

MacDonald, P. J. 145
maladptive styles of attachment 12
Markman, H. 180
Matte Blanco, I. 13
McCullough, L. 144
medical psychotherapy 144–145
Meissner, W. W. 180
melancholia 11
Meltzer, D. 62
mental health professionals (MHPs):
   countertransference by 30–31;
   disclosure by 180–182; duty to
   protect laws and 85–86; patients with
   difficulty in self-disclosure to 47–48;
   personality functioning in patients
   and 23–24; professionals included in
   1–2; projection by patients onto
   19–20; psychodynamic formulation
   skills for 27–28; reassurance by
   142–144
mentalization 16
Milner, M. 172
Mitchell, S. 11, 13, 33
Mitrani, L. 55–56
mother-infant relationship 12, 173, 178;
   addictive behaviour and 63; attachment
   theory and 13–17
mourning 11; somatization of 45

narcissism 11, 30–31, 34, 37, 91,
   93–94, 125
negative capability 122, 175
neurosis 43
neurotic personality 21–22

Newman, C. F. 72
non-thinking patients 149–150

object relations theory 17–20
Oedipus complex 13
Ogden, T. H. 13, 52, 56, 58–59, 172,
   185; on projective identification (PI)
   130; on reverie 178–179
organic ailments 43

pairing 12
paranoid-schizoid position (PS) and
   depressive position (D) 51–52
paraphilias 51–54
parent-child relationship 12; attachment
   theory and 13–17
part-objects 146–147
Pelton, C. L. 145
personality disorders, day treatment
   program (DTP) for: Action Group
   120–121; case example 125–127;
   conclusions on 127–128; introduction
   to 115–119; Large Group 117–118;
   Perspectives for Living Group and
   Life Skills Group 121–122; Problem-
   Solving Group 122–123; Projectives
   Group 119–120; Vocational Group
   123–124; Work Therapy 125
personality functioning 20–24
Perspectives for Living Groups 121–122
Pinsker, H. 144
*Pioneers of Psychoanalysis in South
   America, The* 13
play and creativity 12
positive attachments 13–14
post-traumatic alexithymia 50
precocious maturity 49
Problem-Solving Groups 122–123
projection 21, 30
projective identification (PI) 18–19, 21;
   discussion of therapists experience with
   133–135; introduction to 130–131;
   object relations theory and 135–136;
   in session narrative 131–132
Projectives Groups 119–120
Prosen, H. 145
provocative patients 150–153
psychic conflict 44
psychic trauma 46–47
psychoanalysis 1; aspects of personality
   functioning and 20–24; attachment
   theory in 13–17; child analysis 12;
   Freud as originator of 11–12, 185;
   influential theorists of 11–13, 57; for
   more severe disturbances (*See* severe

Index 195

disturbances); object relations theory in 17–20; paradigm shift with Bion and Winnicott in 42; relational 32–34
Psychoanalysis in Medicine: Applications of Psychoanalytic Thought to Contemporary Medical Care 1–2, 7, 33, 64, 70, 136, 186
psychoanalytic psychotherapy: for addictive behaviour 63–65; for autistic children 55; day treatment programs (DTPs) (*See* day treatment programs (DTPs)); discussion of outcomes of 176–178; for eating disorders 62; group (*See* group psychotherapy); individual (*See* individual psychotherapy); for more severe disturbances (*See* severe disturbances); patient coming alive in process of 174–176; patient history in 166–168; pivotal session in 165, 170–174; professional reflections on 165–166, 182; relational psychoanalysis in 32–37, 169–170, 176–177; for schizophrenia 58–59; session example 34–39; supportive psychotherapy (*See* supportive psychotherapy); of traumatized individuals 50; treatment overview for individual patient in 168–170; the unbidden in 165, 170–174
psychodynamic formulation 12; asking the patient what brings them in and 31–32; introduction to 27–29; using more open-ended non-directive questions that invite patient to elaborate 30; using questions that elicit short, positive or yes-or-no answers 29–30
psychodynamic psychiatry service (PPS), University of Alberta Hospital: changes in approach in 107–108; concepts of group functioning and 110–112; development and challenges in 101–102; evening treatment program (ETP) 99, 100–101, 104; factors contributing to survival and productivity of 108–110; future prospects and conclusions on 112; increasing morbidity in 104–105; integration of psychiatric treatment clinic with 102–103; introduction to 99–100; research and evaluation unit (REU) 100, 101, 105–107; splits within day treatment program and 103; staff relations groups (SRGs) 99,

101, 104; structure and functioning of 100–101
psychosis: and allied conditions 57–59; as thought disorder 12
psychosomatic disturbance 43–47
psychotic personality 21, 23

Quinodoz, D. 23
Quinodoz, J.-M. 11, 12

Rappoport de Aisemberg, E. 43–47, 50
Reading French Psychoanalysis 13
Reading Italian Psychoanalysis 13
reassurance 142–144
Reed, G. S. 13
reflexive function 16
regression 12, 42, 47
relational psychoanalysis 32–37, 169–170, 176–177
repression 146, 174
reverie 44, 135, 165, 173; disclosure of 180–181; types of 178–179
role-responsiveness 133
Rosenfeld, H. 57, 144
Rustin, M. 12

Salter Ainsworth, M. D. 17
Sandler, J. 133
Scarfone, D. 13
schizophrenia 57–58
Searles, H. F. 13, 57
Sechaud, E. 45
Secure Base, A 15
seduction theory 47
Segal, H. 57, 144
self-disclosure 47–48
self-image 18, 34–38
severe disturbances 41–42; addictive behaviour 63–65; autistic disturbance 55–57; eating disorders 59–62; psychosis and allied conditions 57–59; psychosomatic disturbance 43–47; sexual perversions/paraphilias 51–54; in traumatized patients 47–50
sexual abuse 49, 50
sexual perversions/paraphilias 51–54
Shaver, P. R. 17
Simon, R. I. 85–86
skin ego 45
skin symptoms 44–45
SMART goals 123
somatic symptoms 43–47
somatization 45
splitting 19, 21, 146–147
Steinberg, P. I. 109

196 *Index*

Steiner, J. 13
Steinman, I. 58
Stern, D. 13, 33, 165
Stern, D. B. 181
Strange Situation 17
Stuart, M. R. 145
substance abuse 63–65
suicidal intent 91–93
Sullivan, H. S. 1, 13, 57
supportive psychotherapy 141; advice
  giving in 148–149; clarification
  technique in 145–147; confrontation
  technique in 146–147; for coping
  with catastrophic feelings 155–162;
  interpretation technique in 147–148;
  literature on 144–145; non-thinking
  patient and 149–150; provocative
  patient and 150–153; techniques of
  145–148; what is 148–149; what is not
  141–144; what to avoid and what to
  do in 153
symbolic functioning 46–47
sympathetic nervous system 50
Szwec, G. 46

Tarasoff rulings 85–86
Taylor, G. J. 46–47, 50
telepathic dreams 180
terrorism of suffering 49–50
theory of containment 43
Thomson, P. 179
threats of violence 71, 83; case examples
  of 72–76, 88–94; clinical ramifications
  of 86–87; literature review on 72;

management implications of 80–83,
  95–97; against self 91–93; sources of
  77–80; Tarasoff rulings and 85–86;
  to third parties 85–97
touch, issues with 45
transference 18, 20, 52, 63
transformations in K (knowledge) 12
transformations in O 12–13
traumatic progression 49
traumatized patients 47–50
Tustin, F. 55

unbidden, the 165, 170–174
unconscious, the 3
unconscious basis for perversions 52–54
unconscious fantasy 3–4, 179–180

Van de Creek, L. 85
Vapenstad, E. V. 178, 179
Vermote, R. 12, 111
vignettes 5–7
Vocational Groups 123–124

Wachtel, P. 33
Walker, J. I. 145
Waska, R. 64
Werman, D. S. 144
Whipped Cream and Other Delights 170
Winnicott, D. W. 11, 12, 42, 57
Winston, A. 144
Wooldridge, T. 62
Work Therapy 125

Zigmond, D. 145

Printed in the United States
by Baker & Taylor Publisher Services